THE BOOK OF TV LISTS

THE BOOK OF TV LISTS

BY GABE ESSOE

Published in Association with
Stan Corwin Productions

ARLINGTON HOUSE

Westport, Connecticut

THIS BOOK AND ITS COMPANION VOLUME are dedicated to my loving wife, Kelley, who is the most incredible woman I have ever known. She is my safe port in stormy weather, my shade in the heat of day, my glimmer of light when in darkness I have lost my way. I love her for who she is, for the support and love she gives me, and for the two beautiful, wonderful children we have made together—Joshua and Jordan—for they are, at the very least, an improvement on mankind.

"John D. MacDonald Rates 7 TV Mystery Series," Copyright © 1979 by *TV Guide;* reprinted by permission.

"The 10 Worst Children's Shows," Copyright © 1980 by *TV Guide;* reprinted by permission.

"A Baker's Dozen Most Often Broadcast Movies on TV," Copyright © 1977 by *TV Guide;* reprinted by permission.

"Judith Crist's List of the Top 10 TV Movies of 1979," and "Contenders for Number 11," Copyright © 1979 by *TV Guide;* reprinted by permission.

Arlington House/Publishers,
333 Post Road West,
Westport, Connecticut 06880

Library of Congress Cataloging in Publication Data

Essoe, Gabe.
  The official book of TV lists.

  1. Television programs—Miscellanea.   I. Title.
PN1992.9.E85   791.45   80-28175
ISBN 0-87000-497-2

Printed in the United States of America

Designed by Verne Bowman

9 8 7 6 5 4 3 2 1

ISBN 0-87000-519-7

CONTENTS

FOREWORD

The first time I was ever on television was in 1942. Barney Balaban and Sam Katz, owners of the Balaban-Katz theatre chain, had an experimental station in Chicago. Skeets Gallagher and I were starring in a show called "Goodnight Ladies" at the Blackstone Theatre, and our press agent told us about this new gimmick called television. We were invited to come over and appear on it. Not for money, but for the novelty of it and the publicity value, if there was any. There were only about fifty sets in the whole state then. It was a pretty small deal.

So, we went over there and told a few jokes, and I did a few gags with this little wire-haired terrier. And I saw this monitor in the corner, and there were these two ghostly looking creatures on this striated jumpy screen. And the whole thing looked rather green. So I said, "What's that?" And they said, "That's what's going out over the air." I said, *"That's* what's going out over the air?!" And they said, "Yes." And I replied, "It'll never amount to anything."

That was almost forty years ago.

As the technology kept getting better, I was talked into doing some other things. You wouldn't get money. They'd give you a portable washing machine or a television set. There was a lot of barter going on in those early, early days.

Then, finally, it started to catch on in New York, and they built a little network that went out to about four cities, and you could finally

get money for doing TV. I did a number of shows like "The Broadway Television Theatre" in 1952, where you did a live play from 8:30 to 10:30, the same play five nights for a week. I did "Burlesque," "The Nervous Wreck," and "Seven Keys to Baldpate." There were lots of other shows that I did, too, forgotten shows, half-hour things, variety shows, novelty shows, vaudeville programs.

In 1954, Disney came along with "Davy Crockett," and cast me as Fess Parker's sidekick. I never had to look back again. I remember in the days when I was still scrambling, my wife, Nancy, would say, "When are you going to get a steady job?" Well, I eventually managed to get a steady job. What with "The Beverly Hillbillies" (1962–71) and "Barnaby Jones" (1973–80), it's been near twenty years solid. So, now she says, "When are you going to get a vacation?"

I would say that my greatest benefit from television has been a continuity of employment, which is what all actors would like to have. And I've been fortunate, and blessed in that way. I'm grateful for it.

BUDDY EBSEN

TV superstar Buddy Ebsen, best known to viewers for his starring roles on "The Beverly Hillbillies" and "Barnaby Jones."

PREFACE

When I was a boy growing up in Illinois, my father (bless him) worked two jobs to keep food on our table and, often as not, would work deep into the night with my mother, painting our modest little home, or wallpapering or replacing plumbing gone awry. On one occasion, I recall, the two of them worked tirelessly toward dawn, sinking fence posts so we could have a white picket fence encircling our yard that was rich with fruit trees my folks had planted.

The point of this is not that my parents were sublime models of the old-fashioned work ethic, which they definitely were, but rather that there were endless days when they were not as accessible to their children as we wished them to be. Work was often all-consuming and never-ending, and almost always took precedence over pleasure and just being together. Even on weekends.

However, once or twice a year, my folks packed us all (my two older brothers, a younger sister, our German shepherd, and me . . . usually in that order) into our 1949 two-tone blue Pontiac Chief and set out on a family adventure. Those trips were, and remain, highlights of my childhood days. We were together and, as a family, built enviable family ties and memories to look back on and to cherish.

One such outing in the early 1950s stands out. We visited some friends in Chicago; who they were has long been blurred by the years gone by, but what remains indelible is that they had a television set. It was a large console with a salad plate-sized screen, around which the lot of us would huddle in a darkened room, as if engaged in some illicit doings. And hypnotizing us, the little screen sparkled to life-like movement with a boxing match, some wrestling, and commercials for Carling's Black Label beer. Of course, there was snow; in fact, there was more snow than programming then, but it didn't matter. Television had become a reality to us; we, who had only heard about it up to that point, had seen the "radio with moving pictures" with our own eyes. And it was magic, like Disneyland for the first time. And there began a lifelong love affair for me with the medium that changed the world, and all of our lives.

Then when television finally came to our house, it was the grandest event of the decade, by far overshadowing the Presidential election, which was won by Eisenhower (whoever he was). It was the start of a whole new ritual, in which all of us in the family would have dinner, then retire to the living room to vote on which television shows we would watch that evening. To those of you who take television for granted, how can I possibly explain the fantasy and wonder, the dream fulfillment of those evening hours where we were all glued to the set, watching, in glorious black and white, the original runs of "M Squad," "Topper," "Secret File, U.S.A.," "The Millionaire," "I Led Three Lives," "Your Hit Parade," "Captain Video," and the dozens of other shows that became so important at that impressionable age that the whole rest of my waking hours were organized around the programs that I couldn't miss for anything? This book is an affectionate tribute to those early utterly magical moments, and an appreciative nod of acknowledgement to all the men and women—especially the women—who have made television what it is today.

ACKNOWLEDGMENTS:
The Helping Hands

On a project like this, the workload was much more immense than meets the eye. The number of people involved was staggering. A computer would have been extremely helpful in keeping all of the diverse elements quasi-organized: the hundreds of addresses, the phone calls, the photos, the tons of reference books and magazines—not to mention the wads of notes and random scribblings that occurred whenever unpredictable inspiration struck (most often while driving, or in the middle of the night, or in restaurants, or in the bathroom). My office looks like the White House document-shredding station for six months—and still does.

My sanity was preserved only through the help and support of scores of absolutely wonderful people who gave of their time and energies freely and generously. Trying to acknowledge them all adequately is like trying to clip the grass at Forest Lawn with a pair of cuticle scissors. However, I want to publicly state that without their assistance the book you hold in your hands would not have been possible. I'm indebted to: my wife, Kelley, for her creative input and unflagging encouragement; my close friend and mentor, Doug Benton, for his guidance and advice; Stan Corwin, for his patience and inspiration; my agent, Beverly Iser, for opening a lot of doors; Buddy Ebsen, for his friendship and participation; John LeBold, curator of the Hollywood Museum, for photos and research; Bart Andrews, for photos and reseach; Michael Levine and TV News for photos and research; Dwight Whitney, *TV Guide;* Cecil Smith, Los Angeles Times; Richard Lamparski; Larry Frerk, A.C. Nielsen Company; Clint Eastwood, for the first list; Phyllis Diller; Robert Osborne; Kathy Banks, NBC; Dennis Weaver; Vera Miles; Robert Stack; Earl

Holliman; Art Ronnie, Columbia-TV; Monty Hall; Bill Conrad; Carol Burnett; Barbara Brogliatti; Gloria Burke; Peter Marshall; Anton La Vey; Rex Allen; Milton Berle; Dick Martin; Howard Rosenberg; Fred MacMurray; Lou Ferrigno; Gary Coleman; John Michaeli, Hanna-Barbera Inc.; Marty Ingels; Charles Labbe; Don Rickles; Bill Dana; Jo Swerling; Bob O'Neal; Suzy Mallery; Jerry Stanley, NBC; Dr. Laurence Peter; Bob Michaelson; Ron Ely; Mr. Blackwell; David Rose; Lucille Ball; Norman Lear; Mario Andretti; Mel Blanc; Dick Clark; Melvin Belli; my IBM Selectric II, which suffered a lot of abuse without once throwing a temper tantrum; and Shelly Weinstock, for expertly copy-editing everything.

 **"THE NAME OF THE GAME":**
The Ratings Race

Or: *How the Tail Wags the Dog*

CHAPTER

THE 50 HIGHEST-RATED PROGRAMS IN TV HISTORY

CBS-TV's ten-month publicity campaign surrounding the mystery about who shot J.R. Ewing on "Dallas" paid off. When the much ballyhooed episode aired on November 21, 1980, the series episode captured the highest rating ever recorded: 53.3 rating and a 76 percent share of the total viewing audience. British viewers reportedly stayed up all night to catch the disclosure via satellite. Over 100 million people watched the record-breaking telecast.

Though it lost the number one spot on the Top 50 to "Dallas," ABC-TV's milestone miniseries, "Roots," dominates the list, by capturing the number two spot and placing all of its eight segments on the list. Overall, "Roots" averaged a 44.9 rating and 66 share. The final telecast on January 30, 1977, was watched by an estimated 80 million viewers.

The top motion picture is the two-part original "Gone With the Wind" broadcast on NBC in 1976. Sporting events are led by Super Bowl XII in January, 1978. The number one entertainment special is the 1970 Bob Hope Christmas Show. And "The Beverly Hillbillies" remains the most highly watched series of all time, as evidenced by its being on the list an impressive, and unmatched, nine times.

Comedian Bob Hope logged thousands of miles entertaining U.S. troops over-
seas, and in the bargain came up with the highest-rated comedy specials ever.
His Christmas show for 1970 and 1971 both rank in the top eleven most-watched
programs of all time.

David Janssen as "The Fugitive," in a scene with a diminutive Ronny Howard. The final episode is the second highest-rated single episode of a series, watched by approximately fifty million people.

"The Beverly Hillbillies," with Buddy Ebsen, was the most popular show of its time, and is the only series to have nine slots on the Fifty Highest-Rated Shows of All Time.

RANK	PROGRAM	DATE	NETWORK	NIELSEN RATING
1.	DALLAS ("Who Shot J.R.?")	Nov. 21, 1980	CBS	53.3
2.	ROOTS, Part 8 (conclusion)	Jan. 30, 1977	ABC	51.1
3.	GONE WITH THE WIND, Part I	Nov. 7, 1976	NBC	47.7
4.	GONE WITH THE WIND, Part II	Nov. 8, 1976	NBC	47.4
5.	SUPER BOWL XII	Jan. 15, 1978	CBS	47.2
6.	SUPER BOWL XIII	Jan. 21, 1979	NBC	47.1
7.	BOB HOPE CHRISTMAS SHOW	Jan. 15, 1970	NBC	46.6
8.	SUPER BOWL XIV	Jan. 20, 1980	CBS	46.3
9.	ROOTS, Part 6	Jan. 28, 1977	ABC	45.9
9.	THE FUGITIVE (conclusion)*	Aug. 29, 1967	ABC	45.9
11.	ROOTS, Part 5	Jan. 27, 1977	ABC	45.7
12.	BOB HOPE CHRISTMAS SHOW	Jan. 14, 1971	NBC	45.0
13.	ROOTS, Part 3	Jan. 25, 1977	ABC	44.8
14.	THE ED SULLIVAN SHOW (TV debut of Beatles)	Feb. 9, 1964	CBS	44.6
15.	SUPER BOWL XI	Jan. 9, 1977	NBC	44.4
16.	SUPER BOWL VI	Jan. 16, 1972	CBS	44.2
17.	ROOTS, Part 2	Jan. 24, 1977	ABC	44.1
18.	THE BEVERLY HILLBILLIES	Jan. 8, 1964	CBS	44.0
19.	ROOTS, Part 4	Jan. 26, 1977	ABC	43.8
20.	THE 43rd ACADEMY AWARDS	Apr. 7, 1970	ABC	43.4
21.	THE ED SULLIVAN SHOW (Second appearance of Beatles)	Feb. 16, 1964	CBS	43.2
22.	THE BEVERLY HILLBILLIES	Jan. 15, 1964	CBS	42.8
23.	SUPER BOWL VII	Jan. 14, 1973	NBC	42.7
24.	SUPER BOWL IX	Jan. 12, 1975	NBC	42.4
24.	THE BEVERLY HILLBILLIES*	Feb. 26, 1964	CBS	42.4
26.	SUPER BOWL X	Jan. 18, 1976	CBS	42.3
26.	AIRPORT (1970)*	Nov. 11, 1973	ABC	42.3
26.	LOVE STORY (1970)*	Oct. 1, 1972	ABC	42.3
26.	CINDERELLA* (Rodgers & Hammerstein musical with Lesley Warren)	Feb. 22, 1965	CBS	42.3

26. ROOTS, Part 7*	Jan. 29, 1977	ABC	42.3
31. THE BEVERLY HILLBILLIES	Mar. 25, 1964	CBS	42.2
32. THE BEVERLY HILLBILLIES	Feb. 5, 1964	CBS	42.0
33. THE BEVERLY HILLBILLIES	Jan. 29, 1964	CBS	41.9
34. MISS AMERICA PAGEANT	Sept. 9, 1961	CBS	41.8
34. THE BEVERLY HILLBILLIES*	Jan. 1, 1964	CBS	41.8
36. SUPER BOWL VIII	Jan. 13, 1974	CBS	41.6
36. BONANZA*	Mar. 8, 1964	NBC	41.6
38. THE BEVERLY HILLBILLIES	Jan. 22, 1964	CBS	41.5
39. BONANZA	Feb. 16, 1964	NBC	41.4
40. THE 49th ACADEMY AWARDS	Apr. 10, 1967	ABC	41.2
41. BONANZA	Feb. 9, 1964	NBC	41.0
42. GUNSMOKE	Jan. 28, 1961	CBS	40.9
43. BONANZA	Mar. 28, 1965	NBC	40.8
44. BONANZA	Mar. 7, 1965	NBC	40.7
44. ALL IN THE FAMILY*	Jan. 8, 1972	CBS	40.7
46. ROOTS, Part 1	Jan. 23, 1977	ABC	40.5
46. BONANZA*	Feb. 2, 1964	NBC	40.5
46. THE BEVERLY HILLBILLIES*	May 1, 1963	CBS	40.5
46. GUNSMOKE*	Feb. 25, 1961	CBS	40.5
50. BONANZA	Feb. 21, 1965	NBC	40.4
50. GUNSMOKE*	Dec. 17, 1960	CBS	40.4

*Indicates a tie with the immediately preceding show; hence, there is no numerical change in the listing, although the entry does count in the total tally of fifty.

THE HIGHEST-RATED TV SHOW FOR EACH OF THE LAST 30 YEARS

The most common misconception about the A.C. Nielsen ratings is that they are popularity polls. Nielsen has always maintained that they are not. They do not judge a television show's appeal or merits, intrinsic or artistic or social value. None of that.

What the Nielsen ratings do, however, is to estimate the total viewing audience, by way of a carefully selected and controlled cross-section sampling, which then, by extension, represents the entire viewing audience. The resulting ratings figures reveal the percentage of all households tuned into a given program in a given time period (as well as a sophisticated breakdown of the makeup of that audience).

These ratings are not, and were not, intended for use by the three major networks to determine the popularity of their programming, but were developed, rather, as marketing tools for advertisers so that they could more effectively make decisions as to where and how to spend their billions of advertising dollars. Why advertise, for example, on a show that draws a low percentage of the viewing audience?

The object of the networks, then, is to program the shows that will have the highest ratings so that they will attract the biggest share of the advertising dollars. Obviously, a sixty-second commercial on the highest-rating show will cost many times more than the same sixty-second spot on a program that rates low on the Nielsen index.

Consequently, although the Nielsen ratings are not popularity polls as such, they are, nonetheless, a marketing tool, which, by the very virtue of their use in determining how advertising budgets are spent, has become the single key factor in also determining the life and death of any given TV show. Therefore, no matter what Nielsen says, its ratings are a popularity index, because that's how they've come to be used. They're an index that governs the entire TV industry, seen most dramatically in recent years by the cancellation of shows only a few weeks old because of low ratings. This is, in effect, the tail that wags the dog.

The ratings themselves, historically and otherwise, however, are a never-ending source of fascination. Observe: the highest-rated TV shows for each of the last thirty years. These were *number one* for their respective years, followed by network and rating, total seasons on the air, and casts:

1950–51 TEXACO STAR THEATRE, NBC, rating: 61.6, 1948—53, Milton Berle

1951–52 ARTHUR GODFREY'S TALENT SCOUTS, CBS, rating: 67.3, 1948—58, Arthur Godfrey

1952–53 I LOVE LUCY, CBS, rating: 67.3, 1951–57, Lucille Ball, Desi Arnaz, Vivian Vance, William Frawley

1953–54 I LOVE LUCY, CBS, rating: 58.8*

1954–55 I LOVE LUCY, CBS, rating: 49.3

1955–56 THE $64,000 QUESTION, CBS, rating: 47.5, 1955–58, Hal March

1956–57 I LOVE LUCY, CBS, rating: 43.7

NOTE: *The discrepancies in the ratings are due to changes in the way the ratings were calculated rather than in extreme changes in "Lucy's" popularity.*

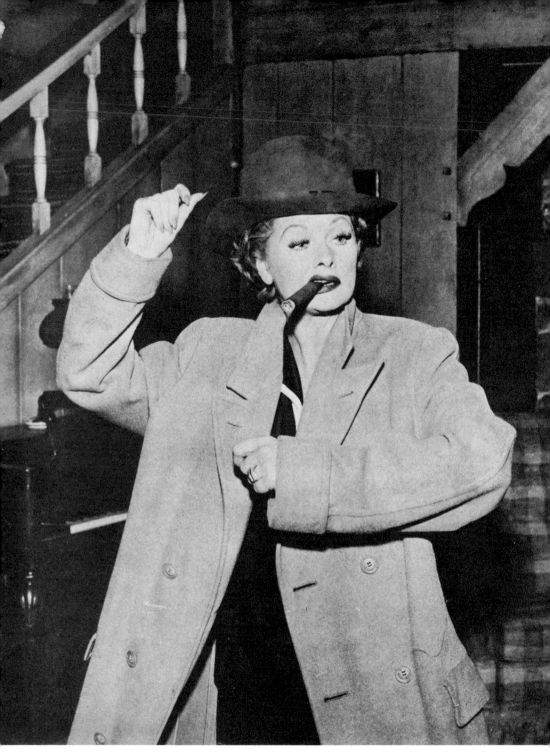

Everybody loved Lucille Ball's clowning on "I Love Lucy" — enough to make her show the number one sitcom for four seasons.

1957–58 GUNSMOKE, CBS, rating: 43.1, 1955–75, James Arness, Amanda Blake, Milburn Stone, Dennis Weaver
1958–59 GUNSMOKE, CBS, rating: 39.6
1959–60 GUNSMOKE, CBS, rating: 40.3
1960–61 GUNSMOKE, CBS, rating: 37.3
1961–62 WAGON TRAIN, NBC, rating: 32.1, 1957–63, Ward Bond, Robert Horton, Frank McGrath
1962–63 THE BEVERLY HILLBILLIES, CBS, rating: 36.0, 1962–71, Buddy Ebsen, Irene Ryan, Donna Douglas, Max Baer
1963–64 THE BEVERLY HILLBILLIES, CBS, rating: 39.1
1964–65 BONANZA, NBC, rating: 36.3, 1959–73, Lorne Greene, Pernell Roberts, Dan Blocker, Michael Landon
1965–66 BONANZA, NBC, rating: 31.8
1966–67 BONANZA, NBC, rating: 29.1
1967–68 THE ANDY GRIFFITH SHOW, CBS, rating: 27.6, 1960–68, Andy Griffith, Don Knotts, Ronny Howard, Frances Bavier

"Gunsmoke," the first "adult" TV Western, featured Amanda Blake, James Arness, Dennis Weaver, and Milburn Stone. It was the only series to tie with the "I Love Lucy" record to capture the number one spot for four seasons and the dramatic series to have lasted twenty years in prime time.

1968–69 ROWAN & MARTIN'S LAUGH-IN, NBC, rating: 31.8, 1968–73, Dan Rowan, Dick Martin, Goldie Hawn, Lily Tomlin

1969–70 ROWAN & MARTIN'S LAUGH-IN, NBC, rating: 26.3

1970–71 MARCUS WELBY, M.D., ABC, rating: 29.6, 1969–76, Robert Young, James Brolin, Elena Verdugo

1971–72 ALL IN THE FAMILY, CBS, rating: 34.0, 1971–80, Carroll O'Connor, Jean Stapleton, Rob Reiner, Sally Struthers

1972–73 ALL IN THE FAMILY, CBS, rating: 33.3

1973–74 ALL IN THE FAMILY, CBS, rating: 31.2

1974–75 ALL IN THE FAMILY, CBS, rating: 30.2

1975–76 ALL IN THE FAMILY, CBS, rating: 30.1

1976–77 HAPPY DAYS, ABC, rating: 31.5, 1974–present; Ronny Howard, Henry Winkler, Tom Bosley, Marion Ross

1977–78 LAVERNE & SHIRLEY, ABC, rating: 31.6, 1976–present, Penny Marshall, Cindy Williams, Eddie Mekka

1978–79 LAVERNE & SHIRLEY, ABC, rating: 30.5

1979–80 60 MINUTES, CBS, rating: 28.2, 1968–present, Mike Wallace, Harry Reasoner, Morley Safer, Dan Rather

10 CONSECUTIVE LISTS OF THE TOP TEN SHOWS FOR THE LAST 10 SEASONS

Working backward from 1979–80 to 1970–71:

1. 1979–80

1. 60 MINUTES
2. THREE'S COMPANY
3. THAT'S INCREDIBLE
4. M*A*S*H
5. ALICE
6. DALLAS
7. FLO
8. THE JEFFERSONS
9. DUKES OF HAZZARD
10. ONE DAY AT A TIME

2. 1978–79

1. LAVERNE & SHIRLEY
2. THREE'S COMPANY
3. MORK AND MINDY
4. HAPPY DAYS
5. ANGIE
6. 60 MINUTES
7. M*A*S*H
8. THE ROPERS
9. CHARLIE'S ANGELS
10. ALL IN THE FAMILY

3. 1977–78

1. LAVERNE & SHIRLEY
2. HAPPY DAYS
3. THREE'S COMPANY
4. 60 MINUTES
5. CHARLIE'S ANGELS
6. ALL IN THE FAMILY
7. LITTLE HOUSE ON THE PRAIRIE
8. ALICE
9. M*A*S*H
10. ONE DAY AT A TIME

4. 1976–77

1. HAPPY DAYS
2. LAVERNE & SHIRLEY
3. ABC MONDAY NIGHT MOVIE
4. M*A*S*H
5. CHARLIE'S ANGELS
6. THE BIG EVENT
7. THE SIX MILLION DOLLAR MAN
8. ABC SUNDAY NIGHT MOVIE
9. BARETTA
10. ONE DAY AT A TIME

5. 1975–76

1. ALL IN THE FAMILY
2. RICH MAN, POOR MAN [limited series]
3. LAVERNE & SHIRLEY
4. MAUDE
5. THE BIONIC WOMAN
6. PHYLLIS
7. SANFORD AND SON
8. RHODA
9. THE SIX MILLION DOLLAR MAN
10. ABC MONDAY NIGHT MOVIE

6. 1974–75

1. ALL IN THE FAMILY
2. SANFORD AND SON
3. CHICO AND THE MAN
4. THE JEFFERSONS
5. M*A*S*H
6. RHODA
7. GOOD TIMES
8. THE WALTONS
9. MAUDE
10. HAWAII FIVE-O

7. 1973–74

1. ALL IN THE FAMILY
2. THE WALTONS
3. SANFORD AND SON
4. M*A*S*H
5. HAWAII FIVE-O
6. MAUDE
7. KOJAK
8. THE SONNY & CHER COMEDY HOUR
9. THE MARY TYLER MOORE SHOW
10. CANNON

8. 1972–73

1. ALL IN THE FAMILY
2. SANFORD AND SON
3. HAWAII FIVE-O
4. MAUDE
5. BRIDGET LOVES BERNIE
6. SUNDAY MYSTERY MOVIE
7. THE MARY TYLER MOORE SHOW
8. GUNSMOKE
9. THE WONDERFUL WORLD OF DISNEY
10. IRONSIDE

9. 1971–72

1. ALL IN THE FAMILY
2. THE FLIP WILSON SHOW
3. MARCUS WELBY, M.D.
4. GUNSMOKE
5. ABC MOVIE OF THE WEEK
6. SANFORD AND SON
7. MANNIX
8. FUNNY FACE
9. ADAM 12
10. THE MARY TYLER MOORE SHOW

10. 1970–71

1. MARCUS WELBY, M.D.
2. THE FLIP WILSON SHOW
3. HERE'S LUCY
4. IRONSIDE
5. GUNSMOKE
6. ABC MOVIE OF THE WEEK
7. HAWAII FIVE-0
8. MEDICAL CENTER
9. BONANZI
10. THE F.B.I.

THE 5 HIGHEST-RATED MINI-SERIES

1. ROOTS (Jan. '77). Rating: 45, share of audience: 66%.
   Twelve-hour adaptation, telecast on eight consecutive nights, of Alex Haley's novel, tracing his African ancestors. All eight telecasts ranked

A former USC student, LeVar Burton catapulted to fame as Kunta Kinte in "Roots," the highest-rated mini-series of all time.

among the fifteen highest-rated single programs of all time! And the final segment topped all shows with a 51.1 rating and a 71 share. Nielsen estimated that some 130 million viewers watched some part of "Roots." Cast included: LeVar Burton (in his acting debut), John Amos, Lou Gossett, Ben Vereen, Ed Asner, Leslie Uggams, Cicely Tyson, Lloyd Bridges, Georg Stanford Brown. Nominated for 37 Emmys and won six, including Outstanding Limited Series.

2. SHOGUN (Sept. '80). Rating: 32.6, share: 51

Twelve-hour adaptation, telecast on five consecutive nights, of James Clavell's novel about an Englishman's adventures in seventeenth-century Japan. Though unquestionably a first-rate production that cost NBC $22 million, in which Richard Chamberlain gave the performance of his career, the ratings were more than a little attributable to the program vacuum on the other networks created by the then nine-week old Hollywood actors' strike. Though a riveting show with top production values, one had to know fluent Japanese to catch all the dialogue. Cast included: Chamberlain, Toshiro Mifune, Yoko Shimada.

3. HOW THE WEST WAS WON (Sept. '77). Rating: 32.5, share: 50

What began as an ambitious TV movie called "The Macahans," which aired in January, 1976, returned as a six-hour sequel entitled "How the West Was Won," which told the saga of the Macahan clan on the frontier. Produced by those wonderful folks who gave us "Gunsmoke," the miniseries again returned in 1978 for an additional twenty hours of the further adventures of the Macahans. The stars of the show were: James Arness, Bruce Boxleitner, Fionnula Flanagan, Vera Miles, William Shatner, and Ricardo Montalban, among others.

4. HOLOCAUST (Oct. '78). Rating: 31.1, share: 49

Four-part, nine-and-one-half-hour dramatization of the persecution and extermination of European Jews by the Nazis during World War II, focusing on the Weiss family who lived in Berlin. Written by Gerald Green, whose subsequent novelization became a best-seller, the gripping drama included: Fritz Weaver, Rosemary Harris, James Woods, Meryl Streep, Joseph Bottoms, Tovah Feldsah, Michael Moriarty, and Sam Wanamaker. Their remarkable achievement won eight well-deserved Emmys.

5. ROOTS: THE NEXT GENERATIONS (Feb. '79). Rating: 30.2, share: 45

A seven-night, twelve-hour sequel to "Roots," which cost $18 million and traced author Haley's ancestors from 1882 to 1967. Although "Roots II" didn't blitz the ratings like "Roots I," the sequel's seven parts all ranked in the week's top eleven programs. It marked Marlon Brando's first dramatic TV role in thirty years; he portrayed George Lincoln Rockwell, leader of the American Nazi Party, who was interviewed by Haley, played by James Earl Jones, for *Playboy* magazine. Others in the cast included: Ben Vereen, Georg Stanford Brown, Henry Fonda, Richard Thomas. Conspicuously absent was LeVar Burton, who was catapulted to fame in "Roots I" but demanded pay equal to Henry Fonda's for a cameo participation. That's gratitude for you.

14 YEARS OF RATINGS FOR THE SUPER BOWL

Literally created by television, for television, the "Super Bowl" is the showdown game between the two conferences of the National Football League, a championship annual event that consistently outdraws practically every telecast show. Initiated in 1967, the Super Bowl became possible after NBC's huge investment in TV rights for the fledgling American Football League in 1964 (a reported $42 million for five years); it led eventually to AFL teams worthy of competing with the long-established National Football League teams (whose games were carried by CBS).

The original agreement stated that both CBS and NBC would carry the first "Super Bowl," and then would alternate on the succeeding games.

The Super Bowl created the climate for the 1970 merger of the two football leagues into one, the National Football League, with two separate conferences.

Super Bowl		Opposing Teams	Network	Ratings	U.S. Households* Total (in millions)
1.	1967	Green Bay/Kansas City	CBS/NBC	41.1	24.4
2.	1968	Green Bay/Oakland	CBS	36.8	25.3
3.	1969	N.Y. Jets/Baltimore	NBC	36.0	24.1
4.	1970	Kansas City/Minnesota	CBS	39.4	23.2
5.	1971	Baltimore/Dallas	NBC	39.9	25.6
6.	1972	Dallas/Miami	CBS	44.2	27.4
7.	1973	Miami/Washington	NBC	42.7	27.6
8.	1974	Miami/Minnesota	CBS	41.6	27.5
9.	1975	Minnesota/Pittsburgh	NBC	42.4	28.2
10.	1976	Dallas/Pittsburgh	CBS	42.3	29.0
11.	1977	Oakland/Minnesota	NBC	44.4	31.6
12.	1978	Dallas/Denver	CBS	47.2	34.4
13.	1979	Pittsburgh/Dallas	NBC	47.1	35.3
14.	1980	Pittsburgh/L.A.	CBS	46.3	36.4

*A household is estimated as 2.2 persons.

2
CHAPTER

"JUDD FOR THE DEFENSE":
The Critics Have Their Say

Or: How You Just Can't Please Everybody

CECIL SMITH'S LIST OF THE 10 ALL-TIME BEST SERIES

When you talk about insightful television criticism, you're bound to be talking about Cecil Smith, the *Los Angeles Times* chief TV critic. Smith, a perceptive man filled with humor and wit, has devoted the last three decades to writing about television for the *Times,* and has also, for a five-year period, covered the emerging L.A. theatre scene as the Los Angeles Music Center came of age. Over the years, he has easily assumed the position of the Dean of West Coast TV Critics. He is a giant in his field, not because he is able to dissect critically (of which he is most certainly capable), but because he always approaches the subject with firm affection, as you would an old friend.

1. PLAYHOUSE 90 ('56–60)
   Dramatic anthology that aired a complete ninety-minute live drama every week. It was the best of its kind.
2. UPSTAIRS, DOWNSTAIRS ('73–77)
   Part of the "PBS Masterpiece Theatre" ('71–present), which has been public television's most popular dramatic anthology series. Hosted by Alistair Cooke, all the productions are made in Great Britain, most by the BBC.

3. THE DEFENDERS ('61–65)
E.G. Marshall and Robert Reed as father-and-son attorneys who atyp-ically occasionally lost a case. They attracted much controversy as well as critical acclaim.

4. VICTORY AT SEA ('52–53)
A documentary series of twenty-six half-hours on naval warfare during WW II. Narrated by Leonard Graves, with a special score by Richard Rodgers.

5. NAKED CITY ('58–59, '60–63)
Ran first as a half-hour series, then returned after a year's absence as an hour show. Cast included: James Franciscus and John McIntire, who was later replaced by Horace McMahon. Filmed entirely in New York, it featured such later greats as Robert Redford, Dustin Hoffman, Jon Voight, Peter Fonda, Sandy Dennis, in their first major TV guest roles.

6. THE SENATOR ('70–71)
Segment of "The Bold Ones" ('69–73). Hal Holbrook was an idealistic politician. Too good to last.

7. OMNIBUS ('52–59)
First major TV project underwritten by the Ford Foundation. Hosted by Alistair Cooke, it presented dramas, musicals, and documentaries; each program usually contained several segments.

8. CIVILIZATION ('70)
Highly acclaimed PBS series that seemed "almost sacrilegious" to Cleve-land Amory who reviewed it for *TV Guide*. It was that good. Hosted by Lord Kenneth Clark. Published as a book which sold 230,000 copies.

9. THE ASCENT OF MAN (Jan.–Apr. '75).
PBS development of mankind series hosted by Dr. Jacob Bronowski. Co-production of BBC and Time-Life.

10. EXPERIMENT IN TELEVISION ('60–71)
Three or four months every year for over a decade, NBC programing executive Tom McAvity produced some of the finest experimental televi-sion, showing what TV was really capable of: musicals, specials, live drama, you name it.

. . . THE 10 RUNNERS-UP

1. M*A*S*H ('72–present)
2. I LOVE LUCY ('51–60)
3. THE LAST WORD ('57–59)
Panel of three celebrities discussed questions about the English language posed by viewers.
4. YOU BET YOUR LIFE ('50–61)
TV's funniest game show emceed by Groucho Marx.

5. YOU'LL NEVER GET RICH ('55–59)
   One of the top sitcoms of the '50s, with Phil Silvers as Sergeant Bilko.
6. BARNEY MILLER ('75–present)
7. THE MARY TYLER MOORE SHOW ('70–77)
8. POLICE STORY ('73–78)
9. MAVERICK ('57–62)
10. STUDIO ONE ('48–58)
    Oldest and most highly acclaimed of the dramatic anthology series; broadcast live from New York until the last half of the last season.

"The Mary Tyler Moore Show," according to *Los Angeles Times* TV critic Cecil Smith is, along with "M*A*S*H," "I Love Lucy," "Barney Miller," and "You'll Never Get Rich," one of the best comedies ever produced for television.

CECIL SMITH'S LIST OF 11 ALL-TIME STINKERS

1. MY MOTHER, THE CAR ('65–66)
   The feeblest sitcom ever.
2. BEACON HILL (Sept.–Nov. '75)
   The biggest flop of the '75–76 season was this expensive, cumbersome, and much-publicized attempt to Americanize "Upstairs, Downstairs."
3. YOU'RE IN THE PICTURE (Jan. '61)
   One of TV's biggest flops and the only one in memory where the star, Jackie Gleason, came on the following week to apologize for the mess.
4. REDD FOXX COMEDY HOUR ('77– 78)
   Hard to believe that Redd Foxx left "Sanford and Son" for this comedy-variety show that had so few laughs it was axed mid-season.
5. THE HOWARD COSELL VARIETY HOUR ('75–76)
   Also known as SATURDAY NIGHT LIVE WITH HOWARD COSELL. But a stinker either way; it didn't last the season.
6. S.W.A.T. ('75–76)
   One of the most violent shows of the decade.
7. SHIRLEY'S WORLD ('71–72)
   Notable example of an unsuccessful TV sitcom featuring a major film star, Shirley MacLaine.
8. KORG 70,000 B.C. ('74–75)
   Essentially a Neanderthal version of "The Waltons"; a live-action Hanna-Barbera entry.
9. MICKEY ('64–65)
   Another example of an unsuccessful TV sitcom featuring a major film star, Mickey Rooney. Like "Shirley's World," it, too, got canceled half-way through the season.
10. THE TAMMY GRIMES SHOW (Sept. '66)
    The first cancellation of the '66–67 season, after only four airings.
11. There are scores of runners-up like PANTOMIME QUIZ ('49–70) and DALLAS ('78–present) that would take a volume to list.

CECIL SMITH'S LIST OF 6 TERRIFIC SHOWS THAT FAILED

1. SLATTERY'S PEOPLE ('64–65)
   Richard Crenna starred as the minority leader in the state legislature, in an effort to make the public understand the legislative process. CBS let it dangle awhile, and then withdrew it prematurely.
2. THE WESTERNER (Sept.–Dec. '60)
   Director Sam Peckinpah's superb series about the realistic West, with Brian Keith as an illiterate cowboy; it deserved more than thirteen weeks from NBC.

3. MY WORLD AND WELCOME TO IT ('69–72)
   William Windom's best work to date in the lead in this whimsical series based on the works of James Thurber. And NBC dropped it to put on "Red Skelton."
4. THE RICHARD BOONE SHOW ('63– 64)
   TV's equivalent of repertory theatre, killed off by stupidity at NBC.
5. THE LAW ('74)
   New York theatre actor Judd Hirsch came west to do this magnificent show. Only four episodes were made, following the TV movie, which were too good for NBC to swallow. Now you can catch Hirsch in "Taxi," which is more the network's speed.
6. EAST SIDE/WEST SIDE ('63–64)
   George C. Scott and Cicely Tyson! And those lunkheads at CBS let them get away.

BART ANDREWS' LIST OF THE 10 WORST TV SHOWS EVER

Author of *The Worst TV Shows Ever* (Dutton; $6.95) and *Lucy & Ricky & Fred & Ethel: The Story of "I Love Lucy"* (Popular Library; $2.50), and a host of trivia quiz books, Bart Andrews is a disgustingly successful writer. In addition to his over two million books in print, he has also written over 150 TV shows: "Bewitched," "The Phyllis Diller Show," "I Dream of Jeannie," "Get Smart," "All in the Family," "The Mary Tyler Moore Show," "He and She," "Maude," and others. Between TV-writing stints, he knocked out nightclub acts for Carol Burnett, Jim Nabors, Bob Newhart, Paul Lynde, Soupy Sales, and others, plus articles and profiles for *TV Guide* and other magazines. Other offenses include three—no, make that four—books upcoming. And the unkindest cut of all from this dastardly Bart is that he's only thirty-six years old. From his credits, he could at least have the decency to be fifty or fifty-five.

1. GILLIGAN'S ISLAND ('64– 67)
   Sherwood ("The Brady Bunch") Schwartz created it in 1964, James Aubrey of CBS bought it, and Americans ate it up for three solid years and ninety-eight half-hour episodes, but that doesn't change the fact that the show was pure drek. Viewers should be ashamed of themselves for watching a show that was so underwritten, unfunny, heavy-handed, and banal. But they aren't. It's still being rerun everywhere to fairly decent ratings, and they've made one sequel-type TV movie—and that's scary.

"Gilligan's Island," with Alan Hale and Bob Denver, is Bart Andrew's choice for the worst television series of all time.

Hokum, callousness, and tragedy combined to make "Queen for a Day," with host Jack Bailey, a successful, but tasteless show.

2. QUEEN FOR A DAY ('55–64)

An enormously successful program that ran for nineteen consecutive years on radio and TV, with Jack Bailey as its hokey host. Every day, three women were paraded shamelessly onstage to tell their tales of woe—dead husband, spastic children, burned down house—only to have a heartless applause meter measure their woefulness. Whoever had the sorriest story won—a washing machine, car, or artificial leg. The losers (in more ways than one) got nothing but a free "Queen for a Day" lunch—a tuna fish sandwich.

3. THE SURVIVORS ('69–70)

Harold Robbins was paid $1 million to write ten pages of storyline for this ABC drama, telecast in 1969. The network would have been better off spending the million on upgrading "The Joey Bishop Show" (by firing

Bishop). Lana Turner, Kevin McCarthy (a fine actor), and Ralph Bellamy could not help this dreary soap opera of finance-and-philandering, other than by quitting. The only thing Miss Turner was worried about was her wardrobe, not the quality of scripts. By Christmas, the series was down the drain, wardrobe and all fifteen episodes.

4. MY MOTHER, THE CAR ('65–66)

This is the classic "Worst TV Show Ever." I don't think there could have been a dumber concept for a TV series: Jerry Van Dyke played a lawyer who goes out one night to buy his wife a "second car," only to return home with a 1927 Porter Jalopy which turns out to be his mother, who has been—get this—reinCARnated. Yup, that's the one joke for this one-joke show that Van Dyke has never lived down. Poor Ann Sothern was stuck in this vehicle (sorry!) which she actually had to audition for (and she won over Eve Arden and Jean Arthur). Grant Tinker, then an NBC executive, bought the show, saying, "It'll be another 'I Love Lucy.'"

5. THE NEWLYWED GAME ('66–74; '77–present)

This was Chuck Barris' second TV offering (the first was "The Dating Game") that lasted on the ABC network for eight years, later going into syndication and making millions in profits for old Chuck baby. Four couples were pitted against each other (for the sake of humiliation only), asked embarassing questions (like "What vegetable would your husband most like to sit on?"), and then urged to make fools of themselves by fighting verbally on camera (as if the divorce rate isn't high enough!). The continuing program proves to us that there is truly no accounting for bad taste.

6. YOU'RE IN THE PICTURE (Jan. '61)

By 1961, Jackie Gleason was established as one of TV's superstars, when you count his success with "The Honeymooners." But he accepted the host chores for a game show on CBS that was so bad it lasted only one night. Yes, at the time, it was some sort of record (since broken). Four celebrities stuck their heads through cutouts in a plyboard scene (a la Atlantic City) and then had to determine the scene or situation they were in based on questions to Gleason. Sound tacky? It was. Gleason came back the following week and actually apologized to the viewing public for perpetrating this game show travesty.

7. SUPERMARKET SWEEP ('65–67)

David Susskind, that *wunderkind* of quality programing (or so he likes us to think) gave us this little paean to greed: a game show that featured three grown men clad in sneakers who ran around a suburban supermarket scooping up groceries and lawn chairs in quest of the highest cash register tally. Not exactly like Susskind's TV productions of "Death of a Salesman" and "The Crucible," but close. What made us nauseous was the fact that there are people still starving in China. . . .

8. THREE'S COMPANY ('77–present)

This may be a perennially popular sitcom—often in the top 10—but it's still pure crap, offensive as they come. It's hard to believe that three writer/producers once connected with "All in the Family" could have perpetrated this low-life series. It's one thing to have bad writing and lousy jokes, but then another to have equally bad acting (except by John Ritter), but this sitcom manages well. When 55 million Americans will stay glued to their Motorolas every week to watch this filthy drivel, then the country is *really* in trouble.

9. THE TAMMY GRIMES SHOW (Sept. '66)

Take a Tony Award-winning actress like Tammy Grimes (who won as Best Musical Actress for "The Unsinkable Molly Brown" on Broadway), and put her into an ill-conceived, ill-produced potboiler like this, and you have the first canceled show of the 1966–67 season. It was the shortest-lived filmed series up to that time. And she had turned down "Bewitched" (not that that was so wonderful, but it was a hit) saying, "It won't work." Then, nearly sight unseen, she accepted George Axelrod's concept for this show. There's still a chance for a decent Tammy Grimes sitcom, but she'd better be more discriminating than she was then. Of the ten episodes completed, only four were ever televised. That's how bad it was!

10. THE JERRY LEWIS SHOW (Sept.–Dec. '63)

There are a lot of mixed feelings about Mr. Lewis. The French think he's a god, for instance. The average American considers him similarly for all his work collecting money for multiple sclerosis. But there is a larger contingent out there who really think he's twenty years too late. He hasn't had a hit movie in about fifteen years and his first TV series, on ABC in 1963, was about the most monumental flop the medium has ever seen. Lewis was given free rein by the network bigwigs to do what he wanted—a two-hour, live variety/talk show every Saturday night. Lewis called the shots, all of them badly. It lasted till Christmas—by then, only Patty and the boys were watching.

Says Andrews: "My book, *The Worst TV Shows Ever*, was the result of some 85,000 hours of TV viewing over thirty years. I've seen everything! I've even written some of the worst TV shows ever! Luckily, some of the best, too."

HOWARD ROSENBERG'S NOMINEES FOR TV'S KING AND QUEEN OF SNORES

TV critic and columnist for the *Los Angeles Times*, Howard Rosenberg relates: "A few of us were sitting around the office the other day, nominating candidates for King and Queen of Snores, performers who would be in a soup line if they had as little income as talent; total wipeouts who were fortunate enough to land in a hit series. The vote was unanimous for:

1. ANSON WILLIAMS (Potsie on "Happy Days") and CHARLENE TIL-TON (Lucy Ewing on "Dallas")

   "I was watching Anson on a 'Happy Days' rerun. He happened to be the focus of that episode, and as I listened to him say his lines vacantly, and sing a song in a voice that seemed to be muffled by a pillow, it occurred to me that you could hang a GONE FISHING sign on him, or BACK IN TEN MINUTES, and no one would know the difference.

   "However, if Anson and Charlene are unable to serve as King and Queen, these are the runners-up:"

2. ERIK ESTRADA ("Chips") and JAYNE KENNEDY ("Speak Up America")
3. MARTIN MILNER ("Adam 12") and SUZANNE SOMERS ("Three's Company")
4. KENT McCORD ("Adam 12") and JACLYN SMITH ("Charlie's Angels")
5. JOHN SCHNEIDER ("Dukes of Hazzard") and SHELLEY HACK ("Charlie's Angels")

CHARLES LABBE'S LIST OF THE 2 WORST TV SERIES ABOUT NAZIS

Captain Labbe is the second in command of the American Nazi Party, headquartered in Cincinnati, Ohio.

1. HOGAN'S HEROES ('65–71), with Bob Crane
   Good comedy and satire, but very poor in its portrayal of Nazis as bumbling and incompetent idiots. Camps were never run like they were shown.
2. COMBAT ('62–67), with Rick Jason, Vic Morrow
   Some nice drama, but too often coarse and unsympathetic to Nazis. One of the better shows featured the young Robert Redford as a Nazi officer.

SALINAS TV VIEWERS SELECT THEIR 6 FAVORITE VINTAGE SERIES FOR RERUNS DURING THE ACTORS' STRIKE

During the July-through-October, 1980 Actors' Strike, a rural newspaper, the *Salinas Californian,* polled its readers to find out what old TV series they would like to see on the air if the new fall shows failed to materialize because of the strike. Despite comments like: "At least we don't have to see the new junk yet," a whopping 212 shows were nominated. But, clearly, only six were runaway choices:

1. THE REAL McCOYS ('57–63). Walter Brennan, Richard Crenna, Kathy Nolan
2. THE MILLIONAIRE ('55–60). Marvin Miller
3. CARTER COUNTRY ('77–79). Victor French, Kene Holliday, Richard Paul
4. BEN CASEY ('61–66). Vince Edwards, Sam Jaffe, Bettye Ackerman
5. LEAVE IT TO BEAVER ('57–63). Hugh Beaumont, Barbara Billingsley, Tony Dow, Jerry Mathers
6. MY LITTLE MARGIE ('52–55). Gale Storm, Charles Farrell, Don Hayden

THE TOP 6 ACTORS ON THE PERFORMER Q

In much the same way that TV programs are measured by Nielsen ratings, TV performers are measured annually in a sort of popularity index—called Performer Q—by a company called Marketing Evaluations, Inc. Based in Port Washington, New York, MEI provides a yearly Performer Q report to about fifty subscribers. The way it works is this: Every April a questionnaire goes to about 1,000 families selected by computer from a roster of 120,000 families registered with Home Testing Institute. The cross-section represents a miniature U.S. population. The results of the testing, which are published every November, are not only costly, but are very guarded. In the November, 1979, Performer Q, the top six were these:

1. JOHN WAYNE
2. ROBIN WILLIAMS of "Mork and Mindy"
3. BOB HOPE
4. ALAN ALDA of "M*A*S*H"
5. ROBERT GUILLAUME of "Benson" tied with:
5. GARY COLEMAN of "Diff'rent Strokes"

The study showed, among other things, that male performers outnumber females three to one during week-night prime-time programing, and five to one on weekends.

THE TOP 4 WOMEN ON TV

1. JEAN STAPLETON of "All in the Family" (rated #11 of all performers)
2. CAROL BURNETT, of "The Carol Burnett Show" (#18)
3. GILDA RADNER, of "Saturday Night Live" (#23)
4. LUCILLE BALL, (#29)

4 WELL-KNOWN PERSONALITIES AT THE BOTTOM OF THE LIST

At the embarrasing end of the Performer Q scale are four undeniably well-known celebrities, whose popularity with viewers is lower than a pill bug's bottom.

1. JANE FONDA
2. MUHAMMAD ALI
3. HOWARD COSELL
4. SHELLEY HACK

Hack, last season's addition to "Charlie's Angels," performed quite poorly. In fact, her popularity rating in her category was one-half the average, while her co-stars Jaclyn Smith and Cheryl Ladd both played at 25 percent above the norm. Unhappily accurate, the Performer Q predicted her inevitable separation from the successful series.

The third line-up of "Charlie's Angels" were Jaclyn Smith, Cheryl Ladd, and Shelley Hack, who replaced Kate Jackson. When the Performer Q came out, Hack rated at the bottom and her demise became a foregone conclusion.

3

CHAPTER

"HULLABALOO":
The Emmy and Other Awards
Or: *The Golden Goddess*
Works in Mysterious Ways

1 SERMON ABOUT THE ILLS OF THE EMMY AWARDS
...3 LISTS ABOUT THE LEADING ACTRESS CATEGORY
...AND 10 LISTS OF THE TOP 12 EMMYS FOR THE PAST DECADE

You don't normally see any kind of organized lists of the Emmy winners. There's a reason for this. The Emmys, at their heart of hearts, lack organization and uniformity—that is, the awards are designated and bestowed on a rather free-form basis, and the categories change from year to year. They are not at all like the Academy Awards, which are the same today as they were, in basics, three decades ago. You know: Best Picture, Best Actor, Best Actress, and so on. We can all recite the categories in our sleep.

Not so with the Emmys. Perhaps to avoid being copycats, the Emmy has done its best to maintain a looser policy. That way an award can be given one year and not the next. For example, in 1950 (Emmy's third year) fifteen awards were given out. That season, Groucho Marx was the Outstanding Personality. The following year, only six

Emmys were voted, and there was no Outstanding Personality. All the TV personalities in 1951 were ordinary.

Then in 1955, forty-one Emmys were awarded (possibly in trying to make up the dearth of awards in 1951); "Lassie" won for Best Children's Series. But enough is enough, and the following year, the number of awards was cut back to twenty-nine, and, wouldn't you know it, there was no Best Children's Series. Yet, had they asked me at the time, I could have named a dozen easily.

Eighteen years later, the wrinkles still weren't quite ironed out. By the 1974–75 season, the Emmy Awards had mushroomed to an all-time high of 128 winners. Apparently though, the following year fewer people deserved recognition, because one-third of the categories were canceled and only eighty-four Emmys for the 1975–76 TV season were handed out. That was the year of the category Outstanding Achievement in Makeup, No Winner. Make that *eighty-three* Emmys handed out.

The constantly changing nature of television is obviously a real problem for the folks in charge of the Emmys, because they seem to have difficulties in clearly defining the award categories. Take, for example, the Leading Actress awards. For the 1973–74 season, the category broke down like this:

1. BEST LEADING ACTRESS IN A COMEDY SERIES
2. BEST LEADING ACTRESS IN A DRAMA SERIES
3. BEST LEADING ACTRESS IN A LIMITED SERIES
4. BEST LEADING ACTRESS IN A DRAMA
5. ACTRESS OF THE YEAR—SERIES
6. ACTRESS OF THE YEAR—SPECIAL

In the previous season, for 1972–73, the same category had been broken down like this:

1. OUTSTANDING CONTINUED PERFORMANCE BY AN ACTRESS IN A COMEDY SERIES
2. OUTSTANDING CONTINUED PERFORMANCE BY AN ACTRESS IN A LEADING ROLE IN:
   A. DRAMA SERIES—CONTINUING
   B. DRAMA/COMEDY—LIMITED EPISODES
3. OUTSTANDING SINGLE PERFORMANCE BY AN ACTRESS IN A LEADING ROLE

A few years later, for the 1975–76 season, the category looked like this:

1. OUTSTANDING LEADING ACTRESS IN A COMEDY SERIES
2. OUTSTANDING LEADING ACTRESS IN A DRAMA SERIES

3. OUTSTANDING LEADING ACTRESS IN A LIMITED SERIES
4. OUTSTANDING LEADING ACTRESS IN A DRAMA OR COMEDY SPECIAL
5. OUTSTANDING LEADING ACTRESS FOR A SINGLE APPEARANCE IN A COMEDY OR DRAMA SERIES

Although the Leading Actress category has more or less finally settled down to a simple variation of the above five awards, indicative of an encroaching stabilization, the total number of Emmys voted in a given year continues to fluctuate. At last count, the total hovered around sixty.

Another disturbing element, at least to me, about the Emmys is that once the television academy membership votes an Emmy to someone, it continues awarding that particular Emmy to the same individual over and over again, to the point where it seems that no one else in that category is capable of outstanding work. And it's just not true. What's more likely the case is that Emmy voters get caught in a rut and vote "like they did last year" without really considering other performers and artists who also deserve recognition. I've enjoyed Carroll O'Connor in "All in the Family" as much as the next guy, but there's no way in hell that he deserves to win five Emmys for Best Leading Actor in a Comedy Series, when such fine talent as Hal Linden, Bob Newhart, Gabe Kaplan, Henry Winkler, Dick Van Patten, and John Ritter, among others, have gone unawarded.

Now, let's take a look at the top Emmy winners. The best way to do this, perhaps, is to select twelve of the most important single awards given each year, and try to fit them into the following conformity:

1. BEST COMEDY SERIES
2. BEST DRAMATIC SERIES
3. OUTSTANDING VARIETY SERIES
4. OUTSTANDING SINGLE PROGRAM
5. BEST LEADING ACTOR IN A COMEDY SERIES
6. BEST LEADING ACTRESS IN A COMEDY SERIES
7. BEST LEADING ACTOR IN A DRAMATIC SERIES
8. BEST LEADING ACTRESS IN A DRAMATIC SERIES
9. BEST SINGLE PERFORMANCE BY AN ACTOR
10. BEST SINGLE PERFORMANCE BY AN ACTRESS
11. BEST DIRECTOR OF A SPECIAL PROGRAM
12. BEST ORIGINAL TELEPLAY FOR A SPECIAL PROGRAM

The above list is *the key* to the following ten lists, which give the Emmy Winners for each of these awards, for ten consecutive seasons, from 1970 through 1980:

1. 1970–71
1. ALL IN THE FAMILY
2. THE SENATOR (segment of THE BOLD ONES)
3. THE FLIP WILSON SHOW
4. ANDERSONVILLE TRIAL (HOLLYWOOD TV THEATRE presentation)
5. Jack Klugman, THE ODD COUPLE
6. Jean Stapleton, ALL IN THE FAMILY
7. Hal Holbrook, THE SENATOR
8. Susan Hampshire, THE FIRST CHURCHILLS (MASTERPIECE THEATRE)
9. George C. Scott, THE PRICE (HALLMARK HALL OF FAME)
10. Lee Grant, THE NEON CEILING (NBC TV Movie)
11. Fielder Cook, THE PRICE
12. Tracy Keenan Wynn, Marvin Schwartz, TRIBES (TV Movie)

2. 1971–72
1. ALL IN THE FAMILY
2. ELIZABETH R (MASTERPIECE THEATRE)
3. THE CAROL BURNETT SHOW
4. BRIAN'S SONG (ABC TV Movie)
5. Carroll O'Connor, ALL IN THE FAMILY
6. Jean Stapleton, ALL IN THE FAMILY
7. Peter Falk, COLUMBO
8. Glenda Jackson, ELIZABETH R
9. Keith Mitchell, "Catherine Howard," SIX WIVES OF HENRY VIII
10. Glenda Jackson, "Shadow in the Sun," ELIZABETH R
11. Tom Gries, THE GLASS HOUSE, (CBS TV Movie)
12. Allan Sloan, TO ALL MY FRIENDS ON SHORE (TV Movie)

3. 1972–73
1. ALL IN THE FAMILY
2. THE WALTONS
3. THE JULIE ANDREWS SHOW
4. A WAR OF CHILDREN (CBS TV Movie)
5. Jack Klugman, THE ODD COUPLE
6. Mary Tyler Moore, THE MARY TYLER MOORE SHOW
7. Richard Thomas, THE WALTONS
8. Michael Learned, The WALTONS
9. Laurence Olivier, LONG DAY'S JOURNEY INTO NIGHT
10. Cloris Leachman, A BRAND NEW LIFE (ABC TV Movie)
11. Joe Sargent, THE MARCUS/NELSON MURDERS (TV Movie)
12. Abby Mann, THE MARCUS/NELSON MURDERS

Mary Tyler Moore won three Emmys for Best Leading Actress in a Comedy Series (as did Jean Stapleton), making it appear that other fine comedy actresses were incapable of doing similar outstanding work.

4. 1973–74

1. M*A*S*H
2. UPSTAIRS, DOWNSTAIRS (MASTERPIECE THEATRE)
3. THE CAROL BURNETT SHOW
4. THE AUTOBIOGRAPHY OF MISS JANE PITMAN (CBS TV Movie)
5. Alan Alda, M*A*S*H
6. Mary Tyler Moore, THE MARY TYLER MOORE SHOW
7. Telly Savalas, KOJAK
8. Michael Learned, THE WALTONS
9. Hal Holbrook, THE PUEBLO (ABC THEATRE Presentation)
10. Cicely Tyson, THE AUTOBIOGRAPHY OF MISS JANE PITMAN
11. John Korty, THE AUTOBIOGRAPHY OF MISS JANE PITMAN
12. Fay Kanin, TELL ME WHERE IT HURTS (G.E. THEATRE Presentation)

5. 1974–75

1. THE MARY TYLER MOORE SHOW
2. UPSTAIRS, DOWNSTAIRS (MASTERPIECE THEATRE)
3. THE CAROL BURNETT SHOW
4. THE LAW (NBC TV Movie)
5. Tony Randall, THE ODD COUPLE
6. Valerie Harper, RHODA
7. Robert Blake, BARETTA
8. Jean Marsh, UPSTAIRS, DOWNSTAIRS
9. Laurence Olivier, LOVE AMONG THE RUINS (ABC THEATRE)
10. Katharine Hepburn, LOVE AMONG THE RUINS

11. George Cukor, LOVE AMONG THE RUINS
12. James Costigan, LOVE AMONG THE RUINS

6. 1975–76

1. THE MARY TYLER MOORE SHOW
2. POLICE STORY
3. NBC'S SATURDAY NIGHT LIVE
4. ELEANOR AND FRANKLIN (ABC THEATRE)
5. Jack Albertson, CHICO AND THE MAN
6. Mary Tyler Moore, THE MARY TYLER MOORE SHOW
7. Peter Falk, COLUMBO
8. Michael Learned, THE WALTONS
9. Anthony Hopkins, THE LINDBERGH KIDNAPPING CASE (NBC TV Movie)
10. Susan Clark, BABE (CBS TV Movie)
11. Daniel Petrie, ELEANOR AND FRANKLIN: THE WHITE HOUSE YEARS
12. James Costigan, ELEANOR AND FRANKLIN: THE WHITE HOUSE YEARS

Considered by many as the only authentic cop show on the air, "Police Story" won an Emmy for the Best Dramatic Series of the 1975–76 Season. Produced by David Gerber for Columbia.

Jack Albertson, with his co-star, the late Freddie Prinz, won a well deserved Emmy for his characterization on "Chico and the Man," for the 1975–76 season.

7. 1976–77
1. THE MARY TYLER MOORE SHOW
2. UPSTAIRS, DOWNSTAIRS (MASTERPIECE THEATRE)
3. VAN DYKE AND COMPANY
4. ELEANOR AND FRANKLIN: THE WHITE HOUSE YEARS (ABC THEATRE)
   tied with: SYBIL (NBC BIG EVENT)
5. Carroll O'Connor, ALL IN THE FAMILY
6. Beatrice Arthur, MAUDE
7. James Garner, THE ROCKFORD FILES
8. Lindsay Wagner, THE BIONIC WOMAN
9. Ed Flanders, HARRY S. TRUMAN: PLAIN SPEAKING (PBS)
10. Sally Field, SYBIL
11. Daniel Petrie, ELEANOR AND FRANKLIN: THE WHITE HOUSE YEARS
12. Lane Slate, TAILGUNNER JOE (NBC BIG EVENT)

8. 1977–78
1. ALL IN THE FAMILY
2. THE ROCKFORD FILES
3. THE MUPPET SHOW
4. THE GATHERING (ABC TV Movie)
5. Carroll O'Connor, ALL IN THE FAMILY
6. Jean Stapleton, ALL IN THE FAMILY
7. Ed Asner, LOU GRANT
8. Sada Thompson, FAMILY
9. Fred Astaire, A FAMILY UPSIDE DOWN (NBC TV Movie)
10. Joanne Woodward, SEE HOW SHE RUNS (G.E. THEATRE)
11. David Lowell Rich, THE DEFECTION OF SIMAS KUDIRKA (CBS TV Movie)
12. George Rubino, THE LAST TENANT (ABC TV Movie)

9. 1978–79*
1. TAXI
2. LOU GRANT
3. STEVE AND EYDIE CELEBRATE IRVING BERLIN

---

*NOTE *To make things more difficult and confusing, during the above '78–79 season awards, the categories were slightly adjusted. The Leading Actor/Actress in a Series was changed by the following added words: "In a Continuing or Single Performance." What this means is that the series regulars now compete with all their guest stars in the Emmy sweepstakes. You no longer have to have your own series to win the Best Performance Emmy on a series. Perhaps it was a move of economy, since it did eliminate two Emmys, those that had been given for Best Actor/Actress for a Single Performance in a Drama or Comedy Series. These were dumped in with the series' leads awards. Not a very fair move, since often the best-written parts in a series are the weekly guest-starring roles which attract high-quality actors. And—how can I say this without sounding overly critical?—it was, well, stupid, as evidenced by the fact that three of the Series' Leads Emmys were won by guest stars that year.*

4. FRIENDLY FIRE (ABC TV Movie)
5. Carroll O'Connor, ALL IN THE FAMILY
6. Ruth Gordon, "Sugar Mama," TAXI
7. Ron Liebman, KAZ
8. Mariette Hartley, "Married," THE INCREDIBLE HULK
9. Peter Strauss, THE JERICHO MILE (ABC TV Movie)
10. Bette Davis, STRANGERS: THE STORY OF A MOTHER AND DAUGHTER (CBS)
11. David Greene, FRIENDLY FIRE
12. Patrick Nolan, Michael Mann, THE JERICHO MILE

10. 1979–80

1. TAXI
2. LOU GRANT
3. IBM PRESENTS BARYSHNIKOV ON BROADWAY
4. THE MIRACLE WORKER (NBC TV Movie)
5. Richard Mulligan, SOAP
6. Cathryn Damon, SOAP
7. Ed Asner, LOU GRANT
8. Barbara Bel Geddes, DALLAS
9. Powers Boothe, GUYANA TRAGEDY: THE STORY OF JIM JONES
10. Patty Duke Astin, THE MIRACLE WORKER
11. Marvin Chomsky, ATTICA (ABC TV Movie)
12. David Chase, OFF THE MINNESOTA STRIP (ABC TV Movie)

10 STARS WHO APPEARED AT THE 32nd EMMY AWARDS SHOW DESPITE THE ACTORS' STRIKE BOYCOTT

Never have so many dressed up so well to honor so many no-shows. The actors' boycott organized by M*A*S*H's Mike Farrell kept practically every actor away from the 32nd Emmy Award Ceremonies on Sunday, September 7, 1980. The hosts (Lee Remick, Michael Landon, and Bob Newhart) didn't show; the presenters didn't show; and only one winning actor showed. Most noticeably absent were the big winners: Ed Asner, Barbara Bel Geddes, Richard Mulligan, Cathryn Damon, and Johnny Carson, as well as Harry Morgan, Loretta Swit, Nancy Marchand, and Stuart Margolin. If everybody was absent or out of town, who did show up? Mostly it was a crowd of disappointed fans, who had hoped that the actors wouldn't try to make an issue of an annual ceremony that honors them and their achievements.

The no-show hosts, Bob Newhart and Michael Landon, failed to make good their commitment to emcee the 32nd Annual Emmy Awards because of the actors' strike. They were replaced at the last minute by Dick Clark and Steve Allen.

However, it wasn't a total wipeout. Some stars did show up:

1. DICK CLARK, emergency emcee
2. STEVE ALLEN, last-minute co-host. Both Allen and Clark announced on the air that they were donating their fees to the Screen Actors Guild emergency strike fund. Allen recalled that his sons had passed an autograph book around at the 1955 Emmys and collected hundreds of signa-

tures. For Sunday night's ceremony, Allen pulled out a piece of paper the size of a matchbook, and said he could get everybody present to sign on it and still have room left over.

3. TOM and DICK SMOTHERS, who led off the evening with some comedy, and then handed out the first two awards. Tom Smothers: "Sure, I support the strike, but I had made a commitment to appear on the Emmy telecast. But even if I hadn't, I would have come anyway. Everyone should have attended. Boycotting the show doesn't help the strike. The performers would have scored more points by being here. After all, this is a show to honor our craft."

4. BARBI BENTON, the prettiest package of the evening: "I was hoping I would be the smallest star here."

5. JIM STAFFORD, co-host of "Those Incredible Animals"

6. RHONDA BATES, co-host of "Speak Up, America"

7. JAYNE KENNEDY, co-host of "Speak Up, America"

8. KAREN LYNN GORNEY, of *Saturday Night Fever* fame

9. DAVID COPPERFIELD, of the TV special, "Magician"

10. POWERS BOOTHE, the only winner present to accept his Emmy. He won Outstanding Performance by an Actor in a Dramatic Special for his powerful portrayal of the Reverend Jim Jones in "The Guyana Tragedy." Said Boothe: "This was my night. How could I not show up?"

5 TANGIBLE RESULTS OF THE ACTORS' BOYCOTT OF THE EMMYS

1. The "Emmy Awards Show" was thirty-second in the Nielsen ratings of the week's sixty-three prime-time shows. It was the smallest audience attracted by the show in recent years, garnering only a 29 percent share, with an estimated 11.6 million homes.

   Said Mike Farrell, who helped organize the boycott: "I don't interpret the low rating as a victory in any way. The intention was simply to support the strike. The point we made is a tremendously strong statement about our unity."

2. The lower-than-expected ratings affected NBC financially. When a program unexpectedly reaches fewer people than anticipated, a network normally offers other commercial time to the advertiser at no additional cost to make up the difference.

3. More happily, NBC, in wanting to show its gratitude to the Smothers Brothers for helping to bail out the Emmy show, boosted its order from one "Smothers Brothers Special" to two, and placed an order for four scripts on a tentative Smothers series.

4. And, NBC gave Steve Allen the go-ahead for six segments of "The Steve

Allen Comedy Hour," to which the network had only committed for one pilot episode. The show then premiered on October 18, 1980.

5. The Academy of Television Arts and Sciences lost $100,000 because of the boycott. Syndication contracts for the TV Awards Show were dropped in fourteen countries for lack of stars, resulting in $40,000 loss of revenues; and $60,000 was lost on the catered banquet which was supposed to have broken even, but nobody attended.

THE 1980 HUMANITAS AWARDS FOR TELEVISION PROGRAMS THAT "COMMUNICATE ENRICHING HUMAN VALUES"

The winners were selected from among 264 entries by the Human Family Institute, which bestows the awards annually with cash prizes totaling $50,000. The money comes from the Lilly Endowment Inc. of Indianapolis.

1. TOP PRIZE
   $25,000 to Stephen Kandel, Barry Neil Kaufman, and Suzi Lyte Kaufman for "Son-Rise," an NBC-TV movie based on the Kaufmans' experiences in transforming their son from autism to normalcy. The judges cited it for "its celebration of the healing power of love."
2. ONE-HOUR CATEGORY
   $15,000 to Sally Robinson for her "Thanksgiving" episode of the ABC series, "Family," in which Henry Fonda appeared as a grandfather whose growing senility posed problems for the Lawrence family. The judges commended "its compassionate treatment of the aging process and the problems it creates for all those involved."
3. HALF-HOUR CATEGORY
   $10,000 to Alan Alda and James Jay Rubinfier for "Dreams," an episode of CBS' "M*A*S*H," which the judges praised for its "hopefilled portrayal of human beings who give of themselves to the point where it hurts, and then some, to help fellow human beings through a situation that could otherwise warrant despair."
4. JOURNALISM CATEGORY
   A nonmonetary award was given for "We're Moving Up! The Hispanic Migration," an NBC News documentary produced by Anthony Potter and reported by Bill McLaughlin. The judges cited its "profound affirmation of the human dignity of the latest and largest addition to the American melting pot as effective audience education."

This was the sixth annual Humanitas Awards, and looking ahead, Ray Bradbury, a trustee of the Human Family Institute, asked rhetorically: "Afraid of the future? I am not. For I feel we go there with our robot friends, and one robot device is television, which is no more and no less than the humanity we program into it. I do not fear futures so much as people who forget that they are the future and must behave so as to insure it."

DON RICKLES' 7 FAVORITE ZINGERS HE DELIVERED ON "THE DEAN MARTIN FRIARS CLUB ROASTS"

1. To ERNEST BORGNINE
   "Look at your face! Was anyone else hurt in the accident? You look like a cab hit you."
2. To LORNE GREENE:
   "I've always wanted to interview a distinguished actor like you. My first question is, 'Are there many flies hanging around your horse?' "
3. To FRANK SINATRA
   "Come right in, Frank. Make yourself at home. Hit somebody."

Comedian with the barbed tongue, Don Rickles is a master roaster on "The Dean Martin Friars Club Roasts."

4. To JOE NAMATH
"You're a great guy to invite to a party. I love the way you sit in the corner all night and pump up footballs."
5. To golfer LEE TREVINO
"Lee, you're a great golfer, except during the lettuce festival—then you fall apart. If you ever stop playing good golf, you'll go back to your old job—selling kaopectate."
6. To LUCILLE BALL
"Lucy, I spoke with your children, and they think of you all the time. They keep wondering how you're going to split up the will."
7. To DIANA ROSS
"If you quit show business, you can become my maid. Do you do windows?"

"The Dean Martin Friars Club Roasts" are occasional specials that grew out of "The Dean Martin Show" ('65–74). The original show was called the "Man of the Week Celebrity Roast," telecast in 1973, in which celebrities seated at a banquet dais tossed comic insults at the guest of honor. This feature of his comedy-variety hour proved so popular that after Martin's regular series ended, the "Roasts" continued on NBC as special events.

DON RICKLES' 6 FAVORITE ZINGERS DIRECTED AT HIM ON "THE DEAN MARTIN FRIARS CLUB ROASTS"

1. DEAN MARTIN
"Don Rickles is the greatest comic in the world. He's the funniest and nicest man in the world. But, you know—I'm drunk, and when I'm drunk, I'm the biggest liar in the world."
2. JOHNNY CARSON
"Don Rickles will always work—as long as there's no one around with talent."
3. PAT McCORMICK
"Don would have gotten here earlier, only he was out walking his rat."
4. MILTON BERLE
"What could you possibly say about Don Rickles that hasn't already been said about hemorrhoids?"
5. FRANK SINATRA
"I like Don Rickles. But that's because I have no taste."
6. BOB HOPE
"There's one thing that can be said about Don Rickles, but I never use that kind of language."

4

"ROOTS":
The Early Years and Other Beginnings

Or: *The B.C. Years—Before Color*

CHAPTER

ED SULLIVAN'S 9 ACTS ON THE TV PREMIERE OF "TOAST OF THE TOWN" ON JUNE 20, 1948

Syndicated columnist Ed Sullivan, who became known as the Great Stone Face because he registered all emotions from glee to disdain with the same seemingly dour expression, was a prime shaper of early television programing. His Sunday night variety show, which premiered as "Toast of the Town" in 1948 and became "The Ed Sullivan Show" in 1955, evolved into an American institution that ran continuously for twenty-four years; a record bested only by "The Tonight Show" and "Walt Disney."

His program smacked of vaudeville, but included ballet, opera, and scenes from Broadway hits, and, with Sullivan's nose for news, he often featured acts and performers who were timely headliners. Among the stars who made their TV debut on his show are Bob Hope, Charles Laughton, Martin and Lewis, Dinah Shore, the Beatles, and Walt Disney. Although Elvis Presley had already appeared on network TV, his appearances on "The Ed Sullivan Show" are best remembered.

Sullivan's total budget for talent on his premiere show was only $400, yet he was able to assemble this lineup:

1. DEAN MARTIN AND JERRY LEWIS, in their television debut, took the lion's share of the talent budget: $200
2. Composers RODGERS and HAMMERSTEIN, singing a medley of their great show tunes
3. Concert pianist EUGENE LIST, playing Chopin
4. Singing fireman JOHN KOKOMAN, from the Bronx
5. Fight referee RUBY GOLDSTEIN, discussing the forthcoming Joe Louis vs. Jersey Joe Walcott heavyweight title bout
6. Dancer KATHRYN LEE, with the six original JUNE TAYLOR DANCERS, then known as the TOASTETTES
7. Comedian LEE GOODMAN
8. Comedian JIM KIRKWOOD
9. A leggy line of COPACABANA CHORUS GIRLS, at $8 each

Former columnist Ed Sullivan premiered on TV on June 20, 1948, with "Toast of the Town," which was renamed "The Ed Sullivan Show." Defining the variety show for television, he managed to stay on the air for twenty-four seasons, making his the third longest-running show in the history of TV.

9 FIRSTS IN SPORTS TELECASTING

1. FIRST SPORTING EVENT ever televised in the U.S. was a college baseball game between Columbia University and Princeton in New York City on May 17, 1939. The announcer was Bill Stern.
2. FIRST HEAVYWEIGHT BOXING MATCH featured Max Baer vs. Lou Nova from Yankee Stadium on June 1, 1939. Sam Taub was the announcer.
3. FIRST MAJOR LEAGUE BASEBALL GAME on the air was a double-header from Ebbets Field between the Dodgers and the Cincinnati Reds on August 26, 1939. Red Barber was the announcer.
4. FIRST COLLEGE FOOTBALL GAME was Fordham vs. Waynesburg on September 30, 1939. Bill Stern announced the game from Triboro Stadium on Randalls Island in New York.
5. FIRST PROFESSIONAL FOOTBALL GAME featured Philadelphia Eagles vs. Brooklyn Dodgers in Ebbets Field on October 22, 1939. Announcer was Allen "Skip" Waltz.
6. FIRST TV NETWORK SPONSOR OF A SPORTING EVENT was Gillette, with the telecast of the Joe Louis vs. Billy Conn Heavyweight Boxing match on June 19, 1946.
7. FIRST NETWORK COLLEGE FOOTBALL TELECAST featured the Army/Navy game in 1945, on a four-city hookup over NBC.
8. FIRST NETWORK WORLD SERIES TELECAST came in 1947 with the New York Yankees vs. the Brooklyn Dodgers in Yankee Stadium on NBC.
9. FIRST SUPER BOWL featured the Green Bay Packers vs. the Kansas City Raiders on January 6, 1967, was carried on both NBC and CBS, and is among the highest-rating single programs in the history of television.

ART LINKLETTER'S LIST OF 10 PERSONALITIES WHO SHAPED EARLY TV

Certainly an important and popular personality who shaped the development of early audience participation television, Art Linkletter made a highly successful transition from radio, where he was already a well-known star. From 1950, he was continuously on TV for two decades, at times in two different shows, all of his own creation. He entertained us with "Life with Linkletter" ('50–52); "House Party" ('52–69), which was the forerunner of the afternoon talk and participation shows; "People Are Funny" ('54–61); "The Art Linkletter Show" ('62–63); "Hollywood Talent Scouts" ('65–66); and went full circle with "Life with Linkletter" ('69–70). His interviews with children on "House Party" made us all agree when he observed, "Kids say the darnedest things." And in the early '60s, he guest-hosted "The To-

The first really zany comedian on TV, Ernie Kovacs was one of a handful of personalities who shaped early television humor.

night Show" before Johnny Carson began his tenure. Linkletter's participation in television was massive, and his influence was greatly felt.

Said Linkletter: "There were a lot of us who had something to do with how early television grew up, but some of us were more important, like these folks":

1. MILTON BERLE, "Mr. Television," the first TV superstar
2. SID CAESAR and his "Show of Shows," a comedy classic
3. LUCILLE BALL, the premiere comedienne in TV history
4. ED SULLIVAN, who defined the variety show for TV
5. ERNIE KOVACS, the first really zany comic
6. OZZIE & HARRIET, preeminent in the wonderfully innocent world of family shows
7. RED SKELTON, one of the world's best clowns
8. JACK BENNY, who successfully crossed over from radio
9. BURNS & ALLEN, a great comedy team, also from radio
10. BOB HOPE, who has lasted longer at the top than any other comedian

ART LINKLETTER'S 10 MEMORABLE EARLY STUNTS ON "PEOPLE ARE FUNNY"

"People Are Funny" began on the radio in 1942, was enormously successful, and twelve years later debuted on TV for a seven-year run. During its first three seasons on television, the radio broadcasts were the soundtrack from the TV show. Later, the TV show was a film of the already-aired radio show. Participants were picked from the audience by host Linkletter and involved in some stunt that showed that people are funny. Sometimes participants were given an assignment during the week and asked to return to tell how they did. In the 1956–57 season, a computer matchup feature was added to the show. The couples that were matched by the computer always got a "homework" assignment.

"Here are ten memorable stunts":

1. We hired an actor to hold interviews for volunteers for a dangerous scientific mission—the first trip to the moon. With hidden cameras we recorded the interviews, which were marvelous. But we had a lot of disappointed volunteers on our hands when they found out it was only a TV show, instead of the real thing.

2. We had lion trainer Clyde Beatty on the show, and we shamed a man into going into the animal cage after a housewife from the audience went in and snapped the whip at the lions. What we didn't tell him was that the housewife was actually Mrs. Beatty. So when he reluctantly went into an empty cage with a chair and a whip, we opened the animal gate and sent in a dozen cats—alley cats.

3. We gave one contestant $250 for letting us put a huge box in his back-yard for a week. When he returned, I told him I'd trade him the box for the $250, but he declined, then nearly fainted when he found out the box contained a power boat and sporting equipment worth about $1,400.

4. A native boy named Klenre on Kwajelein Island found one of the plastic containers we'd dropped over the South Pacific. He won $1,000 and a trip to Hollywood to be on the show.

5. On another show we read love letters that a man had written to a girl friend long before he was married; but it had been something he'd never told his wife about. He admitted the letter sounded familiar, like maybe something he'd written to his wife, but she denied it. That's when we brought out his old girl friend. He almost fell down.

6. We arranged for a bank clerk to run out on the Los Angeles Coliseum football field during an actual game to tackle Bob Waterfield as he started a run. Our photographers were waiting to shoot pictures of him after he accomplished his surprise attack, but some cops grabbed him and off he went to jail. It took us the better part of the day to get him out.

7. To see if people would butt in, we sent a man out to siphon gas from a half dozen cars parked along Sunset near Vine in the middle of the day. No one bothered him.

8. To one man we gave a dream week with a valet, a beautiful secretary, new clothes, a cook, and people to do things for him every time he turned around. When he came back after living the life of a millionaire for a week, he said: "I loved every minute of it, but I'm glad it's over. That sort of thing could get monotonous."

9. One contestant was offered a trip to Hawaii for two if he could go one entire week without breaking a single law. He was sure he could, and said he had when he returned. That's when I pointed out that he'd neglected to break the tax stamp on the top of his pack of cigarettes, which by federal law is supposed to be broken when the product is used. Boy, was he surprised.

10. I told the audience that whoever made the biggest contribution to the Community Chest in the next thirty seconds could hit me in the face with a chocolate meringue pie. A little white-haired lady paid $250 for the privilege to nearly knock me off the stage with a gooey pie on national television. Just goes to show you . . . people are funny!

MILTON BERLE'S NONLIST OF THE COMICS WHO DOMINATED EARLY TV

If any one personality can be said to have dominated the early struggling, virginal years of infant television, it has to be—no contest— Milton Berle. His first appearance was on the debut telecast of "The Texaco Star Theatre" on June 8, 1948. He was already relatively famous for his radio and movie work, but not what you'd call a star. Not even close. But now, on TV, within four months, he was nothing short of a national institution. His comedy/variety show became the most popular hour of the week, and stayed that way through the early years of TV. People stayed home to watch him. He became known as "Mr. Television" and "Mr. Tuesday Night," and it's said that he sold more TV sets than any advertising campaign because people bought the newfangled set just to see this crazy comic everybody was talking about. With all due respect to Davy Crockett hats and Batmania, Uncle Miltie was the first national TV craze.

Said Berle: "Those were wonderful crazy days. But how can I possibly make up a list of the comics who dominated early TV? How can it be *my* list? I mean, if you want to know who the comedians were who made early TV what it was, you can look it up in any of the hundreds of books that have been published.

Milton Berle, "Mr. Television," displays the flamboyant style that made him king of Tuesday nights, and sold more TV sets than RCA because everybody wanted to see him in action.

"There was Sid Caesar, Imogene Coca, Carl Reiner, Howie Morris, Jackie Gleason, Phil Silvers, Jack Benny, Bob Hope, Groucho, Red Skelton, Martha Raye. They're all there in the books. These people are part of history. So it can't be *my* list. I couldn't possibly choose one over another anyway. It's impossible."

22 BIG-NAME MOVIE STARS TODAY WHO STARTED OUT PAYING DUES IN EPISODIC TELEVISION IN FORGETTABLE ROLES

Following each star's name are some of the series on which he/she has guested, and on which you can catch each of them whenever these oldies run in syndication. Watch for them!

1. CHARLES BRONSON—"Alfred Hitchcock Presents," "Gunsmoke," "Laramie," Have Gun Will Travel," "Bonanza," "Fugitive," "Big Valley," "The Virginian," "Dr. Kildare," "Untouchables," "Rawhide," "Combat"
2. ROBERT REDFORD—"Twilight Zone," "Alfred Hitchcock Presents," "Perry Mason," "Maverick," "Naked City," "The Virginian," "Route 66," "Untouchables," "Dr. Kildare," "Cheyenne," "Combat"
3. ROBERT DUVALL—"Twilight Zone," "Alfred Hitchcock Presents," "Outer Limits," "The Virginian," "Untouchables," "Voyage to the Bottom of the Sea," "FBI," "Naked City," "Wild Wild West," "Name of the Game," "Mod Squad," "Hawk," "Combat"
4. MARTIN SHEEN—"Cannon," "Outer Limits," "Columbo," "Mannix," "FBI," "Hawaii Five-0," "Ironside," "Medical Center," "Hawk," "Mod Squad," "Route 66," "Mission Impossible," "Defenders"
5. BURT REYNOLDS—"Love American Style," "FBI," "Gentle Ben," "Flipper," "Route 66," "Branded," "Zane Grey Theater"
6. JACK NICHOLSON—"Dr. Kildare," "Tales of Wells Fargo," "Hawaiian Eye," "Andy Griffith Show"
7. RYAN O'NEAL—"My Three Sons," "The Virginian," "Perry Mason," "Wagon Train," "Bachelor Father," "Dobie Gillis," "Search"
8. KATHARINE ROSS—"Alfred Hitchcock Theatre," "The Virginian," "Gunsmoke," "Big Valley," "Ben Casey," "Loner," "Run for Your Life"
9. WARREN BEATTY—"Suspicion," "Dobie Gillis," "Studio One," "Kraft Theatre"
10. JAMES CAAN—"Alfred Hitchcock Presents," "FBI," "Wagon Train," "Combat"
11. DYAN CANNON—"Medical Center," "77 Sunset Strip," "Untouchables," "Bat Masterson," "Wanted Dead Or Alive"
12. LEE MARVIN—"Twilight Zone," "Dr. Kildare," "Untouchables," "Bonanza," "Wagon Train," "Route 66," "Ben Casey," "The Virginian," "Combat"
13. STEVE McQUEEN—"Alfred Hitchcock Presents," "Trackdown," "Tales of Wells Fargo," "West Point"
14. CLINT EASTWOOD—"Navy Log," "West Point"
15. GENE HACKMAN—"FBI," "I Spy," "Defenders," "Hawk," "Invaders," "Iron Horse"
16. DUSTIN HOFFMAN—"Naked City," "Defenders," "Doctors/Nurses"
17. JON VOIGHT—"Naked City," "Gunsmoke," "NYPD," "Defenders"
18. ANN-MARGRET—"Here's Lucy," "The Flintstones" (voice only for a movie-star character named Ann-Margrock)
19. DONALD SUTHERLAND—"Name of the Game," "The Saint," "Court-Martial"

20. WALTER MATTHAU—"Alfred Hitchcock Presents," "Naked City," "Rogues," "Route 66," "Dr. Kildare," "Eleventh Hour"
21. JACK LEMMON—"Zane Grey Theatre," "Playhouse 90," "Danger," "Alcoa Theatre"
22. PAUL NEWMAN—"Playhouse 90," "Appointment with Adventure," "Danger," "The Mask," "The Web," "Philco Playhouse"

RICHARD LAMPARSKI'S LIST OF 10 TV PERFORMERS FROM THE PAST WHO ARE MOST ASKED ABOUT

Richard Lamparski is a celebrity head hunter, though not in the usual sense. He is not an autograph hound, although he has never been known to refuse one. What he does is locate famous personalities from the past to satisfy that lingering curiosity in us all about what happened to a favorite star of days gone by. Well, Lamparski has made it his business to find out. In the mid-'60s, he created a hugely successful radio show called "Whatever Became of . . . ?," and a few years later turned the radio show's success into a series of equally popular books by the same name. He's still going strong, doing radio shows, telephone interviews, lectures, and in the process has become a bit of a celebrity himself. Perhaps in twenty years, someone will ask: "Whatever became of Richard Lamparski?"

In the meantime, he's still hunting those celebs of yesteryear, and here are the TV stars he's most often asked about:

1. DICK YORK of BEWITCHED ('64–72)
   From 1964 to 1969, he played the husband of witch Samantha Stevens (Elizabeth Montgomery). Personal problems led to his being replaced by Dick Sargent, who stayed with the series to the end in 1972. York has been inactive in acting since.
2. The cast of FATHER KNOWS BEST ('54–60)
   We all know what's happened to Robert Young, who started in the series in radio in 1949. He did "Marcus Welby, M.D." ('69–76) and is now giving Mrs. Olson a run for her coffee money on TV commercials. But what about Jane Wyatt? Elinor Donahue? Billy Gray? Lauren Chapin?

   Jane Wyatt is still occasionally active, and in recent years guested as Mr. Spock's mother on "Star Trek." Elinor Donahue is married to TV producer Harry Ackerman and works constantly; she's been a regular on the following series: "The Andy Griffith Show" ('60–61); "Many Happy Returns" ('64–65); "The Odd Couple" ('72–75); "Mulligan's Stew" ('77); "Please Stand By" ('78–79); "Doctors' Private Lives" ('79). Billy Gray rarely does any acting, and is now a champion motorcycle rider on the dirt bike circuit. And Lauren Chapin has had bouts with drugs and liquor, and is now a Born-Again Christian.

In 1964, struggling actor Walter Matthau had the disease of the week on "Dr. Kildare." Here he is with Raymond Massey, Lee Meriwether, and Richard Chamberlain. Two years later, Matthau became a star in "Fortune Cookie" and won an Oscar doing it.

George Reeves thought it was the greatest thing that ever happened to him when he was cast as TV's "Superman." When the series folded, his career seemed to do the same, and in 1959, he reportedly committed suicide, though some still feel that he was murdered.

3. The cast from SUPERMAN ('51–57)

In June of 1959, George Reeves, who had become world-famous as Superman, shot and killed himself. Since there was no note, his reasons for suicide are now merely speculation; he was frustrated in trying to find work after "Superman" ceased production and he found himself typecast. Both Jack Larson, who played Jimmy Olsen, and Noel Neill, who played Lois Lane, also had trouble finding work thereafter, and have since quit acting. Larson now works in advertising in Los Angeles.

4. The cast of LEAVE IT TO BEAVER ('57–63)

This was one of the classic family comedy series of an era that still clung to innocence. Those of us who grew up with it remember the show as being something special. Following the close of the show in 1963, Jerry Mathers, who played Beaver Cleaver, and Tony Dow, who played his brother, Wally, found it tough to get other work. But now they've found new careers, as a team, doing repertory dinner theatre around the country. Hugh Beaumont, who played Beaver's dad, is retired and living in Minnesota. Barbara Billingsley is no longer very active, but she still does an occasional role, most recently in *Airplane* (1968).

5. BUFFALO BOB SMITH of HOWDY DOODY ('47–60)

Smith created the first popular children's show, and stayed on the air with it for thirteen years. In addition to creating Howdy Doody himself, Smith created such characters as Clarabell Cow, Cornelius Cobb, Chief Thunderthud, who frequently shouted "Kowabunga!", and a host of others. The show always took place in Doodyville, and was live before a group of youngsters sitting in the Peanut Gallery. In 1970, Buffalo Bob toured the nostalgia circuit, appearing at colleges and fairs. Then in 1976, he hosted an updated version of "Howdy Doody." He currently lives in Florida, a wealthy man, and owner of many TV and radio stations.

6. JACK LESCOULIE of TODAY ('52–present)

The show that now brings you Tom Brokaw, originally brought you Dave Garroway and Jack Lescoulie, who remained with the show until 1963, two years longer than Garroway. During his eleven-year "Today" show tenure, he also hosted "Brains & Brawn," 1958; "Meet the Champions," 1956–1957, which consisted of fifteen-minute sports interviews; "Tonight: America After Dark," from January to July 1957; and "1-2-3-Go!" 1961–1962, an educational program that he co-hosted with ten-year-old Richard Thomas, who later became John-Boy on "The Waltons." Today, Lescoulie lives in retirement in Connecticut, though he could get work at the network level if he wanted.

7. MARY HARTLINE of SUPER CIRCUS ('49–56)

As the pert blonde assistant to ringmaster Claude Kirchner, Hartline had quite a following. Today she is a socialite in Palm Beach, Florida.

8. IRISH McCALLA of SHEENA, QUEEN OF THE JUNGLE ('55–56)

Based on the comic book character, this half-hour adventure strip was filmed in Mexico and featured the statuesque McCalla as the leopard-skin-clad female counterpart to Tarzan. Her acting aspirations, she found, were not great; she turned to art, and has been quite successful and happy. Now living in Malibu, she may show up in a special guest part in the planned TV Movie reprise of "Sheena."

9. GUY MITCHELL of THE GUY MITCHELL SHOW ('57–58)
Mitchell was a popular recording artist of the '50s, who wound up with his own musical variety show for the better part of a season. In 1961, he co-starred with Audie Murphy in the short-lived Western series "Whispering Smith." Today, he lives in seclusion in Southern California.

10. FAYE EMERSON of I'VE GOT A SECRET ('52–67)
Fayzie, as she was affectionately known, was an immensely popular quiz and game show celebrity, who was also one of the first network women interviewers. Part of her notoriety was her marvelous cleavage, which she displayed with true bravura. A witty, delightful socialite, she also hosted "Paris Cavalcade of Fashions," 1948–1949. "The Faye Emerson Show," in 1950, and "Of All Things," in the summer of 1956. After "I've Got a Secret" left network TV, she went to Europe for an extended stay—and never came back. When last heard from, she was living in Majorca with no plans of returning.

Buffalo Bob Smith with two of the famous characters he created, Clarabelle the Clown, and Howdy Doody. "Howdy Doody" was the first popular children's show and remained on the air for thirteen years. Today Smith lives in semi-retirement in Florida. (Clarabelle is none other than Bob Keeshan, who went on to his own show as "Captain Kangaroo.")

5
CHAPTER

"LOVE, AMERICAN STYLE":
Sex and the Small Screen

Or: *How I Lost It on the Boob Tube*

THE FIRST 4 TV SHOWS TO FEATURE FRONTAL NUDITY

Even more than violence, nudity is the most censored commodity on television. Only rarely has a TV program or special gotten away with it.

1. STEAMBATH

   A HOLLYWOOD TELEVISION THEATRE Presentation on PBS, was a ninety-minute special, originally aired on May 4, 1973, and then repeated in August 1976. Written by Bruce Jay Friedman, the comedy play was set in a New York City steambath and was controversial for: (1) its portrayal of God as a Puerto Rican steambath attendant and (2) the frontal nudity of Valerie Perrine throughout most of the show. There was so much excitement and argument about the presentation that many PBS stations refused to carry it the first time around, but favorable critical reaction far outweighed the negative. Even so, it was over three years before it was telecast again.

2. CAPTAINS AND THE KINGS

   An installment of NBC'S BEST-SELLERS ('76–77), was an anthology series made up of several serialized novels. Producer Jo Swerling remembers: "We had a lovely young actress named Beverly D'Angelo doing a love scene with Harvey Jason. It was your typical TV shot across her back to Harvey as she lets the negligee drop to the ground, and she's standing

66

there naked. Then we did closeups of Harvey, and then of Beverly. And in Beverly's closeup we put a TV matte on the lens so that our matted field of vision would cut just at the nipple line; that way it was obvious that she was nude but you didn't see any nipple. However, when the show was telecast, there were in the new TV sets variances in the field of vision, and half the sets in the country saw more of Beverly than the other half. The following morning, we got a panic call from Broadcast Standards that we had violated the nudity ban and that more people saw Beverly's nipples than didn't. But nobody complained. Nobody but the censors. The upshot was that we were told not to cut it that close in the future."

3. ROOTS

In January 1977, "Roots" had the distinction of being the first dramatic program on public television to feature frontal nudity. Specifically, in the African sequences there were numerous scenes clearly showing barebreasted African women, nipples and all. The justification was that it was necessary dramatically. NBC head censor, Jerry Stanley, didn't see it that way. "It was not necessary to the show, and if it wasn't necessary, I have to go one step farther and say that it was exploitative." Either way, "Roots" was a production with not only a lot of class, but a lot of clout. There was no real criticism for the nudity, and it opened a lot of doors as far as network programing boundaries were concerned, not only in content, but in form and theme as well.

4. GAUGUIN THE SAVAGE

The CBS biographical film about the French primitive artist almost didn't make its air date because of the concern about too much frontal nudity. Although CBS had told producer Douglas Benton that he could show anything on film that the artist had painted, when the film came in, the censors were shocked at the bare breasts—particularly in one scene on the beach in Tahiti where David Carradine as Gauguin painted his lover. According to a CBS censor: "The Tahitian girl kept swatting flies off her breast, and she kept jiggling. Three times. We felt that once was enough to make the point. Three jiggles was being a little lascivious." But when they asked that two of the three jiggles be cut, the executive producer Robert Wood, a former president of CBS-TV, threatened to withhold the two-and-a-half-hour film. Said Wood: "I think Doug and director Fielder Cook handled the nudity with exquisite taste. The real issue wasn't the bare breast, anyway. Breasts don't mean anything to the networks. It's the nipples they're worried about." Benton shrugged off the attempted censorship as a commonplace occurrence, and the show went on the air intact, three jiggles and all. There was no more said about it. As with "Roots," the scene was very *National Geographic.* Brown skin is okay to show (even under fire), but white skin isn't.

Universal-TV producer Robert O'Neill feels that white skin nudity is just around the corner. "In the next five years, you'll be seeing nudity on commercial television. It will eventually be acceptable. A few years ago, you couldn't say 'damn' or 'hell' on the air, and today it's widespread. The language usage has loosened up, and old Victorian barriers are going by the wayside. And I think it's healthy."

4 WELL-KNOWN STARS WHO FELL OUT OF THEIR DRESSES ON NATIONAL TV

In the early, struggling-for-an-identity, *live* TV days, there were moments of brilliance, of great improvisation, of spontaneity. The unexpected often happened.

1. FAYE EMERSON on THE FAYE EMERSON SHOW (1950)
   Faye Emerson was a very popular TV personality, a socialite who was one of the first female network interviewers, a sort of cocktail-party-circuit, early-day version of Barbara Walters. She was a regular on several quiz shows like "I've Got a Secret" (1952–58), on fashion and talk shows. Part of her attraction, at least to the male populace, was the plunging neckline

One of TV's early sex symbols, Dagmar leans her unmistakable qualifications over fellow panelist Ogden Nash's shoulders on "Masquerade Party" in 1955. Part of the blonde bombshell's legend was created when she accidentally fell out of dress on "Broadway Open House" in 1951.

on her wardrobe. It was her trademark. And on one fateful evening, her trademark slipped, and she exposed her ample self coast to coast.

2. DAGMAR on BROADWAY OPEN HOUSE (1951)
   This statuesque well-endowed "dumb" blonde was made famous on this granddaddy of TV talk shows, which was hosted by comedian Jerry Lester. She read inane poetry with a deadpan expression, sang, and danced. And as she did these things, it always seemed that her strapless gown slipped further and further, until one memorable evening it dropped all the way. The incident didn't damage her popularity one bit. In fact, after "Broadway Open House" closed when Lester left the show because he had been overshadowed by Dagmar, a minor celebrity whom he'd created, she got her own show.

3. JAYNE MANSFIELD on THE ACADEMY AWARDS SHOW (1957)
   The ever-buxom, ever-sensational sex symbol who had grabbed headlines at the Cannes Film Festival with her break-away dress, and who had upstaged Sophia Loren at the Hollywood Golden Globes Award dinner by literally exhaling her abundant assets out of her low-cut dress, did likewise on the seventh Oscar telecast.

4. INA RAY HUTTON on THE INA RAY HUTTON SHOW (1956)
   There were no male guests nor male regulars on Ina Ray Hutton's half-hour musical variety series. She was the conductor of an all-girl band, the first of which she had organized in 1935. For her TV show she assembled some fine musicians, all of whom played to beat the devil, as Ina Ray, always clad in a revealing gown, stirred them onward. On one occasion, as she conducted with exceptional vigor, one breast slipped from its hiding place. Ina Ray didn't miss a beat as she corrected the mishap and kept on swinging.

. . . AND 1 TV GAME-SHOW CONTESTANT

1. On THE PRICE IS RIGHT in the 1976–77 season, when announcer Johnny Olsen called out his famous, "Come on down!" the named contestant jumped from her seat and excitedly ran down the ramp to the stage. And on the way, her blouse snapped open exposing her breasts. The segment was left in the taped show, with an electronically implanted black modesty tape. Remembers host Bob Barker: "She came on down, and they came on out!"

. . . AND 1 HONORABLE MENTION

1. Exhibitionist, sex symbol, and star of a handful of Russ Meyer's X-rated, soft-core pornography films, EDY WILLIAMS has in recent years attended "The Academy Award Shows" in a full-length mink coat, which she then throws open to reveal the skimpiest, tiniest, sexiest bikini covering the barest of essentials, much to the delight of the crowd, photographers, and

Loni Anderson of "WKRP in Cincinnati" came in as the top choice of readers of *Hustler* magazine in its 1980 "Ten Most Wanted Million Dollar Muffs" contest. A dubious honor to say the least.

those of us at home. She deserves an Honorable Mention for effort. Keep trying, Edy.

... AND 1 MAN WHO FELL OUT OF HIS FLY

1. DAVE GARROWAY on THE TODAY SHOW (mid-'50s). The way the story goes is that Garroway, who was unaware that his fly was open, was involved in a musical sketch and inadvertently became an unintentional, coast-to-coast weenie wagger. Although it is difficult to find someone who actually witnessed this event, as it is with all stories of this nature, it is part and parcel of the legend of television. The particulars and the circumstances also vary according to who is telling the story, as, for example, this incident is also accredited to Jack Paar, among others.

MEASUREMENTS OF A DELECTABLE DOZEN TV DISHES

Name	Series	Bust/Waist/Hips
1. LYNDA CARTER	"Wonder Woman"	37½-25-35
2. LONI ANDERSON	"WKRP in Cincinnati"	37¼-24-35
3. CATHERINE BACH	"Dukes of Hazzard"	36-23-35

TV's "Wonder Woman" Lynda Carter inadvertently mixed sex with comic books to become a super sex symbol, attracting as many older viewers as kiddies.

4.	ANGIE DICKINSON	"Police Woman"	35-25-35½
5.	CHARLENE TILTON	"Dallas"	33-25-34
6.	LINDSAY WAGNER	"Bionic Woman"	34-24-36
7.	CHERYL LADD	"Charlie's Angels"	34-22½-33
8.	VICTORIA PRINCIPAL	"Dallas"	35½-24½-34¼
9.	FARRAH FAWCETT	"Charlie's Angels"	35-24-35
10.	JACLYN SMITH	"Charlie's Angels"	35-24-35
11.	CHER	"Cher"	35½-25½-36
12.	STEFANIE POWERS	"Hart to Hart"	36-25-35

MAN WATCHERS, INC. LISTS 10 ALL-TIME TV WATCHABLES

When Suzy Mallery, president and founder of Man Watchers, Inc., presented Burt Bacharach with The Most Watchable Man of the Year Award on "The Merv Griffin Show" in 1976, Merv asked, "What makes him so watchable?" "He's got a good bod," answered Suzy. "He's the new, desirable type of man, sensitive, intelligent, beautiful inside and out . . . plus we like his candle-flickering sexy eyes."

Man Watchers, Inc., an international organization launched in 1974, has over 2,000 members in the U.S., Canada, England, and Australia. Their slogan: "It's our turn-on, now." Members are armed with a man-watching manual called "The Joy of Looking," and a handful of "Well Worth Watching" cards, which are presented to attractive men when they are spied by a card-carrying member.

Man Watching, which is now a full-time project for Mallery, is a far cry from the days when she was Miss Suzy on "Romper Room" for twelve years, as well as on "Suzy Saturn" and "Children's Teacher."

In no particular order:

1. BURT BACHARACH
   Nothing but class, talent, sensitivity . . . and beautiful eyes.
2. PHIL DONAHUE, "The Phil Donahue Show" ('67–present)
   An ideal man, communicative, warm, and handsome too.
3. DAN RATHER, "60 Minutes" ('68–present)
   Classy, intelligent. Great Eyes.
4. JOHN RITTER, "Three's Company" ('77-present)
   Cute, sexy, looks real cuddly.
5. GAVIN MacLEOD, "The Love Boat" ('77–present)
   Radiant smile of a nice person. And some women consider chrome domes irresistible.
6. ALAN ALDA, "M*A*S*H" ('72–present)
   Low-key natural. Warmth of a concerned, caring individual.

7. JOHN DAVIDSON, "That's Incredible" ('80–present) and "The John Davidson Show" ('80–present)
   Wholesome, handsome. Looks great in tight clothes, or any kind of clothes. Great dimple.
8. DAVID HARTMAN, "Good Morning America" ('75–present)
   Great warmth and charm. The more you see him, the more you like him.
9. ROBERT URICH, "Vega$" ('78–present)
   Traditionally handsome, rugged. He's got it all.
10. CLIFTON DAVIS, "That's My Mama" ('74-75)
    Handsome and beautiful body. Super-sensitive mouth.

Man Watchers, Inc.'s president and founder, Suzy Mallery presents a "You're Lookin' Good!" award to Clifton Davis, star of "That's My Mama," in 1975.

... AND 3 TV TURKEYS (WHO SHOULD CLEAN UP THEIR ACTS)

1. MacLEAN STEVENSON, "Hello, Larry" ('79–80)
   ... for his bawdy body and bathroom humor on talk shows.
2. ROBERT BLAKE, "Baretta" ('75–78)
   ... for his attitude toward women, and sometimes men, too, as heard and seen on the talk shows.
3. MR. WHIPPLE, Charmin TV commercials ('76–present)
   ... for having nothing else to do in life but squeeze toilet paper.

9 TV PERFORMERS WHO BECAME FAMOUS FOR APPEARING IN DRAG

1. MILTON BERLE on TEXACO STAR THEATRE ('48–53)
   Uncle Miltie, the supreme vaudevillian, often burlesqued in drag to the amusement of TV viewers who made his show the popular hour of the week in video's Golden Age.
2. FLIP WILSON on THE FLIP WILSON SHOW ('70–74)
   One of the highlights of the show was his flip-side female alter-ego characterization, one cool lady named Geraldine Jones. Not only did "she" have terrific legs—really—and a boyfriend named "Killer," but she popularized the expression, "What you see is what you get!"
3. JAMIE FARR on M*A*S*H ('72–present)
   As Corporal Klinger, Farr seems willing to do anything to get out of the Army, including serving his entire stretch in nylon lingerie. His characterization has added depth and texture to the tableau of supporting players who have made M*A*S*H the most humanly funny sitcom in the history of television.
4. JOHN DAVIDSON on STREETS OF SAN FRANCISCO ('76)
   In a single guest appearance, he created a disturbingly haunting and memorable portrait of a female impressionist who was slowly being overcome by the psychotic personality of a dead film star. His impressions of Carol Channing and others were very good.
5. BILLY CRYSTAL on SOAP ('77–present)
   He portrays a transvestite, who is intent on getting a sex change operation. In one show, when his aunt Mary (Cathryn Damon) surprised him as he tried on one of her dresses, she exclaimed in shock: "Oh, Jodie!" Then taking a hard look at him, she noticed: "Oh, you wear it belted." Crystal takes delight in telling the story about the time he asked the producer for a raise, or something silly like that, and the producer cautioned goodnaturedly: "You better watch your step, or we'll give your character the operation and recast the part as a girl."

uest star Sammy Davis, Jr. is warned to keep his hands off the merchandise by eraldine Jones (Flip Wilson) on "The Flip Wilson Show" in 1973.

6. MAX BAER on THE BEVERLY HILLBILLIES ('62–71)

   He not only played Jed Clampett's (Buddy Ebsen) not-too-bright nephew, Jethro, but also Jethro's sister, Jethrene. At times it was difficult to tell which character was moonlighting as the other in this broad burlesque.

7. ROBERT BLAKE as BARETTA ('75–78)

   He played an unconventional street cop, much of whose work required him to be undercover and in disguise. One of Baretta's frequent disguises was as an old woman. It was both comic and strangely satisfying as hell to see an ''old woman'' *whup* the devil out of those nogoodniks.

8. PETER KASTNER as THE UGLIEST GIRL IN TOWN ('68–69)

   This was an asinine comedy (?) about Hollywood talent agent Tim Blair (Kastner), who disguised himself as a girl model, Timmie Blair, in order to be closer to his girlfriend, an actress who had returned to England. He couldn't afford the trip, and was able to arrange it by posing as a model, in a sort of Twiggy backlash. What can I tell you other than the title tells it like it was.

9. PETER SCOLARI and TOM HANKS are BOSOM BUDDIES ('80–81)

   Peter and Tom are our only tandem entry on this list; in dynel wigs and padded bras, they move into the Suan B. Anthony Hotel for Women—in the name of saving a buck, and because that's what this inept series is all about. The fact that they are surrounded by all those women in an apparently unexpected benefit, a la ''Some Like It Hot.'' But, some like it funny, too, and if this farce about two wolves in she's-clothing is still on the air when you read this, TV viewers are more desperate for new shows (following the actor's strike) than I thought.

... AND 1 HONORABLE MENTION

1. It's not widely known that LASSIE ('54–71), the most famous girl collie in the world, who was a big star on TV surviving four series formats, was actually—hold onto your socks—a *male* dog. A half dozen male dogs, as a matter of fact since the canines would be switched because of age or other problems. Now, this clandestine bit of sex hoodwinkery was only carried too far in the last season when Lassie, in a special seven-part story, met a male collie, fell in love, and bore him a litter of the cutest puppies ever seen on the tube. But if Lassie didn't have the puppies, who did? Had to have been a surrogate bitch, a la ''The Babymaker.''

6 CHAPTER

"THE HOT SEAT":
Network Censors

Or: *The Guys with Scissors Work in Mysterious Ways*

JERRY STANLEY'S LIST OF 3 CENSORSHIP FIRSTS ON "SHŌGUN"

Jerry Stanley, NBC Vice President, Broadcast Standards, West Coast, is, for all practical purposes, the head censor who is ultimately responsible for the day-to-day decisions about what goes—or doesn't go—on the air, as pertains to good taste and responsible broadcasting. Before becoming head censor in 1974, he served NBC in programing from 1956 to 1972, at which time he left the network to go to Universal Studios as a producer for two years.

Says Stanley: "We are the adversary in almost every case. And I hate that image. We, as censors, have a role to play that is very difficult, and we don't profess to be right every time. We try to be, but we make mistakes, too. Sometimes we're too cautious. But we have a responsibility to the 230 individual stations in our network, and if the people get up in arms about what one of our affiliate stations broadcasts, it could lose its license.

"Our object is to present, on behalf of our affiliate stations, on-the-air programing that will not be embarrassing to any of the viewers. And that certainly doesn't rule out any meaningful programing. Going back to 'Sybil' (1976) and 'Case of Rape' (1974), these are examples

of provocative subject matter that we helped get on the air. And with 'Shôgun' (1980), we broke some new ground."

1. For the first time on TV, you saw a man beheaded.
2. For the first time on TV, you heard the expression, "Piss on you!"
3. For the first time on TV, you saw a man literally getting pissed on by another man.

"We permitted these things because we felt that they were properly motivated. The reasoning? Richard Chamberlain as Blackthorn was, for the first time in his life, observing a society that was totally foreign to him: feudal Japan. And, totally foreign to the viewing audience. Consequently, his anger and frustration at the samurai warrior, who had just boiled his friend alive, came with the outburst, 'Piss on you and all your countrymen!' And the samurai's response was so basic and so simple to understand that we felt it had to be done. It was a lesson in morality. You don't say things like that unless you're prepared to back it up, or to suffer the degradation. We got no criticism for that.

"By the same token, were any of our other suppliers to come to us and want to use the same expression, we wouldn't allow it probably, at least not as a general liberty. If given the same kind of justification for it, we'd possibly let it go."

It's this kind of openness and willingness to work creatively with production companies that has made Stanley, and censors like him, more trusted and less of an enemy figure. Though it doesn't always work like that.

JERRY STANLEY'S LIST OF 7 AREAS OF PARTICULAR SENSITIVITY TO NETWORK CENSORS

1. VIOLENCE AND FIGHT SCENES
   "We are sensitive to violence, and won't allow any gratuitous violence. Or too much blood and gore. Certainly nothing that isn't properly motivated. In a fight scene we always ask for ample cutaway shots so that if the fight gets too brutal, we may not want to see the guy get hit as many times as is indicated in the script."
2. BEDROOM SCENES
   "When people are going to have sexual intercourse, we like the scene to play up to the point where they get into bed and then cut away. Or to play the scene after they've had sex, when hopefully one of them is out of bed, or partially dressed."

BC's highest-rating mini-series, "Shogun," with Richard Chamberlain and ɔko Shimada, made some interesting inroads in network television censorship.

3. PROFANITY AND LEWD LANGUAGE

"With dialogue it's rather simple. We eliminate profanity and encourage substitute words. In 'Shôgun' there were a lot of 'goddamns' that we talked to author James Clavell about and he said, 'How about God-cursed?' And we said that was acceptable.

"There seems to be a rampant misconception with some production people about profanity. I've heard actors on talk shows talk about how the censors will trade off three 'hells' for one 'damn.' If they let us cut three 'hells' from the script, we'll let them keep one 'damn.' So they write six 'goddammits' into the script, thinking that it's a bargaining tool, that we'll take out five of them as a sort of justification for our jobs. And it's just not true. Where this sort of misconception arises is that perhaps in the very same script, a 'hell' or 'goddamn' may not be appropriate in one scene, but in a later scene it is. To the inexperienced or unknowledgeable person, it seems that we're trading off.

"In the area of lewd language, we had an interesting experience recently. In a song for 'The Smothers Brothers Special' (1980), Martin Mull did a song in which a lyric said something like, 'I'm goosing her.' We told them to alter it or take it out. And suddenly there was a terrible rhubarb with Tommy Smothers. In the ensuing hassle, we stepped back and asked ourselves is all this worth it for one word in a song that no-body'll probably hear anyway? So we let them have their way. This has worked for us because now we have greater leverage with them on things that really matter."

4. KNIVES AND GUNS THRUST INTO SOMEONE'S FACE

"In working on 'Shôgun,' I found that professionals are willing to listen to what our problems are, not only our problems in relation to their product, but our problems as related to our responsibilities as broadcasters. For example, I watched them film a scene in which a spear was thrust right up next to someone's face. I mentioned that this was bordering on a basic concern about sticking guns and knives into too close proximity of a person's face and neck area. It's repulsive to the viewer and more fright-ening than just a verbal threat with the weapons. They said okay, and I never saw it happen again in the whole twelve hours, even though I had fully expected to. That's responsible film making.

"On the other hand, the opposite side of the coin, is the recent mini-series, 'Alcatraz and Clarence Carnes' (1980). In a prison-riot se-quence, a man shoved a .45 cocked, to a guard's forehead and pressed it there. We wanted it taken out, and they argued and argued. Finally we settled for a reverse shot where the gun wasn't that discernible. And this had been something that we had asked them not to do at the time we read the script. Yet they went ahead and did it anyway. To me, this is where real professionalism comes in."

5. MORAL LESSON: RIGHT WINS OVER WRONG
"We don't necessarily look for retribution, as we used to. Except in children's programing, where we demand it. Wrongdoers must pay for their evil acts. That's very important. Children have to learn the difference between right and wrong. In normal nighttime prime-time programing, those things usually take care of themselves in the dramatic needs of telling the story."

6. NUDITY
"Plain and simple—we don't allow it. There just hasn't ever been enough justification for it. In our 'Marilyn Monroe' (1980) film, in the calendar scenes, we used a still of Catharine Hicks in the famous calendar pose, but it was shot in such a way that though she was obviously naked, nothing was showing. Except for the outline of her buttocks. It was suggested nudity, in a dramatic situation that was necessary for the show, but without showing anything, really. Anything more would have been unjustified.

"In 'Roots' (1977), as a criticism, and it's difficult to criticize such a fine program, they had a couple of early sequences where they showed bare-bosomed black women. I felt it was gratuitous, the 'National-Geographic' syndrome. I don't think it was justified because the story could have been told without it, especially since it was the extras who ran around bare-breasted, and not the stars. If it had been the stars, they might've made a case for it, but as done, it was discriminatory. It just perpetuated this strange set of double standards that allows natives to be shown bare-breasted but not whites."

7. RIFLES WITH TELESCOPIC SIGHTS
"After the J.F.K. assassination, there was a blanket iron-clad rule that no rifles with telescopic lens could be shown on any dramatic program. Today, eighteen years later, the telescopic sights are permitted, but guardedly. We will still not allow any shots through the telescopic sights, absolutely nothing showing anyone in the cross-hairs."

Says Stanley: "There aren't that many areas that we have like this. And the above are really generalities dealing with specifics. It would be impossible to make up a rule book, for example, of all the Do's and Don't's. The basic truth is that we always judge a film at the time we see it on the screen. You can't do it any other way."

11 OUTRAGEOUS CENSORSHIP EXAMPLES

1. During the filming of the seven episodes of "I Love Lucy" in 1952, in which Lucy was pregnant, later giving birth to "little Ricky" on the show, CBS insisted that the word "pregnant" not be used. It was forbidden, though the word "expecting" was deemed acceptable.

2. During the production of "I Dream of Jeannie" ('65–70), Barbara Eden's belly button was censored by NBC Broadcast Standards, who felt that it was "improper" for the younger viewers. TV Producer Doug Benton recalls Eden showing him the flesh-colored divot that fit into her belly button to camouflage it.

3. During the "All in the Family" episodes built around Archie Bunker's newly born grandson, Joey, it was deemed unfit by CBS for Carroll O'Connor to be shown changing little Joey's diapers. That was in December 1975. They did it anyway, with discreet angles, and not a single viewer objected.

4. During the first two seasons of "Happy Days" (Jan. '74–76), ABC censors ruled that Henry Winkler's character of Fonzie couldn't wear his black leather jacket except when he was riding his motorcycle because it made him look like a juvenile delinquent. And this was unacceptable for a youth-oriented sitcom. The way producer Garry Marshall got around it was to have Fonzie's motorcycle appear in all his scenes with him, the leather jacket being a strong character element.

5. On "Rowan & Martin's Laugh-In," NBC censors allowed Henry Gibson in the role of a minister to say: "The fact that the Lord giveth and the Lord taketh away does not make him an Indian giver." But they drew the line at: "I don't understand members of my flock who on Saturday sow their wild oats and on Sunday pray for crop failure."

6. When producing "The Story of Esther" for ABC for telecasting on Easter Sunday 1979, Universal-TV producer Robert O'Neill was told that nowhere in the story could words such as "lust," "harem" and "eunuch" be used in the show, though these are specifically words used in the Biblical telling of the story of Esther. Said O'Neill: "We were opposite Disney and '60 Minutes,' the traditional children's hour, and the network people felt that those words were unacceptable in a children's program, though on '60 Minutes' the words and subject matter are unbelievable."

7. One of the most famous and ludicrous censorships in TV history came on January 6, 1957. The event was Elvis Presley's third appearance on "The Ed Sullivan Show." Because of protests from clergy and PTA members about Elvis' "lascivious and suggestive" hip-swinging style allegedly being an immoral influence on America's teenagers, CBS got the brainstorm of showing the rock singer only from the waist up and in closeups. They weren't willing to cancel his appearance because Elvis had already been paid and because he assured high ratings. It was ludicrous because he'd already appeared in full-length view not only on "Ed Sullivan," but on "Stage Show," "The Steve Allen Show," and "The Milton Berle Show."

8. As hard to believe as it is, even PLAYHOUSE 90, generally considered to be television's finest hour (and a half) was not immune from the inane

"Look, Ma, no belly button." At least, that's the way the censors wanted it on Barbara Eden's sitcom, "I Dream of Jeannie." A truly outrageous censorship example.

The three little noses all in a row belong to Dick Smothers, Jimmy Durante, and Tom Smothers, in a comic lookalike sketch on "The Smothers Brothers Show," which accounted for the CBS censors' high budget allowance for anti-acid tablets.

outrageousness of censorship dictates. In 1959, "Judgement at Nuremberg," with Claude Rains, Melvyn Douglas, and Maximilian Schell, was irritatingly hamstrung by the CBS mandate that all references to "gas" ovens be struck. The rationale? The sponsor of the program was the American Gas Association. And in this instance, the AGA gave everyone connected with the production about the Nazi criminal war trials a healthy case of gas.

9. Already at war with THE SMOTHERS BROTHERS COMEDY HOUR, CBS censors held their snipping shears at the ready. So when Pete Seeger, blacklisted from television for nearly two decades because of his political beliefs, appeared on the show in 1967, one of his songs, "Waist Deep in the Big Muddy," was cut. Although the lyrics are about a soldier who died during WW II following stupid orders from a commanding officer, CBS thought it might be construed as an insult to then President Lyndon Johnson. At the end of the season, CBS canceled the "Smothers Brothers" altogether.

10. Created and sold as a sophisticated, adult comedy, FAY, starring Lee Grant, lasted only six weeks in the fall of 1975. The reason was that, in its infinite wisdom, NBC scheduled the sitcom smack in the middle of the

family viewing hour. So, Broadcast Standards quickly went to work deleting such offensive words as "stretch marks" and "diarrhea" from the show. Not that these words would have made the show a hit, but their deletion certainly didn't suddenly transform the adult-oriented sitcom into a family program. The rock-bottom ratings proved that.

11. Bob Dylan had been signed to appear on THE ED SULLIVAN SHOW in 1963 and chose for his number a song entitled "Talkin' John Birch Society Blues." Reportedly Sullivan liked the humorous tune about a man who begins beating the bushes everywhere for Communists, and voiced no objection. However, CBS censors, antsy about anything political, nixed the selection and asked Dylan to do something else. When Dylan refused, he was allowed out of his contract by "mutual agreement."

CECIL SMITH'S LIST OF 10 LUNKHEAD DECISIONS BY THE NETWORKS AND OTHER GOVERNING POWERS

1-6. The first six of this list have to be the entire "List of 6 Terrific Shows that Failed" (presented earlier in the book).

7. NBC's decision to cut off the telecasting of the end of a tied championship football game to run its production of a TV movie, "Heidi," in 1968.

8. NBC fouling up the production of "Born Free" (Sept.–Dec. '74) by insisting it control the program from here even though it was being filmed in Kenya, Africa. Columbia had a hand in this dumbness, too.

9. The FCC's bumbling lack of control of broadcasting over the years and the nitwit way it originally doled out TV licenses.

10. The Nixonization of Public TV when his White House administrators emasculated PBS by decentralizing allotment of funds.

Smith: "And this doesn't even scratch the surface, but it is indicative of the types of things those in power are capable of doing."

PRODUCER DOUGLAS BENTON'S LIST OF 5 CHANGES REQUESTED BY THE NETWORK CENSORS

Hugely prolific, nearly to the point of being creatively promiscuous, producer-director-writer Douglas Benton has, since his early beginnings as story editor on "The General Electric Theatre" in 1953, amassed over 400 prime-time television shows to his credit, one Emmy for "Columbo," and a total of six Emmy nominations. His major producing efforts include: "Dr. Kildare" (1961–66); "The Girl from U.N.C.L.E." (1966–67); "Cimarron Strip" (1967–68); "Ironside" (1968–71); "Columbo" (1971–72); "Hec Ramsey" (1971–

Producer Doug Benton confers with stars Angie Dickinson and Earl Holliman on the set of Columbia TV's "Police Woman." The show was not without its censorship problems.

72); "The Rookies" (1973–74); "Police Woman" (1974–78); and dozens of TV Movies, including the controversial and highly rated "My Undercover Years with the Ku Klux Klan" and "Gaugin, the Savage."

Says Benton: "Here's some stuff we had to change at the request of the censors. I'm sure there are more and better ones, but these are the things that come immediately to mind":

1. THRILLER
   "The hero (Lawrence Harvey) tells the heroine, 'I'll see you in Washington.' Then he gives her a passionate kiss, which she reciprocates. We *cut* immediately to a stock shot of the Washington Monument. At that point, the censor said no way. It's obviously phallic symbolism.

2. DR. KILDARE
   "The good doctor (Richard Chamberlain) had just been chosen to represent the residents and interns on the medical council. Another intern, an Oriental, was supposed to say, 'Congratulations on your election.' The censors made us change his line.

3. THE GIRL FROM U.N.C.L.E.
   "Agent Stephanie Powers was staked out in a tree watching evil-doers Margaret Leighton and Michael Wilding conduct some diabolical scientific experiment. Fellow agent Noel Harrison appeared on the roof of the building and managed to swing down on a telephone line, and as the

script said: 'He makes a perfect landing in the crotch of Stefanie's tree.' The censors made us change the script, even though we tried to explain that it was only a scene description.

4. CIMARRON STRIP
"Marshal Stuart Whitman was supposed to go into a hotel and order chicken. We had to reshoot the scene for the censors because he had ad libbed, 'Kentucky fried.'

5. POLICE WOMAN
"Sergeant Angie Dickinson luxuriates in her bubble bath, while on the phone to her partner Earl Holliman. After elaborating about the bath, she teasingly invites him over. His reply was: 'I'm coming.' The censors requested a retake, and Earl then said, 'I'll be right over."

GEORGE C. SCOTT'S LIST OF 4 EXAMPLES OF RESTRICTIONS AND CENSORSHIP DURING THE PRODUCTION OF HIS "EAST SIDE/WEST SIDE" SERIES

When asked in a *TV Guide* interview in 1964 about his experience in TV series work, Scott, whose "East Side/West Side" (1963–64) had just been canceled, replied that he would never again do a series, and that he was going to advise everybody to stay off television.

"Mostly my problems were with CBS, and with the restrictions they wished to place on the show, and constantly did. There was constant blue-penciling of material by the Program Practices Department of the network, constant interference with the creative effort of people on the show. It was a policy which was highly restrictive.

1. "For example, they never consulted us about the sequence in which the segments would be aired; we'd simply be given a list of the order in which they would be shown. I was highly incensed about this, because it prevented our preserving the novelistic concept. The characters couldn't grow in a linear fashion.

2. "An episode called 'Who Do You Kill?' dealt with the death of a child in Harlem from rat bites. We shot some brilliant scenes of rats in Harlem, but these were cut out. We had the villain but couldn't show him. Their reason? They thought it might be offensive to the sponsor, or to the public, or to someone; I never found out who.

3. "In a segment called 'No Hiding Place,' a story about blockbusting by unscrupulous real estate operators, there was a scene in which I ask a black woman, played by Ruby Dee, to dance. The scene was edited out of the script by CBS. I insisted it be put back in. It was, and we shot it. Then, it was cut out of the footage by the network.

4. "Another time in a segment about politics in Greenwich Village, we were shooting a rally in Washington Square. A beatnik-type is making a speech and a group of Italians call out insults like "pidocchio" which means "louse" in Italian. My character, Brock, leaps to the platform for an impassioned speech, saying: 'You like to call names, do you? How about the names your parents were called when they first came to this country, names like "wop" and "guinea." ' Then Brock says sardonically, trying to show the stupidity of bigotry: 'Everybody knows that all Italians are gangsters, and all gangsters are Italians.' Well, the setup lines with the words 'wop' and 'guinea' were cut because somebody thought they might offend somebody, but the part about Italians being gangsters was left in. This ruined the entire sardonicism and changed the whole meaning of the speech. As a result, I got hundreds of letters from Italians complaining about what I'd said. All because of some stupid jerk who made stupid cuts in the final footage."

THE 8 MOST OFFENSIVE AND IMMORAL SHOWS ON THE AIR

In mid-1980, a grass-roots church-and-clergy campaign to "Clean Up TV" was launched from the Joelton, Tenn., Church of Christ, aimed at national advertisers who support objectionable TV shows. The Reverend John Hurt, minister of the Joelton church, said that the following shows are the most offensive because of their "presentation of scenes of adultery, sexual perversion, or incest, as well as material which treats any form of immorality in a joking or otherwise favorable light."

1. SOAP—ABC
2. THREE'S COMPANY—ABC
3. DALLAS—CBS
4. SATURDAY NIGHT LIVE—NBC
5. CHARLIE'S ANGELS—ABC
6. THE NEWLYWED GAME—Syndicated
7. THE DATING GAME—Syndicated
8. THREE'S A CROWD—Syndicated

The campaign spread rapidly across the South to some 20,000 congregations, representing over a half-million churchgoers, who wrote letters to advertisers warning them of a boycott. Said Reverend Hurt: "We're not trying to censor anything, but are simply exercising our right not to allow TV sponsors to use our money to support material which we feel is offensive."

4 CONCESSIONS MADE BY DESILU STUDIOS TO THE ITALIAN-AMERICAN ANTI-DEFAMATION LEAGUE ABOUT "THE UNTOUCHABLES" SERIES

Almost from the start, "The Untouchables" (1959–63) drew not only high ratings, but also a lot of heat from the Italian-American community, which protested that the show "unfairly stereotyped Italian-Americans as gangsters." Toward the end of the second season, which "The Untouchables" finished as the eighth most popular show on the air, the series sponsor, L&M cigarettes, came under direct attack. Brooklyn

"The Untouchables," with star Robert Stack and Paul Picerni, was at war not only with Al Capone and the Mafia, but also with the Italian-American Anti-Defamation League and the PTA.

longshoremen threatened to stop handling L&M shipments and the Federation of Italian-American Democratic Organizations announced that it was launching a boycott of L&M products. The pressure was so great that L&M withdrew sponsorship not only from "The Untouchables," but from two other ABC series as well, "Adventures in Paradise" and "Asphalt Jungle."

On St. Patrick's Day, 1961, came peace. Desi Arnaz, whose Desilu Studios made the series; Quinn Martin, the show's producer; ABC representatives; and the chairman of the Italian-American Anti-Defamation League agreed on these four points:

1. There would be no more fictional hoodlums with Italian names in future productions.
2. There will be more stress on the law-enforcement role of "Nick Rossi" (Nick Georgiade), Eliot Ness's (Robert Stack's) right-hand man in the show.
3. There will be emphasis on the "formidable influence" of Italian-American officials in reducing crime.
4. There will be emphasis on the "great contributions" made to American culture by Americans of Italian descent.

13 SERIES TO HAVE BEEN ATTACKED FOR EXCESSIVE VIOLENCE

As early as 1954, there have been Congressional inquiries into television violence, which, because of the medium's constant presence in the home, may have serious and far-reaching harmful effects. Over the past two decades, dozens of theories about these effects have been run up the flagpole.

The most organized drive to reduce objectionable and gratuitous violence came in the mid-1970s, with even the U.S. Surgeon General getting into the action. The findings of an exhaustive (three-year) and expensive ($1-million) governmental report stated: "The overwhelming consensus is that televised violence does have an adverse effect on certain members of society." Statistics estimated that by the age of 15, the average child will have probably witnessed over 14,000 killings, muggings, rapes, robberies, and other acts of violence on TV shows. The fear is that a child who is a heavy television watcher can become desensitized to violence in the real world, and accept it as normal. And that the more violence and aggression a youngster sees on television, regardless of his age, sex, or social background, the more aggressive he is likely to be in his behavior and attitudes.

Among the series that have been singled out for their excessive use of "action" (a euphemism for violence) are these:

1. THE UNTOUCHABLES ('59–63). Robert Stack; produced by Quinn Martin
2. WHISPERING SMITH (May–Sept. '61). Audie Murphy; p: Richard Lewis
3. MOD SQUAD ('68–73). Michael Cole, Peggy Lipton, Clarence Williams III, Tige Andrews; p: Aaron Spelling
4. MISSION: IMPOSSIBLE ('66–73). Peter Graves, Martin Landau, Barbara Bain, Greg Morris, Peter Lupus; p: Bruce Geller
5. ROOKIES ('72–76). Michael Ontkean, Georg Stanford Brown, Kate Jackson; p: Aaron Spelling and Leonard Goldberg
6. S.W.A.T. ('75–76). Steve Forrest, Robert Urich, Mark Shera; p: Aaron Spelling and Leonard Goldberg. Generally criticized as one of the most violent shows of the decade.
7. KOJAK ('73–78). Telly Savalas, Kevin Dobson, Dan Frazer; p: Matthew Rapf
8. MANNIX ('67–75). Mike Connors, Gail Fisher; p: Bruce Geller
9. HAWAII FIVE-0 ('68–80). Jack Lord, James MacArthur; p: Leonard Freeman
10. STARSKY AND HUTCH ('75–79). David Soul, Paul Michael Glaser; p: Aaron Spelling and Leonard Goldberg
11. QUEST (Sept.–Dec. '76). Kurt Russell, Tim Matheson; p: David Gerber
12. CANNON ('71–76). William Conrad; p: Quinn Martin
13. EISCHIED ('79–80). Joe Don Baker; p: David Gerber

3 TELEVISION SHOWS THAT ALLEGEDLY INSPIRED REAL-LIFE VIOLENCE

Jerry Stanley, NBC Vice President, Broadcast Standards and Practices said: "I remember reading in *TV Guide* about how inmates watched the latest crime and police shows to learn some new techniques. We try to make sure that we don't add to the situation. For example, when a private eye like James Garner on "The Rockford Files" jimmies a door with a credit card, we never allow a closeup of exactly what he does. And if you've tried it out of curiosity, you know that it can't be done—unless you know the trick to it.

"In regards to violence, we go to great pains to eliminate those things in our programs that we feel could, even in the remotest possibility, be imitated by impressionable youngsters."

But even with the hard work of such dedicated network watchdogs as Jerry Stanley, there occasionally arises a real-life incident which seems to spring from an imitation of a television incident:

1. BORN INNOCENT (1974)

   TV Movie with Linda Blair, which depicted a graphic shower rape scene in which she was assaulted with a broom handle by other juvenile girls in a detention home. The scene was allegedly the source for an assault with a Coke bottle on an adolescent girl by three teenagers in San Francisco. Subsequent telecasts of the film have not included the scene in question.

2. DOOMSDAY FLIGHT (1966)

   TV Movie about a blackmailer who had rigged a bomb with an altitude-activated detonator that would go off if the plane descended below 4,000 feet, which allegedly inspired a rash of similar bomb threats. Rod Serling's incredible invention, unfortunately, was entirely workable.

3. KOJAK (1977)

   An episode in which minors are used as hit men because they wouldn't get prosecuted for murder like an adult, allegedly inspired a similar shooting in New York.

7

"THE REAL McCOYS": The Stars Do Their Thing

Or: *Glamorous Tidbits and Weird Doings*

CHAPTER

DWIGHT WHITNEY'S LIST OF 13 STAR-INTERVIEW SUBJECTS—AND WHAT IT TOOK TO GET THEIR STORIES

Dwight Whitney, a magazine writer's magazine writer, is the sort of guy with whom you feel genuinely comfortable, even after just a few minutes. Comfortable enough to share your private thoughts and concerns. His casual and warmly interested demeanor is the big tipoff as to how he's been so highly successful in the personality profile business, which, as often as not, masticates and spits out writers by the mouthful. In truth, he wears well, like an old sweater or a favored pair of broken-in shoes.

And he writes the same way: insightful, perceptive, lively, and always with humor and wit, which, depending on the subject, can be outrageous or bloodletting. He is a man of all words.

Whitney is the Hollywood Bureau Chief of *TV Guide,* where he began temporary work some twenty-three years ago: "March 18, 1958. That's when I came to work for this 'pamphlet.' I thought I was too good for this outfit. I was a big-time journalist. But *Colliers* had just folded and I needed some grocery money. Laddie Marshack, with whom I'd worked on *Colliers,* and also on *Life,* had gone to work for them doing their pictures. She called up and said, 'Hey, they need somebody. Are you interested?' So I went over, thinking I'd work for them six or eight weeks, until I could get something respectable. And the first thing I knew, I looked around and this thing was taking off. *Colliers* had already folded; *Saturday Evening Post* was next; then *Look;* and then—horror of horrors—*Life!* And what was going through the ceiling? This little old pamphlet. So I finally caught on that things had changed.

"Doing a list like this puts an unreal slant on things because the interviews that most readily jump to mind are the ones that were the roughest, and took the greatest finessing. So, it's important to note that the good guys by far outnumber the bad guys. And it's kind of an interesting hooker that all the stars who've given me a notably rough time have all made for marvelous stories.

1. FRANK SINATRA

"He's the toughest interview there is. Unless he likes you. And if he's pressed, he doesn't like you. When he wants to be charming, there's nobody more charming. Trouble is he doesn't want to be charming very often, especially not with the press. He kept me waiting for three months, put me off about six times before I finally got to him, then he made me wait for an hour. Then he held up his own TV Special rehearsal—he had Howard Koch, the producer, there, musicians, the director—he had a million bucks worth of talent wait while he did this interview with me. What it must have cost them? All these guys sitting around on that rehearsal stage, cooling their heels while Sinatra did his ego trip. But it made a great story. I told it exactly as it happened, how the guys looked, what the people said—without any editorial comment. It made for a powerful story. Sinatra is the most difficult, and yet frequently the best.

2. JIM DRURY

"He was difficult in a different sense than Sinatra. Since he was hot as "The Virginian," he decided that he was a star and he was going to act like one. He gave me a very rough time. I'd say, 'Jim, how'd you get into this business?' and he'd say, 'That's a personal question.' So I'd say, 'Are you a Los Angeles guy, or what?' And he'd say, 'That's a personal question. Ask me about my art.' So, I'd ask about his career, and he'd say, 'Look it up in the record.' And so I began writing down all these replies, and I came out with this piece about this strong, silent, 'Smile when you say that, stranger' kind of guy; and I began looking it up in the record. I got lucky. I came up with the people who were willing to give me the life story of this kid. His father turned out to be a professor of marketing at Columbia University. I remember getting him on the phone and explaining the problem. I can still hear him laughing. He said, 'Oh,

Frank Sinatra shares the spotlight on one of his TV specials with Ella Fitzgerald. "Ol' Blue Eyes" has a reputation as being not only a tough interview, but also as being a hard man to get a picture of. He's not fond of the press.

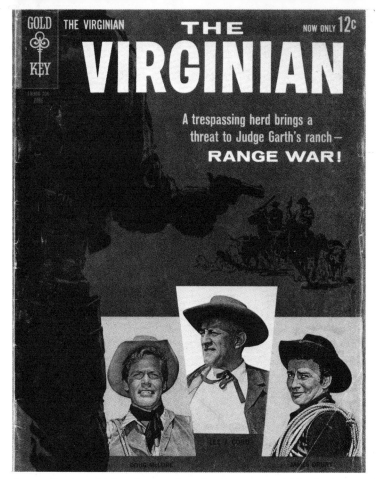

James Drury, who has been referred to by actors who've had to work with him as "James Dreary," became a star on "The Virginian." And it went straight to his head. His hat size grew with every season the show remained on the air.

Jimmy . . . he always wanted to be the Garbo of the Sagebrush,' and that became the title of the piece. Then I got hold of his divorced mother, and some other people, and got all the details of his rather checkered career. And I played it all against his standoffish answers. It turned out to be very funny stuff, a portrait of someone dead bent on making an ass of himself.

3. BOB HOPE

"I find him a difficult interview. He's a wonderful man, but he needs a script. You can go along like what Al Martinez did for the last story we did on Bob, and listen in on what he says to other people, and get a story that way. But you can't sit him down and say, 'Bob, I'd like you to tell me about Al Jolson,' or 'What was it like in the old days?' No chance. Bob's not good at that. He got furious at me once after I did a story on him in which I treated him like a human being instead of a guy who walked on water. I mentioned that Dolores was a practicing Catholic and how the house was full of men of the cloth a lot. And that he and Dolores had separate bedrooms.

4. JACK LORD

"Jack decided that he was bigger than *TV Guide.* And that was okay with me because I wasn't anxious to do a story about him. He was a guy who had once been a very good actor, and really sold out. He wouldn't be interviewed except on his own set of conditions: 1) he had to be on the cover all by himself; no girls, no palm trees, no supporting players, no Jimmy MacArthur, just Jack. 2) He had to have copy approval, and all kinds of incredible nonsense. Our management was fed up with those kinds of demands, so we just ignored him. So three years went by and 'Hawaii Five-0' got very big, and it really became impossible not to do a story any longer. My boss called me and said he knew the guy was intolerable, but could I get a story on him without his blessings or coop- eration? I said I wasn't sure, but when I started calling around, I got lucky. I began running into all kinds of people who knew Jack. You could throw a piano and hit the nearest guy dying to tell all about him. Then I went to Hawaii, interviewing everybody in town, Jack's friends, his enemies; and I didn't even try to get on the set. And the more I didn't try to get on the set, the more frantic the network became. I remember talking to the show's producer, Lenny Freeman, in the Kahala Hilton, and Lenny saying, 'You gotta understand I've got fifteen million dollars riding on this show and a star who's impossible.' He might've said, 'Please be kind,' but he didn't. I was in Hawaii for five and a half days, and on the fourth day, Jack decided that he'd better talk to me. I ended up spending an hour and a half in his trailer, with him reading me poetry by e.e. cum- mings. Getting this story sort of surpassed being difficult, because here was this guy who said 'forget it' and 'you're banned from my set.' But I spent five terrific days in Hawaii, and came away with enough material for several pieces.

5. DEMOND WILSON

"When somebody makes a damn fool of himself, you're bound to get a good story, if your ear is sharp enough and if you write down what he says and do it straight. Because he can't help but reveal himself. That was the case with Demond on 'Sanford and Son.' But unfortunately the show went off the air before the story got printed. And it was devastating. Yet it was just the things he'd said, nothing more. I didn't make anything up.

6. REDD FOXX

"I know Redd and I've talked with him, but somehow I've never inter- viewed him, though I've worked on some stories other people have done about him. He wouldn't be difficult for me to write about because there's so much emotion there. Anyone who feels as deeply and gets as angry as Redd does, you don't have any problems with. And Redd is an angry man. I mean he really hates whitey. He may make jokes about it, but he's still making whitey pay for all the indignities he suffered in those two-bit nightclubs where he had to dress in the toilet. He wanted whitey to tear out the wall at NBC to give him a window in his dressing room. And you can do a story about that. That is an understandable feeling. I can relate to that, and I can talk to that man.

7. CHAD EVERETT

"Chad falls into that category of actors who have this ego, guys who are perfect and never have a hair out of place. The technique is to let them have all the line they will take. You say, 'Oh, you write poetry, Mr. Everett. I hear it's terrific.' 'Oh, you did?' And you're off and running with him, but you have to be suddenly very interested in poetry, and all those other avante garde things that Chad does. And he writes the story for you.

8. JACK KLUGMAN

"Now he's the exact opposite of guys like Everett. I had a great time with Jack. I did him and Tony Randall in tandem. And they're very different and complemented each other nicely. It was a fun story because these are guys who in real life somewhat parallel the roles they played on 'The Odd Couple.' Klugman really is a racehorse aficionado who drinks beer and wears his baseball cap backwards. And Randall really does turn on to opera and likes his champagne chilled to the proper degree.

9. MORT SAHL

"He was difficult because he talked so fast, and his sentence structure was so convoluted, and so intellectualized. I couldn't get the quotes down fast enough. I can relate better to Red Skelton, whose comedy has humanity in it. I never found anything funny in Mort. Satiric, yes. It wasn't because he wasn't pleasant, because he was; it was just that he never struck any chords with me.

10. MARY TYLER MOORE

"I had trouble with her, actually. Not because she wasn't as nice as pie, but because I find her so tightly controlled. Anybody who is that controlled is difficult in an interview unless you can loosen them up. But not Mary; she held it all in. She was always perfect. That was her image and she lived up to it. There wasn't any real emotion that came crackling out of her, even. As long as she played the controlled Mary Richards on the controlled 'Mary Tyler Moore Show,' it worked, but when she tried the variety show, it didn't.

11. ELVIS PRESLEY

"This *was* a goodie. Colonel Parker, the manager, made it absolutely impossible to work with Elvis. He wouldn't let you in for the taping of Elvis' TV special. You had to wait outside in the line with folks just in from Des Moines. And all of NBC couldn't do anything about it; they had to wait in line, too. NBC told the Colonel that he couldn't do this to *TV Guide*. And he said, 'Oh, I can't?' And he did. When I finally got to Elvis, I had him for all of about two minutes. He was very stiff and I couldn't get much from him at all. I had to go to the press conferences to get quotes there. Colonel Parker was absolutely outrageous in the way he handled the press, and he was laughing at you while he did it.

12. LARRY HAGMAN

"Larry's an old friend. I've done a lot on him. We first met when he was playing second fiddle to Barbara Eden on 'I Dream of Jeannie.' He'd do the work and she'd waltz in and pay off the scene. After the series finished, Larry fell on some bad times. We'd see him on the beach in Malibu, and his kids went to school with our kids. And when he made his big success in 'Dallas,' I did a piece on him. And it was real satisfying because I love Larry. He's one of my favorite people.

13. BARBARA STANWYCK

"She an old-fashioned movie queen up to her eyeballs. And old-fashioned movie queens never tell the truth about anything. She's used to being interviewed by the fan magazines, and making up her script as she went along. At the same time, she's always been very guarded about her personal story, which is one of the most dramatic in the business. If you go and look it up in the library, you come off with a terrific tale about an orphan who made good. Frank Capra can tell you tales about Barbara Stanwyck that are really moving. Capra recognized her qualities and could verbalize what they were. 'Any girl who can make me cry,' he said after auditioning her in the mid-1920s, 'has something I want.' "

5 ACTORS TO BE REGULARS IN 2 TV SERIES SIMULTANEOUSLY

It's plenty tough for an actor to land a regular continuing role in a series, much less to be working regularly in two shows at the same time. However, it is possible.

1. NANCY WALKER: "Rhoda" and "McMillan and Wife"
   As Mildred, his maternal and meddling housekeeper (have you ever known a TV housekeeper who wasn't?), Nancy Walker worked for Rock Hudson on "McMillan and Wife" from 1971 to 1976. When "Rhoda" spin off from "The Mary Tyler Moore Show" in 1974, she was cast as Valerie Harper's mother, a role she continued for two seasons, while simultaneously appearing regularly on "McMillan."

2. LEE MAJORS: "Owen Marshall" and "The Six Million Dollar Man"
   While playing Arthur Hill's assistant on "Owen Marshall," Majors made the TV-Movie pilot for "The Six Million Dollar Man" (Mar. '73). Highly successful, the bionic man became a monthly feature on "The ABC Suspense Movie" for the rest of the '72–73 season; while Majors continued his role as "Owen Marshall's" second banana, which he'd begun at the start of the series in 1971. By fall 1973, he'd dropped out of "Marshall" in favor of "The Six Million Dollar Man," which then continued through

1978. On "Owen Marshall," Majors was replaced by Reni Santoni, who, in turn, was replaced four months later by David Soul.

3. RICHARD ANDERSON: "The Six Million Dollar Man" and "The Bionic Woman"
   In the role of O.S.I. chief and Lee Major's boss, Oscar Goldman, Anderson suddenly found himself happily stuck with double duty when "Six Million Dollar Man" spun off into a sister series, "The Bionic Woman." Anderson played the same role in the spinoff, which starred Lindsay Wagner.

4. MARTIN E. BROOKS: "The Six Million Dollar Man" and "The Bionic Woman"
   He played bionics expert, Rudy Wells, on both series.

5. JENNIFER DARLING: "The Six Million Dollar Man" and "The Bionic Woman"
   She was Callahan, Oscar Goldman's secretary, on both shows.

... AND THE ONLY 5 ACTORS EVER TO PLAY THE SAME CONTINUING ROLES SIMULTANEOUSLY ON 2 DIFFERENT NETWORKS

There was a great deal of interplay between "The Six Million Dollar Man" and "The Bionic Woman"; Lee Majors and Lindsay Wagner guested often on each other's series. So, when ABC dropped "Bionic Woman" at the end of the '77–78 season, NBC picked up the show for another first-run year. The five regulars then played the same continuing roles simultaneously on both ABC and NBC:

1. LEE MAJORS
2. LINDSAY WAGNER
3. RICHARD ANDERSON
4. MARTIN E. BROOKS
5. JENNIFER DARLING

DENNIS WEAVER'S LIST OF 17 ACTORS TO LEAVE A HIT SERIES

In 1962, when Dennis Weaver made it clear that he was leaving "Gunsmoke" (1955–79) to try for more challenging parts, he shocked the TV community and home viewers at large. Why would anyone want to leave a hit show? No one had ever done it before. It seemed like a crazy thing to do. However, he made two pilots for new series, but neither sold, so he remained on "Gunsmoke" for another two seasons, until 1964, when his third pilot, "Kentucky Jones" (1964–65) sold. It lasted one season. After that, he guested on various TV series, made a handful of films, and starred in the following shows:

Dennis Weaver as "McCloud," in the "kind of role I left 'Gunsmoke' to get. I wanted to be a leading man, instead of a second banana."

"Gentle Ben" (1967–69), "McCloud" (1970–77), and "Stone" (1979–80).

Says Weaver: "The interesting thing is that no one is indispensable. All of us are dispensable, and the proof is that a successful series goes on, no matter who leaves for whatever reason. I think that all of us on this list learned that . . . and some of us were luckier than others.

NO. 1221

DELL
15¢

BONANZA

NOVEMBER

When Pernell Roberts left 'Bonanza,' he just didn't get the roles he wanted. Times were tough for a long time. It's a dangerous thing to leave a hit series, if you want some security.

"I think that had I known in 1964 what I know now, I probably would have thought long and hard about leaving 'Gunsmoke.' See, I thought that every series you got into was a hit. That was the only experience I'd had. So, when 'Kentucky Jones' folded in one year, it was an eye-opener. I was lucky that I got a couple of pictures, and 'Gentle Ben,' and then 'McCloud.' You know, 'McCloud' was the kind of part that I left 'Gunsmoke' to get. I wanted to be a leading man, instead of a second banana."

1. PERNELL ROBERTS—"Bonanza" ('59–73)
   Roberts played the eldest son, Adam, of Ben Cartwright (Lorne Greene); the other two sons were Hoss (Dan Blocker) and Little Joe (Michael Landon). Roberts quit the Ponderosa Ranch in 1965, explaining that he'd "grown tired of the role and wanted to do more serious acting." A friend of his at the time said that "when Lady Luck smiled, Pernell kicked her in the teeth." Says Weaver, "For fifteen years, Hollywood said that he'd made a damn fool mistake, but the cream always rises to the top, and here he is back again in a hit series, 'Trapper John' ('79–present)." It's a spinoff from M*A*S*H ('72–present). Roberts: "I now want security. It's called covering your rear end."

2. FARRAH FAWCETT—"Charlie's Angels" ('76–present)
   One of the original three Angels (the other two were Kate Jackson and Jaclyn Smith), Farrah quickly became the most popular and left the show at the end of the first season to do films. There were lawsuits which culminated in her agreeing to do a limited number of additional "Angels" episodes. Her replacement was Cheryl Ladd, introduced on the series as her younger sister. "The first time I ever saw Farrah was on a 'McCloud,' in the same show that John Denver did his first acting job. She played a hooker, and I thought she was very attractive. But I had no idea she was going to be the sensation she became. No way. Just goes to show you that you never know how the public is going to react. And that the right part, and the right show, and the right publicity make all the difference in the world. I think her popularity took her by surprise, and if she was honest about it, I think she'd tell you that she left too soon. She evidently wasn't ready for films, to carry the lead roles. But that also depends on the material you have to work with."

   Rumors abounded that Farrah was going to return to "Charlie's Angels" after her film career didn't take off. Only lackluster box office receipts resulted from *Somebody Killed Her Husband* (1978), *Sunburn* (1979) , and *Saturn 3* (1980).

People thought Pernell Roberts was crazy to leave fellow co-stars Lorne Greene, Michael Landon, and Dan Blocker in "Bonanza." Unswayed, Roberts struck out on his own, and fourteen years later found himself in another series, "Trapper John, M.D."

3. KATE JACKSON—"Charlie's Angels" ('76–present)
   She was the second Angel to fly the coop, primarily because she found the show unchallenging, and was eager to develop new properties with her freshly married husband, Andrew Stevens. Their first such joint venture was a breezy update of "Topper," a 1979 TV movie, aimed at a series. But it didn't sell. Kate Jackson was replaced on "Charlie's Angels" by Shelley Hack, an ex-model who couldn't act and was axed after one season. She, in turn, was replaced by Tanya Roberts for the '80–81 season.

4. McLEAN STEVENSON—"M*A*S*H" ('72–present)
   As Colonel Henry Blake, Stevenson seemed an indispensable member of an excellent cast that made the show a hit. He was lured away from the CBS series by rival network NBC, which promised him his own show. That kind of thing is hard to turn down. Since leaving M*A*S*H in 1975, he's had three mediocre series: "The McLean Stevenson Show" ('76–77), "In the Beginning" (Sept.–Oct. '78), and "Hello, Larry" ('79–80). The surprise was not that Stevenson didn't score on his own, but that his departure didn't affect M*A*S*H's popularity one iota.

5. WAYNE ROGERS—"M*A*S*H" ('72–present)
   Several months after Stevenson's departure, Rogers, who played Trapper John, failed to show up for work. And was never seen again. Disappointed that his contractual agreement, in which he was supposed to be the star of the series (long before Alan Alda was signed for the role of Hawkeye Pierce), was unfulfilled, he exited. His first effort thereafter was as private eye Jake Axminster in "City of Angels" (Feb.–Aug. '76). Although a Chinatown (1974) knockoff, "City of Angels" should have been given a better chance; it was one of producer Jo Swerling's and creator Steve Cannell's best co-ventures (another of their collaborations was "Baretta"), Rogers has since gotten good reviews in his new hit comedy series "House Calls" ('79–present).

6. LARRY LINVILLE—"M*A*S*H" ('72–present)
   The third to leave the series, Linville departed in 1977, tired of being the butt of the jokes. Since then he's co-starred in the ill-fated, badly done "Grandpa Goes to Washington" ('78–79).

7. GARY BURGHOFF—"M*A*S*H" ('72–present)
   Burghoff was the last of the original cast, and the most recent, to exit the show, wanting to try his hand as a Las Vegas entertainer. Reviews have not been good. Burghoff was the only member of the movie M*A*S*H (1970) cast to have gone into the series, and it was disappointing to see him go. However, "M*A*S*H" keeps going strong, held together by Alan Alda, a superb supporting cast, Larry Gelbart, and sensitive well-written scripts.

8. SUSAN ST. JAMES—"McMillan and Wife" ('71–77)
   She departed the series in a contractual dispute in 1976, and has since

Susan Saint James split from Rock Hudson and "McMillan and Wife," and, ironically, the following season the series was cancelled.

concentrated on films like *Outlaw Blues* (1978), among others. Nancy Walker also left the same year to star in her own series, "Blansky's Beauties" (Feb.–May '77), as did John Schuck to co-star in "Holmes and Yoyo" (Sept.–May '77), leaving Rock Hudson to carry the series, which was retitled "McMillan." He became a widower to explain the loss of St. James (in a car accident), and new supporting characters were added, but the series lasted only one more season. Says Weaver, "It appears that when Susan left the show it died, but the truth of the matter was that 'McMillan' had been suffering from faltering ratings, and may have died anyway, whether she'd stayed on or not. The first time I met her was on 'McCloud.' She played a lead opposite me, and that show led to her getting 'McMillan' the following year."

9. ROB REINER and SALLY STRUTHERS—"All in the Family" ('71–79)
Reiner and Struthers, who played Mike and Gloria, the son-in-law and daughter, respectively, of Archie Bunker (Carroll O'Connor) left the smash series in 1976 to pursue ventures of their own. Reiner developed an extremely short-lived series, "Free Country" (July–July '78); and Struthers has appeared in several TV Movies. "All in the Family" continued to be a hit show, much to Norman Lear's credit, but the departure of Jean Stapleton as Edith Bunker in 1979 irrevocably altered the show. A shift was then made from Archie's home life to his bar and the show was retitled "Archie's Place" ('79–present).

10. MIKE EVANS—"The Jeffersons" ('75–present)

Evans played Lionel Jefferson on "All in the Family" for four seasons ('71–75) and stayed in the role when "The Jeffersons" spun off into its own show. After one season, Evans began feeling anxious and asked to be set free from his contract. Norman Lear, ever benevolent, complied. "It was a terrible mistake," Evans admitted four years later, and with the help of Sherman Hemsley, who plays George Jefferson, Lionel's father, Evans got back on the show. And he's very happy about it. He's the only actor even to have left and been able to go back. So much for Thomas Wolfe.

11. TONY MUSANTE—"Toma" ('73–74)

In a rather unusual move, Musante, who starred as David Toma, a real-life undercover cop, quit his surprise hit series because he didn't like "the weekly grind of production." Recasting the role with Robert Blake, it was originally to be called "Toma Starring Robert Blake," but despite strong similarities in the lead role, a number of changes in the format resulted in a new series titled "Baretta" ('75–78). Says Weaver, "Hats off to creator Steve Cannell, who, incidentally, created and produced 'Stone,' my last series. He also did the same on 'The Rockford Files.'"

12. RON HOWARD—"Happy Days" ('70–present)

Howard was wooed from the ABC comedy hit by NBC with a highly lucrative deal to produce-direct-star in projects that he developed with partner Anson Williams, who left the series concurrently at the end of the '79–80 season. The focus on the show is now on "The Fonz" (Henry Winkler), and although he's a strong character, the future of the show is questionable. Howard: "It's been clear for a long time that directing is my obsession. At ABC, the focus was on 'Happy Days' and my directing would have been a little bone tossed in reluctantly. At NBC they believed I would be an asset as a producer and director." Weaver: "And it looks like he's gonna do it, too. His first TV movie, 'An Act of Love' (1980) did real well, and his second, 'Skyward,' with Bette Davis, which he directed, is coming up."

13. RICHARD THOMAS—"The Waltons" ('72–present)

The Waltons' John-Boy, Richard Thomas, left the series in 1977 to pursue a film career. He landed a substantial role in "Roots II" (Feb. '79); delivered a wonderful perfomance in *September 30, 1955* (1978), a film about the death of James Dean, which failed to do any box office; another TV movie, "All Quiet on the Western Front" ('79); and, most recently, "To Find My Son," a 1980 TV Movie.

14. JOHN AMOS—"Good Times" ('74–79)

In this spinoff from "Maude" ('72–78), Amos got tired within two seasons of doing situation comedy. In 1976, he left the series and landed the role of the adult Kunta Kinte in "Roots" (Jan. '77).

15. ROBERT HORTON—"Wagon Train" ('57–65)

Fed up with Westerns, Horton rode away from one of the most popular series of the day in 1962 and wasn't heard from until he resurfaced in another Western series, "A Man Called Shenandoah" ('65–66). Then, after a handful of guest appearances, he dropped out of sight again.

16. LEE J. COBB—"The Virginian" ('62–71)

When his contract ran out in 1966, Cobb would not renew it. He'd made a pile of money, and, essentially a movie actor anyway, he had always considered the series to be beneath him. Weaver: "And by all visible means, it didn't seem to hurt his career any. The series producers were just as happy, since he hadn't been a very pleasant man to work with." Although he did an occasional TV show until his untimely death in 1976, he concentrated on films like *Our Man Flint* (1966), *Coogan's Bluff* (1968), *The Exorcist* (1973), among others.

17. MICHAEL DOUGLAS—"The Streets of San Francisco" ('72–77)

Douglas left this hit show at the outset of the '76–77 season, to be replaced by Richard Hatch, and the show went into the barrel. The spark between Douglas and co-star Karl Malden couldn't be duplicated. Douglas, meantime, had produced *One Flew Over the Cuckoo's Nest* (1975) and has since produced and starred in *The China Syndrome* (1979). He ain't hurting. But his departure, uniquely, killed one of the better crime shows on the air.

4 SERIES ACTORS ADMIRED BY GEORGE C. SCOTT IN 1964

Because of the unpleasant experience with his series, "East Side/West Side" ('63–64), George C. Scott left television with a sour taste in his mouth, and told *TV Guide* that TV series acting tends to lessen an actor's abilities. Yet, at the same time that he insisted "anyone who has any legitimate desires and aspirations should stay out of television," he admitted that there were a few TV actors he admired.

1. E.G. MARSHALL, "The Defenders" ('61–65)

"I admire him for the magnificent control of himself; both on and off the screen. I admire him for his perseverance, for his wonderful facility to keep fresh what must be an extremely taxing role."

2. RICHARD BOONE, "The Richard Boone Show" ('63–64)

"I admire what Dick Boone was trying to do; I don't say he achieved it by any means. I admire some of his people . . . ."

3. LAURA DEVON, "The Richard Boone Show" (63-64)

4. BETHEL LESLIE, "The Richard Boone Show" ('63–64)

"I think they're all better actors now, and that's a good thing to say about a TV series. Most actors come out worse."

George C. Scott admired Richard Boone's valiant effort at creating a TV repertory company with "The Richard Boone Show" (1963–64). Here, on the "Hec Ramsey" set in 1973, Boone seems preoccupied in something other than his acting technique.

4 ODIOUS OMENS ON FARRAH FAWCETT'S OPENING NIGHT OF "BUTTERFLIES ARE FREE" IN THE BURT REYNOLDS DINNER THEATRE IN JUPITER, FLORIDA, JULY 25, 1980

1. When Farrah first appeared on stage, an obese blonde lady sitting in the front row of tables began yelling insults and, believe it or not, bird calls.
2. When Farrah continued undaunted, this same lady, who'd been dipping her snoot in champagne all evening, raised her dress and "flashed" the actress and her co-star, Dennis Christopher (who reacted, even though playing a blind character).
3. Nearby, also in the front row of tables, a man in a white suit began throwing up. (Everybody's a critic.)
4. Then, still another patron, perhaps because there was more action in the audience than on stage, fainted.

However, according to theatre critic John Huddy: "Miss Fawcett, the actress the critics love to hate, provided a page from an old Hollywood movie. You know the scene: the luckless actress, given one last shot in a play, stuns the jaded audience with her talent and nerve . . . she is a pro, with fine comedic instincts and the ability to turn on a dime."

CAROL BURNETT'S LIST OF THE 1 MOST SIGNIFICANT TV PRESENTATION ABOUT TEENAGE DRUG ABUSE

TV's queen of comedy, Carol Burnett, has had to face the teenage drug problem head-on. Her daughter, Carrie, was deeply involved with drugs. Says Burnett: "Well, to begin with, my husband, Joe Hamilton, and I were totally uneducated about drugs. I had no idea that Carrie was doing everything but angel dust, LSD, and heroin. I just thought she was going through some kind of teenage lethargy. When we did find out, the usual hassles took place: negotiations, cajoling, threatening, punishing, begging, crying, yelling. We took her to doctors to scare the hell out of her, and that didn't work. Finally, Joe and I reached bottom, long before Carrie did, and we said, 'Okay, we love you enough to let you hate us.' We sent her to Houston to a drug program we heard about called the Palmer Drug Abuse Program. And it took. The other things we tried did not. And I advise other parents not to wait as long as we did. Carrie has been sober for over a year now.

"There's one point I'd like to stress. The government says that sixty percent of high school seniors are now experimenting with drugs. If you want to know the truth, the percentage is much higher than that. And that's why our schools seem to be turning out kids who can't read or write. If something isn't done, in ten years or so, we're going to have a nation of rutabagas."

1. THE DEATH OF RICHIE (1977)
   Director: Paul Wendkos; Ben Gazzara, Robby Benson, Lance Kerwin, Eileen Brennan, Charles Fleischer, Clint Howard. A family is torn apart by the teenage son's drug addiction, and Gazzara, the straight-laced father, is driven to kill the boy. The intelligent script was based on Thomas Thompson's nonfiction book, *Richie.*

CATHY LEE CROSBY'S LIST OF 50 HOLLYWOOD STARS COMMITTED TO FIGHTING DRUGS

Testifying before the House Select Committee on Narcotics Abuse and Control in September, 1980, Cathy Lee Crosby, hostess of "That's Incredible (1980–present) and former tennis pro, lashed out at the government's heavy-handed anti-drug campaign. She said that they overemphasize marijuana control and use "scare tactics, over-whelming statistics, and lies." Describing herself as a one-time "social dabbler" in drugs, Cathy Lee called for a more honest approach in high school narcotics education. She also produced a list of 181 athletes and actors who, as Friends of Narconon, are willing to partici-pate in educational and promotional activities to change peer pressure from pro-drug to anti-drug. "One effective way to combat peer pres-sure," says Crosby, "is with celebrity pressure." And here are fifty well-known celebrities who feel the same way:

1. CATHERINE BACH
2. JOE DON BAKER
3. KAREN BLACK
4. JOYCE BULIFANTE
5. MICHAEL CALLAN
6. ROBERT CARRADINE
7. JACK CARTER
8. SCATMAN CROTHERS
9. JOHN DAVIDSON
10. WILLIAM DEVANE
11. CLIFF DE YOUNG
12. PHYLLIS DILLER
13. KEVIN DOBSON
14. GREG EVIGAN
15. LOU FERRIGNO
16. LEIF GARRETT
17. CINDY GARVEY
18. ANDY GIBB
19. ROBERT HAYS
20. MARILU HENNER
21. RON HOWARD
22. BRUCE JENNER
23. JAMES EARLE JONES
24. HAL LINDEN
25. DEAN PAUL MARTIN
26. KENT McCORD
27. DONNA MILLS
28. TED NEELY

29. PAT O'BRIAN
30. RANDI OAKES
31. ROBERT PINE
32. JOAN PRATHER
33. PRISCILLA PRESLEY
34. ROB REINER
35. SUSAN RICHARDSON
36. JOE SANTOS
37. MICKEY SPILLANE
38. PARKER STEVENSON
39. BARRY SULLIVAN

40. FRAN TARKENTON
41. JOSH TAYLOR
42. CHARLENE TILTON
43. ELLEN TRAVOLTA
44. TANYA TUCKER
45. HERVE VILLACHAIZE
46. RALPH WAITE
47. JON WALMSLEY
48. PAT WAYNE
49. CARL WEATHERS
50. HENRY WINKLER

8

"I'VE GOT A SECRET":
The Way the Stars Really Are

Or: How Private Can Their Private Lives Be?

CHAPTER

DR. LAURENCE J. PETER'S LIST OF 15 WHO REACHED THEIR LEVEL OF COMPETENCE AND WENT BEYOND TO ACHIEVE THEIR PETER PRINCIPLE

Dr. Peter's best-selling book, *The Peter Principle,* identified the universal truth that: in every hierarchy, an individual tends to rise to his level of incompetency. Peter: "In other words, the cream rises until it sours.

"In television, sometimes levels are achieved rapidly; while others work away at it for years—until their ultimate potential is surpassed."

1.	FRED SILVERMAN	9.	ANITA BRYANT
2.	FARRAH FAWCETT	10.	HOWARD COSELL
3.	McLEAN STEVENSON	11.	PAUL MICHAEL GLASER
4.	DICK VAN DYKE	12.	SUSAN ANTON
5.	ROBERT BLAKE	13.	JAMES AUBREY
6.	STEVE MARTIN	14.	RICHARD BOONE
7.	JOHN BELUSHI	15.	RON LIEBMAN
8.	HENRY WINKLER		

BOB MICHAELSON'S LIST OF THE 6 HARDEST-TO-PHOTOGRAPH, MOST UNCOOPERATIVE TV STARS

One of the foremost of the Hollywood paparazzi photographers is Bob Michaelson. At forty-five, after having pounded the bricks for years clutching his Rollei, he now runs his own agency with a staff of twenty cameramen nationwide. His agency sells over 10,000 celebrity photos in a single year.

Says Michaelson: "To be a successful paparazzi, you have to have guts. You have to be determined and willing to wait five hours in the rain for a good shot. You don't have to be a great photographer, or an artist, or even a good newsman, just have the will to win."

Among the TV celebs who are often as determined not to be photographed at every turn are:

1. FRANK SINATRA
2. CARROLL O'CONNOR
3. REDD FOXX
4. ERIK ESTRADA
5. MISS PIGGY (without makeup)
6. ALAN ALDA

Anita Bryant, songstress and former Florida orange juice queen, achieved her Peter Principle when she campaigned against gay liberation in the name of God. (Have you noticed how some of the most heinous things in history have been done in the name of God?)

Dinah Shore, whose real name is Frances Shore, has made Mr. Blackwell's Worst Dressed Women list many, many times.

MR. BLACKWELL'S 9 WORST-DRESSED WOMEN ON TV

On the first Tuesday of every January for the past eighteen years, Hollywood fashion designer Mr. Blackwell separates the wheat from the chaff, the chic from the goats, in his annual list of the World's Ten Worst-Dressed Women. As much an institution as Groundhog Day, the tart-tongued designer zings out his winners' dubious qualifications at the ladies he feels have violated fashion's prime purpose—to glorify womanhood.

1. LONI ANDERSON (WKRP), 3rd Worst Dressed, 1979. "Gravity could be her worst enemy, and she dresses to prove it."
2. DOLLY PARTON ("The Dolly Parton Show"), Worst Dressed, 1978. "A ruffled bedspread covering king-sized pillows."
3. SUZANNE SOMERS ("Three's Company"), 2nd Worst Dressed, 1978
4. FARRAH FAWCETT ("Charlie's Angels"), Worst Dressed, 1977
5. LINDA RONSTADT (TV guest star), 2nd Worst Dressed, 1977
6. CHARO (frequent TV guest star), 3rd Worst Dressed, 1977
7. LOUISE LASSER ("Mary Hartman, Mary Hartman"), Worst Dressed, 1976
8. ANGIE DICKINSON ("Police Woman"), 3rd Worst Dressed, 1976
9. DINAH SHORE ("Dinah"), She's made the list many, many times "Most of the stars are wonderful. They know it's all good, clean fun. Except Dinah. I've tried to do her show and she has flat zeroed me out."

21 TV STARS AND THEIR REAL NAMES

Changing a name when embarking upon a career was a practice begun in the Golden Age of Hollywood, when the major studios would put an actor under contract and then build him into a star from the soles of his feet to the color of his hair; and this often included name changes as part of the new identity. It's not done too much anymore, unless an actor's real moniker, like, for example, Krekor Ohanian, is too much of a jaw breaker. Here are twenty-one well-known names, and the identities they came into this world with:

1. EVE ARDEN—Eunice Quedens
2. JACK BENNY—Benjamin Kubelsky
3. GEORGE BURNS—Nathan Burnham
4. GENE BARRY—Eugene Klass
5. MIKE CONNORS—Krekor Ohanian
6. ROBERT BLAKE—Michael Gubitosi
7. ROCK HUDSON—Roy Fitzgerald
8. DAVID JANSSEN—David Meyer

9. MICHAEL LANDON—Eugene Orowitz
10. JERRY LEWIS—Joseph Levitch
11. LEE MAJORS—Lee Yeary
12. DEAN MARTIN—Dino Crocetti
13. KARL MALDEN—Malden Sukilovich
14. STEFANIE POWERS—Zofja Federkiewicz
15. DINAH SHORE—Frances Shore
16. DAVID SOUL—David Solberg
17. JAMES STACY—Maurice Elias
18. CONNIE STEVENS—Concetta Ann Ingolia
19. DANNY THOMAS—Amos Jacobs
20. REDD FOXX—John Sanford
21. BEA ARTHUR—Bernice Frankel

10 TV STARS REVEAL HOW THEY EXERCISE AND KEEP IN SHAPE

1. ROBIN WILLIAMS, "Mork and Mindy" ('78–present)
   "I jog whenever I can, usually in the hills near my home. And I do yoga exercises twice a week. When I'm at work at Paramount, I roller skate from set to set."
2. LYNDA CARTER, "Wonder Woman" ('76–79)
   "I jog about a mile and a half to two miles in the morning. Then I come home and do floor exercises. I also work out in my complete gym, which has a stationary bicycle as well. Sometimes I'll play tennis instead, but I do exercise in some way every day."
3. CHERYL TIEGS, TV commercials
   "In New York, I skip rope in my apartment, and in California I run on the beach and swim in the ocean."
4. VALERIE HARPER, "Rhoda" ('74-78)
   "I jog four times a week, and work out every day on parallel bars and weights in my living room. I also do stretching exercises, as well as cut calories and drink lots of juices."
5. PERNELL ROBERTS, "Trapper John, M.D." ('79–present)
   "I run. It's a wonderful way to unwind and to keep fit."
6. RODNEY DANGERFIELD, "The Dean Martin Comedy Hour" ('72–73), frequent guest on talk and variety shows
   "I go to a gym every day for aerobic exercises, like bicycle riding and stretching. I don't go in too much for that heavy stuff, though I did try jogging once. My doctor told me to jog five miles a day. A week later I called him and said, 'Doctor, what do I do now? I'm thirty-five miles from home.' "

7. ANDY KAUFMAN, "Taxi" ('78–present)

"Meditation, yoga, and wrestling women—in that order. I'd wrestle women every day if I could, but I can't get enough matches. Heterosexual wrestling is a wonderful way to exercise—and to get to know your date better."

8. SUZANNE SOMMERS, "Three's Company" ('77–present)

"I keep in shape with an insane, nonstop hectic schedule, which often keeps me running seventeen hours a day, including rehearsing for my Vegas show. I encounter enough stress during a single day to keep my heart pumping and my body burning calories."

9. CATHY LEE CROSBY, "That's Incredible" ('80–present)

"I fill my life with sports, like wind-surfing, high-wire and trapeze acrobatics. I love tennis. I'm competitive with myself. I enjoy being a jock—it's fun."

10. CHEVY CHASE, "Saturday Night Live" ('75–present)

"In the afternoon, I run, not jog, for up to seven miles, and then speed sprint for a hundred yards several times. That really gets the heart pumping and the blood circulating."

LOU FERRIGNO'S LIST OF THE 6 BEST-BUILT TV ACTORS

Ever since its premiere in March 1978, "The Incredible Hulk" has captivated viewers with its Jekyll-and-Hyde transformation of David Banner (Bill Bixby) into a massive green monster who is driven by rage, and who, in the person of Lou Ferrigno, bursts not only through walls, but right out of his clothes. (The wardrobe budget on the show reads like the national debt.)

Although too modest to claim the number 1 spot on his list for himself—at 6'5" and 260 pounds, with a 56" chest, 32" waist, and 21" biceps—the Hulk's alter ego is unquestionably the best-built TV actor around. (Unless you consider 5'10" tall Lynda "Wonder Woman" Carter, but that's another list . . .)

1. LOU FERRIGNO, "The Incredible Hulk" ('78–present)

"I wasn't going to say myself, but if you insist, I really am the best-built guy on TV."

2. BRUCE LEE, "The Green Hornet" ('66–67)

"For a little guy (5'10") he was the best proportioned, with great definition."

3. STUART DAMON, "General Hospital" ('76–present)

"His physique impresses me."

Lou Ferrigno, and his alter-ego, "The Incredible Hulk." No one would argue the fact that he's the best built actor on TV. At least, not with Lou.

4. CLINT WALKER, "Cheyenne" ('55–63)
   "He's always been in good shape. If he hadn't been, that skiing accident where the ski pole went into his heart would've killed him."
5. ROBERT CONRAD, "The Wild, Wild West" ('65–70)
   "He works out all the time and keeps himself in good shape."
6. RON ELY, "Tarzan" ('66–69)
   "He's pretty well-built for such a tall guy (6'4")."

SALARIES OF 17 SERIES STARS

ACTOR/ACTRESS	SERIES	SALARY
1. PETER FALK	"Columbo"	$350,000 per 2-hr. episode
2. JAMES GARNER	"Rockford Files"	100,000 per 1-hr. episode
3. ROBERT CONRAD	"Sloan"	100,000 per 1-hr. episode
4. CARROLL O'CONNOR	"All in the Family"	100,000 per ½-hr. episode

5. KARL MALDEN	"Skag"	75,000 per 1-hr. episode
6. ROCK HUDSON	"McMillan & Wife"	75,000 per 1½-hr. episode
7. LARRY HAGMAN	"Dallas"	70,000 per 1-hr. episode
8. CLAUDE AKINS	"Sheriff Lobo"	50,000 per 1-hr. episode
9. HENRY WINKLER	"Happy Days"	50,000 per ½-hr. episode
10. ANGIE DICKINSON	"Police Woman"	40,000 per 1-hr. episode
11. ROBIN WILLIAMS	"Mork & Mindy"	35,000 per ½-hr. episode
12. SUZANNE SOMERS	"Three's Company"	30,000 per ½-hr. episode
13. LONI ANDERSON	"WKRP In Cincinnati"	20,000 per ½-hr. episode
14. ROBERT GUILLAUME	"Benson"	20,000 per ½-hr. episode
15. PAM DAWBER	"Mork & Mindy"	15,000 per ½-hr. episode
16. ROBERT WALDEN	"Lou Grant"	12,500 per ½-hr. episode
17. DONNY MOST	"Happy Days"	12,000 per ½-hr. episode

MICHAEL LEVINE'S LIST OF THE 10 MOST SOUGHT-AFTER ADDRESSES OF TV STARS

Michael Levine, twenty-six, is the author of the best-selling *How to Reach Anyone Who's Anyone* (Price/Stern/Sloan $4.95), which has been referred to by critics as the *Guinness Book of Addresses*. It contains 3,200 addresses of notables so you can write directly to the source, whether it's the president of Revlon, or Howard Cosell. In his exhaustive research and letter-writing, certain names popped up more often as the most desirable addresses to have:

1. MISS PIGGY of "The Muppet Show"
2. LARRY HAGMAN of "Dallas"
3. HOWARD COSELL
4. LONI ANDERSON of "W.K.R.P. In Cincinnati"
5. CHARLIE'S ANGELS (whoever they happen to be at the time)

Miss Piggy, in all her glory, on "The Muppet Show." Her address is the most sought-after among TV stars, according to Michael Levine, address expert.

6. LUCILLE BALL
7. WALTER CRONKITE
8. GARY COLEMAN of "Diff'rent Strokes"
9. BARBARA WALTERS
10. MIKE WALLACE of "60 Minutes"

DENNIS WEAVER'S LIST OF 10 TV ACTORS WHO'VE BEEN BITTEN BY THE SINGING BUG

"In each of us, I think, there's a secret desire to be something in addition to what we are," says Dennis Weaver, of "Gunsmoke" (1955–64) and "McCloud" (1970–77) fame. Weaver's secret leanings have surfaced in recent years, when he began singing and playing guitar on TV specials and variety shows. Weaver recalls: "My first interest and involvement with singing came in 1958, when Milburn Stone, Amanda Blake, and I put together a trio, a singing act for our personal appearances. Two years later, we broke the house record for the Albuquerque Arena during the New Mexico State Fair. We had a lot of fun, and we were in demand for personal appearances." Weaver fulfilled a long-time ambition when he recorded an album called "The World Needs Country Music," in 1979. And it seems that he's not the only actor to be bitten by the singing bug.

Dennis Weaver comes out of the closet as a Country and Western singer. He's recorded a hit album, "The World Needs Country Music," and does singing gigs.

1. JIMMY GARNER

   Recently recorded an album in Nashville with Waylon Jennings. Since his "Rockford Files" series ('74–80) ceased production in early 1980, he's had the time to pursue other interests. "But, Jimmy, recording with Waylon is like betting on a pat hand. It's cheating a little bit. You haven't gone out and done it on your own. . . . I remember when he sang at the Emmy Awards ceremonies the first year I was nominated for an Emmy; must've been 1957. Jim Arness was also nominated that year. We sat there and listened to him; I think it was his first year on 'Maverick,' and I was surprised. He wasn't bad."

2. JIM NABORS

   Best known for his Gomer Pyle characterization on "The Andy Griffith Show" ('63–64) and on "Gomer Pyle USMC" ('64–70), is also known for his incredible singing voice, thanks to his many albums and TV guest appearances. "It's hard to imagine that his speaking voice, which is sort of Southern country, and his singing voice, which is a beautiful light operatic tenor, come out of the same person."

3. TELLY SAVALAS

   He traded his "Kojak" ('73–78) badge and lollipop for Sinatra-type strings for his albums, "Telly" and "Telly Savalas." "In fact, when I was in England on a tour, he had a number-one song on the charts over there."

4. DAVID SOUL, from "Starsky and Hutch" ('73–79)

   Used to appear on the "Merv Griffin Show" wearing a hood and billed as the Mystery Singer. "When I was touring in England in 1977, he had just had a number-one record, called 'Don't Give Up on Us,' which was the title cut of his album. He recorded another called 'Playing to an Audience of One.' "

5. JOHN TRAVOLTA

   Did a stylized version of "Barbara Ann" on "Welcome Back, Kotter" ('75–79), which led directly to his first album, "John Travolta."

6. ROCK HUDSON from "McMillan & Wife" ('71–77)

   Turned friend Rod McKuen's tunes into an album: "Rock Hudson Sings the Songs of Rod McKuen."

7. LYNDA CARTER, TV's "Wonder Woman" ('75–79)

   Proof that men aren't the only ones bitten by the bug. In 1979, she recorded her first album,"Country and Western."

8. BOBBY SHERMAN of "Here Comes the Brides" ('68–70)

   Capitalized on his huge teenage following to record and sell a truckful of albums and singles.

9. CHAD EVERETT

   Tried out his vocal chords in an album called "Chad," while starring in "Medical Center" ('69–76).

10. DICK CHAMBERLAIN

Scored a huge success in the "Shôgun" mini-series (Sept. '80), and recorded a half-dozen albums during his tenure on "Dr. Kildare" ('61–66). They're now collectors' items.

CATHY LEE CROSBY'S LIST OF 8 OF THE MOST INCREDIBLE *THAT'S INCREDIBLE* STORIES

Along with dimpled John Davidson and former football pro Fran Tarkenton, Cathy Lee Crosby cohosts "That's Incredible" (1980–present), a highly controversial series hit. Crosby's incredible background would qualify her to be on the show if she weren't already a regular: She was a former teenage tennis pro, has a degree in psychology, is an accomplished aerialist, and declined becoming one of "Charlie's Angels."

Admits Crosby: "I love my show. It offers a better way of entertainment. Fran, John, and I are like the Three Musketeers, encouraging people to develop their potential." And, yes, along with all of America, she has been personally touched and impressed by some of the people and stories to have been featured on "That's Incredible."

1. Yogi Coudoux Paulin displayed his unbelievable ability in a 2 x 2-foot box underwater at the Oakwood apartments in Burbank, California.
2. Sheila Holzworth, the blind girl from Des Moines, Iowa, runs track. Before being blinded in a freak accident, she was a running star and now keeps running with the aid of a radar.
3. One-legged athletic star Carl Joseph is a nineteen-year-old high school senior in Madison, Florida, who participates in football, basketball, and track.
4. The paraplegic who climbed the Himalayas in a wheelchair.
5. The new energy developed by Consumers Solar Electric Power. Their solar cells power cars at about half the cost of gasoline. Hopefully, they will be available to the public sometime in 1981.
6. The new medical procedure that saves snake bite victims' lives through transfusions. Twenty-four-year-old James Lee of Monroe, Louisiana, was bitten and flown to Florida, where he was saved by a transfusion from Bill Hasst.
7. The Bungee Jumpers who jumped off the 1,000-foot bridge at Royal Gorge, Colorado, attached to bungee cords, under the leadership of David Kirke from Oxford, England.
8. Darven Miller drowned in icy water and was pronounced legally dead for thirty minutes; then he was brought back to life through CPR (Cardiac Pulmonary Resusitation) by Commander David Smith.

9

CHAPTER

"MUSICAL CHAIRS":
Fun and Games and Music
Or: *How Many Notes To Identify This Chapter?*

MONTY HALL'S LIST OF 10 MEMORABLE DEALS ON "LET'S MAKE A DEAL"

Television host/emcee extraordinaire, Monty Hall has been an even more enduring fixture on the tube than the NBC peacock. His initial national prominence on early audience participation shows "Strike It Rich" (1955) and "Keep Talking" (1958) led eventually to "Let's Make a Deal," which premiered in 1963 and has been running ever since, first on NBC, then ABC, and currently in syndication.

1. THE MOST PAINFUL DEAL
   A little Italian woman named Rosa, five feet tall and just as wide, got excited when she won a prize and wanted to throw her arms around me. The arms were too short, and the clenched fists caught me on both sides of my jaw, rendering me *non compos mentis* for about five minutes.

2. THE "WHERE DID IT GO?" DEAL
   I asked a woman if she would trade the curtain for what was inside the box of chicken. She agreed. I lifted up the box lid, and there was a beautiful watch case, and inside the beautiful watch case . . . nothing! The $2,500 watch had been lifted backstage! I assured the woman that it was supposed to be there, and would receive it as advertised.

3. ANOTHER "WHERE DID IT GO?" DEAL

   We opened up the curtain to reveal our model, Carol Merrill, standing with a tether rope—but the baby elephant that was supposed to have been there was gone. At the sound of the door opening, trumpeting his last farewell, he had bolted from the stage and from the studio, and was last seen galloping down Prospect Avenue.

4. MY FAVORITE PRIZE DEAL

   We arranged for a private sleeper and dining car for eight people to be attached to a cross-country train which would end up at a siding in Montreal, Canada, for Expo '67. That's my idea of a dream vacation.

5. THE "WATCH IT, BUDDY" DEAL

   A married couple wins a car. The woman throws her arms around me and kisses me, and her husband follows suit. After the laughter subsides, he says: "I always said I'd do that if I got on the show!"

6. "WATCH IT, BUDDY" PART 2

   Man wins prize . . . kisses me. No wife. No story. No explanation. Suspect.

7. THE "OOPS, I'M SORRY" DEAL

   I walk down the aisle, look to my right, but make a deal with the woman on my left. Woman on the right, in frustration, starts hitting me with a stuffed tiger. After the show, she apologizes to the audience and to me,

Monty Hall has been making deals on "Let's Make a Deal" for fourteen years. And some of them have been pretty interesting.

saying: "My goodness, I'm an attorney and I lost my head. Can we edit it out of the show?" We didn't.

8. THE "NEVER FORGET YOUR TRADE" DEAL
A little man wins a car, jumps six feet into the air, and on his descent, grabs my lapel, saying: "I'm a tailor. Nice piece of material you have there."

9. THE QUICK-THINKING DEAL
Man with mask and flippers is offered $500 if he can produce a pool ball. Using his noodle and remembering a previous deal behind the door, he runs across the set, flippers flapping, and removes a pool ball from a pool table, flips back triumphantly, and collects his $500.

10. THE "MATCH MADE IN HEAVEN" DEAL
A couple who had been waiting for tickets for two years finds out their tickets are for the evening of their wedding day. And would you believe it, they came to the show. And would you believe this—they won the Super Deal worth $30,000! What a wedding present!

PETER MARSHALL'S LIST OF 21 ONE-LINERS FROM "HOLLYWOOD SQUARES"

Hosted by Peter Marshall since its debut in 1966, "Hollywood Squares," a durable, fast-paced celebrity-studded game show, has been a hit in both daytime and nighttime versions. Often, the quiz element, with the two vying contestants, has been distinctly secondary to the hilarious quips and one-liners from the stars in the huge tic-tac-toe squares. The regulars have included Paul Lynde, Rose Marie, Charley Weaver (Cliff Arquette), Jonathan Winters, John Davidson, and others.

1. According to *Movie Life* magazine, Ann-Margret would like to start having babies, soon, but her husband wants her to wait awhile. Why?
PAUL LYNDE: He's out of town.

2. Dennis Weaver, Debbie Reynolds, and Shelley Winters star in the movie *What's the Matter with Helen?* Who plays Helen?
CHARLEY WEAVER: Dennis Weaver—that's why they ask the question.

3. What are "dual purpose cattle" good for that other cattle aren't?
PAUL LYNDE: They give milk . . . and cookies, but I don't recommend the cookies.

4. Who stays pregnant for a longer period of time, your wife or your elephant?
PAUL LYNDE: Who told you about my elephant?

5. When a couple have a baby, who is responsible for its sex?
CHARLEY WEAVER: I'll lend him the car. The rest is up to him.

Host Peter Marshall hasn't missed a single taping of "The Hollywood Squares" in its entire run of fourteen years. He's won numerous Emmys for his work on the show, which itself has a total of twenty-seven Emmy Awards to its credit, more than any other show of its kind in the history of TV.

6. Robert Young recently stated, "I never, never give . . ." something to his fans who ask for it. What?
PAUL LYNDE: A hysterectomy.

7. James Stewart did it over twenty years ago when he was forty-one years old. Now he says it was "one of the best things I ever did." What was it?
MARTY ALLEN: Rhonda Fleming.

8. Jackie Gleason recently revealed that he firmly believes in them and has actually seen them on at least two occasions. What are they?
CHARLEY WEAVER: His feet.

9. Before a cow will give you any milk, she has to have something very important. What?
PAUL LYNDE: An engagement ring.

10. According to Robert Mitchum, one thing has ruined more actors than drinking. What?
CHARLEY WEAVER: Not drinking.

11. When the Lone Ranger finished with a case, he left something behind. What?
PAUL LYNDE: A masked baby.

12. True or false: Some African Watusi tribesmen greet guests by running toward them at full speed, then high-jumping over them.
CHARLEY WEAVER: This is sometimes terribly embarrassing to tall guests.

13. You're on your first visit to Japan, and you head right for the Kabuki. Why?
PAUL LYNDE: It was a long plane ride.

Paul Lynde, the unequalled master of the one-liner zingers on "Hollywood Squares," had his own series briefly. "The Paul Lynde Show" also featured Jane Actman, John Calvin, Elizabeth Allen, and Pamlyn Ferdin, and was on for one season, 1972–73.

14. If you're going to make a parachute jump, you should be at least how high?

   CHARLEY WEAVER: Three days of steady drinking should do it.

15. Do female frogs croak?

   PAUL LYNDE: If you hold their little heads under water.

16. You've been having trouble going to sleep. Are you probably a man or a woman?

   DON KNOTTS: That's what's keeping me awake.

17. Is there any such thing as an F cup in bra sizes?

   PAUL LYNDE: Yes, it sleeps four.

18. True or false: Many people sleep better in their street clothes than they do in their pajamas.

   PAUL LYNDE: Yes. We call them winos.

19. According to the *World Book,* is it okay to freeze your persimmons?
    PAUL LYNDE: No. You should dress warmly.
20. According to psychologists, when a child begins to get curious about sex, what is the one question he will most ask his mommy and daddy?
    PAUL LYNDE: Where can I get some?
21. Your baby has a certain object which he loves to cling to. Should you try to break him of his habit?
    JOAN RIVERS: Yes. It's daddy's turn.

PETER MARSHALL'S LIST OF HIS 5 ALL-TIME FAVORITE GAME SHOWS

1. JEOPARDY ('64–79)
   "My all-time favorite." Developed by Merv Griffin and produced by his production company, the game here involved three contestants who competed for cash by answering questions uncovered on a board of thirty squares, containing five answers in each of six categories. Art Fleming hosted the series, both on NBC and in syndication.
2. COLLEGE BOWL ('59–70)
   Two four-member teams from different colleges and universities competed on this fast-paced quiz show for $1,500 in scholarship funds and the right to return the following week; the losing team took back $500 to its school. Allen Ludden hosted from '59 to '62; then Robert Earle to the end of the run.
3. HOLLYWOOD SQUARES ('66–present)
   "It's a lot of fun for me. I enjoy watching it as well as doing the show." Hosted by Marshall, this durable show, in which two contestants play tic-tac-toe on a huge gameboard by matching answers with the celebrity in each of the squares, features regulars like Paul Lynde, George Gobel, Madame and Wayland, and others. Merrill Heatter and Bob Quigley are executive producers. Kenny Williams is the announcer.
4. PASSWORD ('61–present)
   Although the game has gone through several format changes, the basic concept is still winning by supplying a word or phrase. Now called "Password Plus," it features two competing celebrity and contestant teams. Allen Ludden hosted the game through 1975. A Mark Goodson-Bill Todman production.
5. TO TELL THE TRUTH ('56–77)
   Developed by Goodson-Todman who also gave us "What's My Line," "I've Got a Secret," "Match Game," "Password" among others, "To Tell the Truth" featured a panel of four celebrities who tried to determine which of three guests was telling the truth. Bud Collyer hosted the network versions on CBS; the syndicated show was hosted by Garry Moore and by Joe Garagiola for the last few months.

NORMAN LEAR'S LIST OF A BAKER'S DOZEN ARCHIE BUNKERISMS

Much in the way that "All in the Family" permanently altered the course of television comedy, Archie Bunker as portrayed by Carroll O'Connor may have permanently enriched the English language. In addition to popularizing such expressions as "dingbat," "stifle yourself!" and "meathead," Archie has raised the use of malapropisms to an art. A malapropism is the humorous use of the wrong word, a word that sounds like the right word but is ludicrous in its misapplication—hereafter known as an Archie Bunkerism. Lear: "Archie's command of the language is legionary."

1. There's somethin' rotten in Sweden, Edith. Call it a father's intermission . . . but I smell a rat.
2. What am I, a clairvoyage or somethin'? How do I know what's in the box?
3. This political precussion is over.
4. What you see here is a pigment of your imagination.
5. The Mets winnin' the pennant . . . that would be a miracle. Yeah . . . like the immaculate connection.
6. You and that Reverend Bleedin' Heart Felcher up there in his ivory shower.
7. Cold enough to freeze a witch's mitt.
8. You're invading the issue.
9. That's as funny as a rubber crotch.
10. I received your leaflet at my home residence and the words "substantial profit" fought my eye.
11. I always said those two was right outta science friction.
12. You're taking it outta contest.
13. Well, goodbye and good ribbons.

THE TEASING 20 "PHAMOUS PHRASE" MATCH-UP LIST

What sort of trivia/nostalgia/reference/entertainment-type book would this be if there wasn't at least *one* match-up quiz? Well, it just so happens that there are *three*—count 'em—and this happens to be one of them.

The quiz concerns unforgettable expressions foisted on us by our favorite shows over the years, "phamous phrases," which were made unforgettable through sheer repetition. Beware in taking the test, however, because the match-up isn't necessarily a one-to-one match.

Robert Blake on talk shows may express some outspoken opinions, but as TV's "Barretta," he created some "phamous phrases," which everyone picked up on.

Some of the TV series on the right will have more than one "phamous phrase" to come out of it, and some won't have any but are merely red herrings. Good luck, and remember, if you're caught taking this quiz, we will disavow any knowledge of your activity.

"PHAMOUS PHRASE"	SERIES SOURCE
1. Sit on it.	a. ALICE
2. Kiss my grits.	b. BARNABY JONES
3. An' that's the name of that tune.	c. BARETTA
4. And away we go.	d. BATMAN
5. Who was that masked man?	e. THE DAVE GARROWAY SHOW
6. What you see is what you get.	f. THE ED SULLIVAN SHOW
7. And you can take that to the bank.	g. THE FLIP WILSON SHOW
8. Nanoo, nanoo.	h. GET CHRISTIE LOVE
9. We have a really big shew tonight.	i. GUNSMOKE
10. Peace.	j. HAPPY DAYS
11. You wouldn't like me when I'm angry.	k. THE INCREDIBLE HULK

12. Be careful, Matt	l. THE JACKIE GLEASON SHOW
13. The devil made me do it.	m. LAUGH-IN
14. Here come de judge.	n. LAVERNE & SHIRLEY
15. You're under awest, sugah.	o. THE LONE RANGER
16. Mom always liked you best.	p. MORK & MINDY
17. I dood it!	q. OZZIE & HARRIET
18. Holy moley!	r. THE RED SKELTON SHOW
19. Look that up in your Funk & Wagnalls.	s. POLICE WOMAN
20. I don't mess around, boy.	t. THE SMOTHERS BROTHERS SHOW

ANSWERS

1j, 2a, 3c, 4l, 5o, 6g, 7c, 8f, 9t, 10e, 11k, 12i, 13g, 14m, 15h, 16r, 17r, 18d, 18m, 20q

DICK CLARK'S LIST OF 50 TOP MUSICAL STARS WHO MADE THEIR FIRST NATIONAL TV APPEARANCE ON *AMERICAN BANDSTAND*

"American Bandstand" (1957–present), which began as a local show in Philadelphia in 1952, is notable as TV's longest-running musical program and also as the first network series devoted exclusively to rock 'n roll music. Dick Clark, then a popular Philadelphia disc jockey, became host of the show in 1956, set the simple format, and made "Bandstand" a national hit. Many of the hundred or more teenagers who filled the studio each day and danced on the air were regulars and became celebrities, receiving lots of fan mail. Over the years, almost every major rock star appeared at least once. Many got their start on "Bandstand." For example, on the 1957 Thanksgiving show, two New York teenagers who called themselves Tom and Jerry lip-synced their new record, "Hey, Schoolgirl." They're better known today as Simon and Garfunkel. Some Philadelphia artists like Fabian, Bobby Rydell, Dion & the Belmonts, Frankie Avalon, and others, all owed their careers to exposure on "Bandstand."

Explains Dick Clark, the youthful-looking host of the show: "There have been over 8,500 musical appearances made by several thousand artists on 'American Bandstand' since its debut twenty-eight years ago. Among those various performers, hundreds made their first national appearance on the program. Some of the artists who debuted on TV on our show may surprise you. They include the following, which, because of space limitations, could be no longer than a list of fifty . . . and in alphabetical order."

1. PAUL ANKA
2. FRANKIE AVALON
3. CHUCK BERRY
4. JAMES BROWN
5. CAPTAIN & TENNILLE
6. THE CARPENTERS
7. JOHNNY CASH
8. CHUBBY CHECKER
9. COASTERS
10. SAM COOKE
11. CREEDENCE CLEARWATER REVIVAL
12. JIM CROCE
13. BOBBY DARIN
14. NEIL DIAMOND
15. DION & THE BELMONTS
16. FATS DOMINO
17. THE DOORS
18. DRIFTERS
19. THE EVERLY BROTHERS
20. FIFTH DIMENSION
21. FOUR SEASONS
22. FOUR TOPS
23. GLADYS KNIGHT & THE PIPS
24. BILL HALEY & THE COMETS
25. BUDDY HOLLY
26. JACKSON FIVE
27. JEFFERSON AIRPLANE
28. BRENDA LEE
29. JERRY LEE LEWIS
30. LOGGINS & MESSINA
31. THE MAMAS & THE PAPAS
32. BARRY MANILOW
33. JOHNNY MATHIS
34. TONY ORLANDO & DAWN
35. THE PLATTERS
36. THE RASCALS
37. OTIS REDDING
38. HELEN REDDY
39. MARTY ROBBINS
40. SMOKEY ROBINSON AND THE|MIRACLES
41. LINDA RONSTADT
42. NEIL SEDAKA
43. THE SHIRELLES
44. SIMON & GARFUNKEL
45. THE SUPREMES
46. THE TEMPTATIONS
47. THREE DOG NIGHT
48. CONWAY TWITTY
49. DIONNE WARWICK
50. STEVIE WONDER

DAVID ROSE'S LIST OF 12 MEMORABLE THEMES FROM TELEVISION SHOWS

During his twenty-seven years with Red Skelton, first on radio, then for two decades on TV's "The Red Skelton Show" (1951–71), David Rose and his orchestra became one of the most celebrated names in the music field. In addition to scoring dozens of motion pictures and winning two Academy Award nominations, Rose was equally busy with additional TV assignments. He composed music and conducted for the major stars: three years with Bob Hope, specials and variety shows for Bing Crosby, Julie Andrews, Dean Martin, among others; and for his musical direction on the unforgettable "An Evening with

For twenty years, Red Skelton served up guests stars like Fernando Lamas on "The Red Skelton Show." But for twenty-seven years, through radio and TV, he used the memorable David Rose composition, "Holiday for Strings," as his theme music.

Fred Astaire" (1959), he won an Emmy. Rose also claimed two additional Emmys for scoring on "Bonanza" (1970) and "Little House on the Prairie" (1979).

1. "THIS IS TODAY," by Ray Ellis—"The Today Show" ('52–present)
   "My all-time favorite. This is the best theme on TV."
2. "HOLIDAY FOR STRINGS," by David Rose—"The Red Skelton Show" ('51–71)
   "We used this theme for Red for twenty-seven years. I guess that makes it memorable."
3. "THE PETER GUNN THEME," by Henry Mancini—"Peter Gunn" ('58–61)
4. "THOSE WERE THE DAYS," by Lee Adams and Charles Strouse—"All in the Family" ('71–79)
5. "SUICIDE IS PAINLESS," by Johnny Mandel—"M*A*S*H ('72–present)
6. "MISSION IMPOSSIBLE," by Lalo Schifrin—"Mission: Impossible" ('66–73)
7. "BONANZA," by Jay Livingston and Ray Evans—"Bonanza" ('59–73)
8. "DRAGNET MARCH," by Walter Schumann—"Dragnet" ('52–70)
9. "BATMAN," by Neil Hefti—"Batman" ('66–68)
10. "ROUTE 66," by Nelson Riddle—"Route 66" ('60–64)
11. "STAR TREK THEME," by Alexander Courage—"Star Trek" ('66–69)
12. "ELIOT NESS THEME," by Nelson Riddle—"Untouchables" ('59–63)

22 HIT THEME SONGS FROM TV SERIES, THE RECORDING ARTISTS, AND THEIR HIGHEST POSITION ON THE MUSIC CHARTS

1. DRAGNET, 1953; Ray Anthony; shot up to #3.
2. ZORRO. 1958; The Chordettes; #17.
3. PETER GUNN, 1959; Ray Anthony; #8.
4. MR. LUCKY. 1960; Henry Mancini; #21.
5. BONANZA, 1961; Al Caiola; #19.
6. DR. KILDARE, 1962; Richard Chamberlain; #10.*
7. BEN CASEY, 1962; Valjean; #28.
8. ROUTE 66, 1962; Nelson Riddle; #30.
9. HAVE GUN WILL TRAVEL: "Ballad of Paladin," 1962; Duane Eddy; #33.
10. BEVERLY HILLBILLIES: "The Ballad of Jed Clampett," 1962; Flatt & Scruggs; #44.
11. SECRET AGENT: "Secret Agent Man," 1966; Johnny Rivers; #3.
12. BATMAN, 1966; The Marketts; #17.

*NOTE: Only the stars of "Dr. Kildare" and "All in the Family" recorded their theme songs. All the others were recorded by the composers or outside musicians.

"Peter Gunn," which starred Craig Stevens and featured Hope Emerson, boasted original jazz themes by Henry Mancini. The music was as popular as the show. Several successful record albums were released, and the "Peter Gunn Theme" became the third TV theme song to hit the best-selling charts.

13. MISSION: IMPOSSIBLE, 1968; Lalo Schifrin; #41.
14. HAWAII FIVE-O, 1969; The Ventures; #4.
15. ALL IN THE FAMILY: "Those Were the Days," 1971; Carroll O'Connor and Jean Stapleton; #43.
16. S.W.A.T., 1975; Rhythm Heritage; #1.
17. THE ROCKFORD FILES, 1975; Mike Post; #10.
18. WELCOME BACK, KOTTER: "Welcome Back," 1976; John Sebastian; #1.
19. HAPPY DAYS, 1976; Pratt & McClain; #5.
20. BARETTA: "Keep Your Eye on the Sparrow," 1976; Rhythm Heritage; #20.
21. LAVERNE & SHIRLEY: "Making Our Dreams Come True," 1976; Cyndi Greco; #26.
22. CHARLIE'S ANGELS, 1977; Henry Mancini; #45.

10

CHAPTER

"PEOPLE ARE FUNNY":
TV's Specialty Is Humor

Or: *Almost Anything Can Be Funny . . .*
At the Time

LUCILLE BALL'S FAVORITE 10 . . . ER . . .
20 "I LOVE LUCY" EPISODES

"I Love Lucy" ('51–60) was television's first bonafide hit situation comedy series. Its success is unparalleled. During its six-season tenure, "I Love Lucy" ranked first for four years, second once, and third once.

Lucille Ball and Desi Arnaz.

(Its last three seasons on prime-time were as occasional hour-long episodes on "The Lucy-Desi Comedy Hour.")

"I Love Lucy" pioneered major breakthroughs in the way TV was produced. The decision to film it, rather than do it live from New York like other shows at the time (as CBS wanted it done), was not only a stroke of genius, but had far-reaching effects. Filming made it possible to have high-quality prints of all episodes for endless syndication, which made millions for Lucille Ball and Desi Arnaz, whose company, Desilu, produced and owned the series. "I Love Lucy" is by far the most successful series ever in worldwide syndication and has never stopped running in reruns. This set the pattern for all of television, and resulted in the eventual shift of TV production from New York to Hollywood's filming facilities. The use of three cameras to film before a live audience was also an "I Love Lucy" first.

The basic concept of the show was simple: Desi played Ricky Ricardo, a band leader whose wife, a wacky redhead named Lucy, made life unpredictable and crazy with her perpetual schemes to break into show business. Their landlord neighbors, best friends, and comedy foils, the Mertzes, were played by William Frawley and Vivian Vance. The plots of the individual episodes were superb, the gags inventive, but the ingredient that made it all work was the masterful clowning of Lucille Ball, the first lady of TV, an unequaled talent and comedienne.

While everyone has favorite episodes of "I Love Lucy," there are so many memorable ones that trying to list the best is indeed difficult. Even CBS programing executives had a tough time. Over the summer of 1958, in a series of reruns entitled "The Top 10 Lucy Shows," there were not ten, but thirteen episodes. Understandable. Lucille Ball, too, has her favorite ten shows . . . or . . . ah, make that favorite twenty shows:

1. "THE ADAGIO"—Show #12, original telecast December 17, 1951
   Lucy tries to learn an apache dance number for an upcoming show at the Tropicana.
2. "THE BALLET"—Show #19, February 18, 1952
   Lucy tries desperately to learn ballet for a new nightclub revue. She ad-libbed brilliantly when her foot accidentally caught in the ballet practice bar during the live filming.
3. "THE FREEZER"—Show #29, April 28, 1952
   Lucy and Ethel acquire a huge walk-in freezer and order two sides of beef, unaware of the enormity of their order.
4. "LUCY DOES A TV COMMERCIAL"—Show #30, May 5, 1952

One of Lucille Ball's favorite episodes of "I Love Lucy" is this one, entitled "Lucy and John Wayne," in which she and Ethel (Vivian Vance) steal Wayne's cement footprints from the Grauman's Chinese Theatre. Their "souvenir" breaks, and they're unable to return it as Ricky (Desi Arnaz) insists. So, they try to duplicate them, and all Lucy is able to manage at first is her own tush-print.

Lucy connives to appear in a commercial on the TV show Ricky is emceeing. As she rehearses the pitch, sampling the vitamin syrup with each try, she gets progressively drunk, because the elixir is mostly alcohol.

5. "SAXOPHONE"—Show #40, September 22, 1952

   Lucy's attempts to make Ricky jealous enough not to go out of town on a series of one-nighters without her backfire when he hires three actors to pose as her lovers.

6. "LUCY GOES TO THE HOSPITAL"—Show #56, January 19, 1953

   Despite a series of mishaps, Lucy gives birth to Ricky Ricardo, Jr. (This episode was seen by more people than any other TV episode of its time, and is one of Desi Arnaz' favorites, too.)

7. "THE CAMPING TRIP"—Show #64, June 8, 1953

   To discourage Lucy and Ethel from wanting to go on a summer camping trip, Ricky and Fred hatch a scheme to take them on a trial weekend trip in order to make them hate the outdoors.

8. "THE GIRLS GO INTO BUSINESS"—Show #68, October 12, 1953

   Certain that they'll be rich overnight, Lucy and Ethel go into a dress shop business as partners.

9. "EQUAL RIGHTS"—Show #70, October 26, 1953

   After an argument about Lucy and Ethel wanting to be treated like men, the foursome go to dinner and request separate checks. When the girls are unable to pay, they have to wash dishes.

10. "THE MILLION DOLLAR IDEA"—Show #79, January 11, 1954

    Having spent her house budget through June 12, 1978, Lucy decides she has to make some money before Ricky catches on. She and Ethel decide to market a salad dressing.

11. "MERTZ AND KURTZ"—Show #102, October 11, 1954

    When Fred wants to impress his old vaudeville partner, Lucy agrees to pose as Fred and Ethel's maid.

12. "L.A. AT LAST"—Show #114; February 7, 1955

    Finally arriving in Hollywood to start Ricky's movie career, Lucy goes celebrity hunting at the Brown Derby where she accidentally dumps a tray of desserts on William Holden. Later, Ricky brings Holden back to their hotel room to meet Lucy, who, in embarassment, disguises herself with a putty nose and glasses. The nose grows and catches on fire before she's exposed. (This putty nose routine is Lucille Ball's favorite comedy bit, and the script received an Emmy nomination.)

13. "HARPO MARX"—Show #124, May 9, 1955

    When Lucy promises to have movie stars at an open house to impress a near-sighted friend, she and Ethel steal her friend's glasses and fool her with movie star masks. Then, unexpectedly, Harpo Marx shows up at Ricky's request and runs into Lucy in Harpo disguise.

14. "LUCY AND JOHN WAYNE"—Show #129, October 10, 1955

    In an effort to replace John Wayne's footprints to the Grauman's Chinese Theater, Wayne is repeatedly imposed upon to stick his hands and feet into wet cement because something always fouls things up. (This was Wayne's first episodic television appearance; his second and last episodic TV role was eleven years later on "The Lucy Show.")

15. "LUCY MEETS CHARLES BOYER"—Show #146, March 5, 1956
Forewarned by Ricky, Charles Boyer pretends to be a lookalike when Lucy and Ethel swoop down on him in their usual movie star assault. (This was on their trip to Europe.)

16. "LUCY MEETS BOB HOPE"—Show #154, October 1, 1956
In attempting to talk Bob Hope into appearing at Ricky's new nightspot, the Club Babalu, she causes him to get hit in the head by a foul ball at a Yankee baseball game.

17. "LUCY MEETS ORSON WELLES"—Show #155, October 15, 1956
When Orson Welles agrees to appear at a benefit at the club, Ricky tries to get Lucy out of town on a vacation. But in shopping for the trip, Lucy encounters Welles in a department store.

18. "LITTLE RICKY'S SCHOOL PAGEANT"—Show #163, December 17, 1956
When little Ricky's kindergarten class runs short of cast members for its annual play, Lucy, Ricky, Fred, and Ethel are drafted.

19. "LUCY AND THE LOVING CUP"—Show #164, January 7, 1957
When Ricky pokes fun at Lucy's new hat, she jokingly puts on a loving cup which is to be presented to jockey Johnny Longden at a dinner that night. And the loving cup won't come off!

20. "LUCY RAISES CHICKENS"—Show #171, March 4, 1957
At the same time that *House & Garden* magazine plans to do a photo layout of the Ricardos Connecticut home, Lucy has decided to start raising chickens to keep Ricky from going broke.

CAROL BURNETT'S 4 ALL-TIME FAVORITE COMEDY SERIES

In an era in which variety shows were rapidly disappearing from television, "The Carol Burnett Show" (1967–78) survived for more than a decade. Surrounded by regulars Harvey Korman, Lyle Waggoner, Vicki Lawrence, and Tim Conway, Burnett created a versatile and uniquely consistent comedy/variety program. But she was no novice to TV comedy. She had already been a featured regular in "Stanley" (1956–57), a situation comedy with Buddy Hackett; then "Pantomime Quiz" (1958–59); "The Garry Moore Show" (1958–67); and "The Entertainers" (1964–65).

Burnett: "These are my favorite comedy series. They're in no particular order; they're just the best."

1. SID CAESAR'S YOUR SHOW OF SHOWS ('50–54), Caesar, Imogene Coca, and Carl Reiner

Movie star Fred MacMurray made "My Three Sons" the second longest-running situation comedy — twelve seasons. Two of his three sons were played by Stanley Livingston and Tim Considine.

2. I LOVE LUCY ('51–61), Lucille Ball, Desi Arnaz, Vivian Vance, and William Frawley
3. THE DICK VAN DYKE SHOW ('61–66), Van Dyke, Mary Tyler Moore, Rose Marie, Morey Amsterdam, and Carl Reiner
4. THE MARY TYLER MOORE SHOW ('70–77), Moore, Ed Asner, Ted Knight, and Gavin MacLeod

FRED MacMURRAY'S LIST OF 4 CLASSIC FAMILY-CENTERED TV COMEDIES

Movie superstar Fred MacMurray made television history with his classic "My Three Sons" (1960–72) family situation comedy series. Second only to "Ozzie and Harriet" as network TV's longest-running sitcom, "My Three Sons" was as much a weekly moral lesson about family ties, love, responsibilities, consideration, and all the wonderful things that carry true value, as it was a comedy. What was important

arol Burnett, clowning on "The Carol Burnett Show," followed Lucille Ball as ✓'s premier comedienne. Her variety show was on the air for over a decade.

about the show was that it made you feel good to watch it; and you wanted your children to see it with you.

MacMurray: "When we began, I never dreamed that it would stay on the air as long as it did. But I'll tell you what made it work, and why people stayed with the show so devotedly—everybody grew into a great big family. The crew, the staff, the cast, they all cared about everyone else involved. And it showed on the screen."

1. OZZIE AND HARRIET ('52–66)

   "A real classic of its kind. I think it worked because the Nelsons really were a family—Ozzie, Harriet, David, and Ricky. We all watched the two boys grow up, like on 'My Three Sons,' and they became part of our families, even if only once a week. It was a real pleasant show. Rick's singing didn't hurt either."

2. FATHER KNOWS BEST ('54–62)

   "Robert Young is great, and had he stayed with the show, who knows how long it would have gone on. Again, the family unit was strong, and you got to like them and to care about them. That's really the secret. And over the years, the characters all learned from each other, and became better people."

3. THE DONNA REED SHOW ('58–66)

   "This was really a wholesome show. With Donna Reed were Carl Betz, Paul Petersen, and Shelley Fabares. This show, like the other two, all dealt with little but important domestic problems, and maybe helped a few people out there along the way. If a series can do that, it's saying a lot."

4. MY THREE SONS ('60–72)

   "If for no other reason than I had a great time doing it, 'My Three Sons' should be on this list. But I do in all honesty feel that the show had a lot to offer, and it was nicely received over the years. I worked with a lot of great people—Don Fedderson, the late Bill Frawley, Bill Demarest, Don Grady, Beverly Garland, Meredith MacRae, Tim Considine, many others—and I'm grateful we were as successful as we were."

RED SKELTON'S 3 FAVORITE CONTEMPORARY COMEDIANS

The greatest comic and clown in memory, Red Skelton was active in vaudeville from boyhood, before beginning his successful radio show in 1941. Three years earlier, he'd made his film debut in *Having a Wonderful Time,* and went on to make such comedy classics as *Whistling in Dixie* (1942) and *Merton of the Movies* (1947). His radio show segued right into television as "The Red Skelton Show," which premiered in 1951 and ran for twenty years. In its final season, his show ranked 7th for the year, a hit to the end.

Ozzie and Harriet Nelson, taking a break from their hugely successful series, "Ozzie and Harriet," guest with TV's top clown, Red Skelton on "The Red Skelton Show."

Skelton has always believed that laughter keeps you young. He loves to laugh, almost as much as he likes making people laugh. And he enjoys some of the newer comedians:

1. DAVID BRENNER, who occasionally hosts "The Tonight Show"
2. STEVE MARTIN, the irrepressible comic with "Saturday Night Live" roots
3. GEORGE BURNS, who's hot again after a full and complete career in movies and TV. "Burns is an old friend. His humor is about age. We all laugh, but we lie when we do."

DICK MARTIN'S 9 MEMORABLE MOMENTS FROM "LAUGH-IN"

"Rowan & Martin's Laugh-In" (1968–73) is one of television's classic comedy/variety shows undeniably funniest hours. First seen as a one-time special in the fall of 1967, it was such an enormous success that a series was kicked off the following January. Not only was it an overnight sensation, but it was highly innovative, a genuine, ingenious breath of fresh fare, starting trends in comedy that other programs

Dan Rowan and Dick Martin bestow yet another Flying Fickle Finger of Fate Award on their smash comedy-variety show, "Laugh-In." They innovated TV comedy and set new trends in humor.

would imitate for years to come. The show created a host of new stars: Goldie Hawn, Ruth Buzzi, Joe Anne Worley, Lily Tomlin, Henry Gibson, Judy Carne, Arte Johnson, Gary Owens, and more. It made household names of the comedy team of Dan Rowan and Dick Martin. A typical skit between them went like this:

Dick tells Dan about his trip to Rome.

DICK: I stood on the spot where Caesar killed Brutus.
DAN: Caesar didn't kill Brutus.
DICK: Oh. I'm glad he pulled through.
DAN: No, no. You're got it wrong. Brutus killed Caesar.
DICK: I heard it the other way around.
DAN: You heard that Caesar killed Brutus?
DICK: That's funny. So did I.

The pace was wonderfully fast, and a deft blend of tape with live bits and guests. Some of the memorable features of the show were: The Flying Fickle Finger of Fate, "Laugh-In" News, the Cocktail Party, Mod Mod World, New Talent Showcase, the Joke Wall—with cast members popping out to deliver one-liners, or to get hit in the face with a bucket of water, or to get a pie in the face. A sample of the one-liners from the Joke Wall:

JO ANNE WORLEY: Boris says capitalism doesn't work—but then, neither does Boris.
GOLDIE HAWN: If Dinah Shore married John Byner, she'd be Dinah Byner.
ARTE JOHNSON: If Ida Lupino married Don Ho, she'd be Ida Ho.
JUDY CARNE: If Sybil Burton married Ish Kabibble, she's be Sybil Kabibble.

Says Martin: "Making 'Laugh-In' was some of the best fun I've ever had, and to have people love it was just icing on the cake. Here are some funny moments that come back to me:

1. "Larry Hovis came on the show dressed in a Ku Klux Klan white robe and asked Sammy Davis, Jr. for his autograph. I'll never forget the sight of the two of them, with Sammy giving him an autograph.
2. "Richard Nixon agreed to a guest tape shot. He looked right into camera and solemnly declared: 'Sock it to me!'
3. "One of the most brilliant ad-libs I've ever seen was when Peter Sellers tried to explain the game of cricket to Goldie Hawn. There was no script, we just stood them in front of the camera and turned it on. Cricket, it seems, is just like croquet, only it's totally different. He had us all crying, we were laughing so hard.
4. "We gave the Flying Fickle Finger of Fate to the Pentagon five times for various acts of oversight, stupidity, callousness, and whatever. After the

fifth one, the Pentagon sent us a letter, saying that after five times, perhaps it was time to retire them as a recipient. It showed that they had a sense of humor, so we didn't give them any more.

5. "I had this running gag about being a dyed-in-the-wool John Wayne diehard. So we got him to come on the show in a pink—yeah, pink— bunny costume. Can you imagine a six-foot-six fluffy pink bunny that looks like John Wayne? He knocked 'em dead.

6. "Steve Lawrence and Richard Dawson did a bit where they tried to out-Groucho each other. They both do a great Groucho Marx, with mustache, glasses, cigar, and the whole bit. They went right on doing it after the show was over. We were in stitches.

7. "We once gave the Flying Fickle Finger of Fate to a close friend of mine, the then Los Angeles Police Chief Ed Davis. He'd just made headlines by saying that the way to stop plane hijackings was to have a gallows waiting at the airport for the hijacker, and to lynch him right there. We gave him the Finger of Fate for helping to expedite justice. It's one of his most prized possessions. He keeps it right there on his desk.

8. "Gene Hackman and I once did a running sight gag where we were two convicts digging our way out of prison with teaspoons, á la *The Great Escape*. They'd keep cutting back to us during the show, and we kept getting nowhere and nowhere.

9. "We gave the Flying Fickle Finger of Fate to the City of Cleveland because their Kioga River caught on fire, it was so polluted."

DICK MARTIN'S 7 CATCH PHRASES TO COME OUT OF "LAUGH-IN"

1. You bet your bippy
2. Sock it to me
3. Here come de Judge
4. Beautiful downtown Burbank
5. Look that up in your Funk & Wagnalls
6. Verrrry interesting
7. Ring my chimes

BUDDY EBSEN'S LIST OF 5 MEMORABLE MOMENTS DURING THE TENURE OF "THE BEVERLY HILLBILLIES"

When 6'3" Buddy Ebsen, already known to everyone in America from Walt Disney's limited "Davy Crockett" series (1954–56) and "Northwest Passage" (1958–59), debuted in "The Beverly Hillbillies" in

September 1962, the series shot to the top of the Neilsens like greased lightning. The show's thumping success sent more serious-minded viewers and critics to the wailing wall, moaning "What is television coming to?" However, as respected TV reviewer Gilbert Seldes wrote in *TV Guide:* "The single simple, and to some people outrageous, fact is that 'The Beverly Hillbillies' is very funny."

The basic premise of the show was tried and true: the country mouse comes to the city and has humorous adjustment problems. Only in this case, it was an entire clan, the Clampetts, transplanted from their oil-rich Ozark soil to the posh and exclusive Beverly Hills community. Played by Ebsen, Irene Ryan, Donna Douglas, and Max Baer, Jr., the Clampetts became the most popular TV family. During its nine-year run (1962–71), "The Beverly Hillbillies" was the number-one program for two seasons and hovered around the top ten thereafter. Typical of the humor was this exchange:

The runaway sensation of the '60s was "The Beverly Hillbillies," which more than any other show typifies that TV decade. Sure, it was corny, but it was the kind of corn that people just ate up. The regulars included Irene Ryan, Buddy Ebsen, and Donna Douglas.

JED (Ebsen): We're gonna be shooting some wild game called golf.

GRANNY (Ryan): What in tarnation is a golf?

JED: I dunno, but they must be thicker'n crows in a corn patch around here, because everybody in Beverly Hills shoots 'em.

Says Ebsen: "It was a daily joy to work with the congenial people connected with the show. It's such a vast memory and so many wonderful things happened, that it's hard to pick things out:

1. "In the second or third week of the show, we saw in the paper that we were number one. That was a thrill!

2. "It used to be fun every week because we were up against a lot of good shows. And occasionally, maybe once a month, Bob Hope would load up a special and try to knock us off in the ratings. He never succeeded. He'd load up with all the hot performers and he never topped us.

3. "I remember once as Irene and I stood in the foyer in the middle of the mansion. We suddenly looked at each other and said, 'Seven years?! Where'd the time go?' It seemed just like yesterday that we'd started the show.

4. "CBS decided in 1971 that they didn't want to be the hillbilly network anymore and they canceled all the bucolic shows. That was the year we were axed, along with a lot of other good rural comedies.

5. "I saw a list of the twenty highest-rated individual shows ever, and "Beverly Hillbilles" is on it twice. And most of the other shows on it are football games or specials. We must have been doing something right."

Upcoming: Ebsen is currently in development on a TV special which will reprise his two highly successful series, "The Beverly Hillbillies" and "Barnaby Jones." In the planned Movie of the Week, Nancy Kulp, who played secretary Jane Hathaway on "Hillbillies," hires Barnaby Jones to locate the Clampetts, who are mysteriously missing from Beverly Hills. Watch for it!

CAROL BURNETT'S 2 MOST MEMORABLE AND RICHEST AREAS FOR HUMOR ON "THE CAROL BURNETT SHOW"

Though now concentrating more on movies and theatre, Carol Burnett claims that television is still her first love. "TV is the country's most powerful medium, and I found that out very early in my career. When I appeared on 'The Garry Moore Show' in 1958, I did the opening number from my Broadway show 'Once Upon a Mattress,' and the play ran for a year on the strength of that appearance."

Burnett's appearances on Moore's show while doing the musical led to her becoming a regular on his program from 1959 to 1962. Five years later she had her own weekly variety show, "The Carol Burnett Show" (1967–78). She and her multi-talented zany co-stars, Harvey Korman, Vicki Lawrence, Lyle Waggoner, and Tim Conway, delivered some of TV's funniest spoofs of virtually everything under the sun. Burnett was to the late '60s and '70s what Lucille Ball was to the '50s and early '60s.

1. ALL OF THE MOVIE SPOOFS DONE THROUGH ELEVEN SEASONS
   "By the time we started doing movie sendups, the movies themselves had a kind of nostalgia that was campy. Those thirty-year-old Betty Grable and Dan Dailey, Alice Faye and Tyrone Power, Grable and Victor Mature 20th-Century-Fox musicals often turn out to be serious tear jerkers with a show business backdrop—soap operas really. All we had to do was to add a bit more tongue-in-cheek humor and it was a spoof. We didn't have to do much at all. We once did a whole hour on *The Dolly Sisters,* which was funny as hell, and in places we practically copied the movie word for word, scene for scene. We also did a lot of takeoffs on movies in which people were shot. For instance, we had scenes from *The Little Foxes* and *The Postman Always Rings Twice* that ended in cartoon deaths. We kidded death a lot, with humor."

2. ALL OF "THE FAMILY" SKETCHES WITH EUNICE AND MAMA
   "We started doing 'The Family' sketches—with Eunice and Mama and Ed—in the sixth season, and it was a gold mine for us. You know, Vicki Lawrence was only twenty-six when she first began doing Mama, and that took a consummate young character actress. We all still want to get into those characters more deeply, and I really want to get my teeth into Eunice and take the time to explore what's wrong with her, and what makes her funny and what makes her sad. We're going to do it, too. Dick Claire and Jenna McMahon, who created 'The Family,' are writing a two-hour special about those characters."

NORMAN LEAR'S 4 SPINOFFS FROM "ALL IN THE FAMILY"

In terms of its impact on the American public and on the nature of television comedy, Norman Lear's "All in the Family" (1971–79) was the most influential sitcom in the history of broadcasting since "I Love Lucy" (1951–57).

The man responsible for "All in the Family" is Norman Lear, who with partner Bud Yorkin, pioneered the new trend in more realistic TV sitcoms. A comedy writer (who wrote the "All in the Family" pilot) and director-producer, Lear has an impressive background. His credits include: "The TV Guide Awards Show" in 1962; "The Henry Fonda Special," of 1963; "The Andy Williams Show" (1965–66); and such memorable films as *Come Blow Your Horn* (1963), *Divorce American Style* (1967), *The Night They Raided Minsky's* (1968), and *Cold Turkey* (1971).

Although "All in the Family" pioneered videotaping before a live audience, its groundshaking breakthrough was in the areas of character development and the treatment of such heretofore taboo subjects as bigotry, abortion, rape, homosexuality, wife-swapping, menopause. For the first time such expressions as "spic," "coon," "smart-ass," "jungle bunnies," "chinks," and other racial and religious slurs were routinely spoken. These casually, though passionately, strewn epithets were the outspoken calling cards of the central character, Archie Bunker, portrayed with style and dimension by Carroll O'Connor. In voicing his bigotry, he allowed us to laugh at it and ourselves in the bargain by showing the absurdity of prejudice.

As brilliant as O'Connor was his supporting cast: Jean Stapleton as his foggy-headed wife, Edith, whom he called Dingbat; Sally Struthers as his daughter, Gloria; and Rob Reiner as his son-in-law, Mike, who was as vocally aggressive about his liberal views as Archie was in his red-neck views. The two seemed organically incapable of passing each other without an argument.

"All in the Family" was a controversial hit that zoomed to the top in its second season, and held that spot for five years. No other show has beat that record: "I Love Lucy" and "Gunsmoke" come the closest with four years apiece in the number-one spot. Another record held by the show is the number of series that have spun off from it. Lear: "It's not unusual for a successful program to give birth to another show, but beyond one is rare."

1. MAUDE ('72–78)
   Grew out of Beatrice Arthur's appearances on "All in the Family" as Edith's cousin in 1971. Others in "Maude" included Bill Macy, Conrad Bain, and Rue McClanahan.
2. THE JEFFERSONS ('75–present)
   In this spinoff, Archie's black neighbors, the Jeffersons, moved from Queens to Manhattan's East Side, with stars Sherman Hemsley, Isabel Sanford, and Mike Evans.
3. GOOD TIMES ('74–79)
   This was the first spinoff of a spinoff, sort of a second generation from "All in the Family," from which is descended by way of "Maude." The show starred Esther Rolle, who'd been Maude's maid, and who moved to

Chicago for her own series. The cast included Jimmie Walker, John Amos, BerNadette Stanis, and Ralph Carter.
4. ARCHIE BUNKER'S PLACE ('79–present)
This is both a continuation of "All in the Family," and also a spinoff, in that only Carroll O'Connor remains from the original cast. The setting has been changed from a domestic comedy, and the action now takes place in a bar, Archie's Place, which he co-owns with partner Martin Balsam. Despite changes in format and the loss of major supporting characters, Archie Bunker continues to pull strong ratings.

JOHN RITTER'S LIST OF HIS 5 FAVORITE CURRENT COMEDY SERIES

Affable John Ritter is a good example of an overnight success who's been plodding away in the film business for over a decade. A veteran of a handful of Disney comedies and dozens of TV shows, Ritter parlayed his boyish charm to stardom in "Three's Company" (1977–present), and also starred in the feature *Hero at Large* (1980), an outrageous comedy with heart.

Says Ritter: "With comedy, everything is timing. I follow my instincts and try not to go for the pratfalls but for the real humor. All my life, I've known that I could make people laugh. It's nice to be able to do that on a weekly basis and get paid for it."

1. LAVERNE AND SHIRLEY
2. HAPPY DAYS
3. MORK & MINDY
About the above three, Ritter says: "We all know each other and we like to watch each other's work. It's a lot of fun."
4. THREE'S COMPANY
"This one's got some great people in it. I especially like that young good looking male lead . . . what's his name? . . ."
5. M*A*S*H
"The timing and delivery, the writing . . . it's fabulous."

. . . AND 3 FAVORITES FROM DAYS GONE BY

1. I SPY ('65–68)
"I never missed it. If I had time, I'd catch the reruns in the afternoon."
2. THE ANDY GRIFFITH SHOW ('60–68)
"I really liked Don Knotts on this show."
3. I MARRIED JOAN ('52–55)
"She used to get into some wild screwball situations. It was a real funny show."

# 11

CHAPTER

"HAVE GUN, WILL TRAVEL":
Action and Adventure Shows
Or: How Can We Squeeze in Another Fight or Car Chase?

JOHN D. MacDONALD RATES 7 TV MYSTERY SERIES

A past president of the Mystery Writers of America, John D. Mac-Donald is one of the most successful mystery and crime novelists of our times. In addition to a whole slew of Travis McGee private-eye adventures, he has also crafted such best sellers as *Condominium.* In rating a fistful of television mystery series for *TV Guide,* he viewed them with the basic question in mind: Could he have gotten away with it in a book? Most often the answer was no.

1. QUINCY ('76–present), Jack Klugman
   ". . . shouting profundities at the top of his lungs, annoying everybody he approaches, creating unnecessary conflict because he is too loud and impatient to make a reasonable request. I could use him in a novel as an obstacle to the hero, or as comic relief. But as a lead? No way."
2. HART TO HART ('79–present), Robert Wagner and Stefanie Powers
   "The two-hour preseason opener was so glacial that one felt he had to watch he screen closely to see if anything was moving at all. It was stupefyingly dull to watch these two plastic young people flit about their vulgar possessions."
3. EISCHEID ('79–80), Joe Don Baker
   ". . . was reminiscent, in its best moments, of 'Naked City.' I could not get

away with Eischeid as a lead character, except possibly as a small-time political hack in Alabama. Plots reasonably well-knit. Could sustain book use."

4. CHARLIE'S ANGELS ('76–present), Jaclyn Smith, Kate Jackson, Cheryl Ladd

   "The three interchangeable neoprene lovelies cavort to be looked at. The words they mewl and coo, and the gruntings they get in response, make no sense. Nor, I suspect, are they meant to."

5. HAWAII FIVE-O ('68–80), Jack Lord

   "The plots, except when they bend over backwards to endanger McGarret, have seemed coherent. . . . but it is full of speeches and turns of phrase used only in early comic strips. One thing I must note, however, is its consistency. In books or in TV series, loyalty comes from consistency. Stinkers alternating with gems turn us off."

6. KATE COLUMBO (Feb.–Dec. '79), Kate Mulgrew

   "This series exemplifies the worst failure of television believability."

7. THE ROCKFORD FILES ('74–80), James Garner

   "Finally, a plaudit. In believability, dialogue, plausibility of character, plot

Suzanne Lederer and Joe Don Baker in the short-lived, hard-hitting police drama, "Eischeid," which, says mystery novelist John D. MacDonald, was reminiscent of "Naked City."

coherence, 'Rockford' comes as close to meeting the standards of the written mystery as anything I found.''

BUDDY EBSEN'S 4 FAVORITE PRIVATE DETECTIVES

Premiering mid-season on January 28, 1973, "Barnaby Jones" (1973–80) is eactly one-half season short of tying with "Mannix" (1967–75) as the longest-running private detective series on television. TV superstar Buddy Ebsen, who became a household name as Jed Clampett on the classic bucolic comedy "The Beverly Hillbillies" (1962–71), portrayed the detective with dimension—an older man with quaint, irresistible country charm and trigger-quick wit. Ebsen and his supporting cast, Lee Merriwether and Mark Shera, were an engaging threesome who made the show a highly watchable hit.

Ebsen: "When 'Barnaby Jones' was rushed into being, it was to fill a vacant slot on CBS's schedule. It was an hour slot that had had two half-hour shows, 'The Sandy Duncan Show' and 'Anna and the King,' and in the middle of the season their ratings were unsatisfactory, so Fred Silverman, who was head of programing at CBS then, wanted something in a hurry to replace them. At the time, I had just been booked to guest on 'Cannon' as a private eye, a character similar to Barnaby, with the hopes that it might be a spinoff. When this emergency occurred, Silverman made an executive decision, and instead of my appearing as a guest on 'Cannon,' Bill Conrad became a guest on the first of thirteen 'Barnaby's.''

1. CANNON (1971–76), starring William Conrad
   " 'Cannon' has to be number one for sentimental reasons. He really started me in the business. And while he was on the air, we sometimes had interplays between the two shows.''
2. MANNIX (1967–75), starring Mike Connors
   "I liked the show, and Mike's son and my son were in the same carpool. We used to take turns driving the kids to school.''
3. HUMPHREY BOGART (1899–1957)
   "He's my all-time favorite private eye, hands down. Bogey only made one television show, 'The Petrified Forest' in 1955 on 'Producer's Showcase,' but you can catch his classic p.i. films on the Late Show. He plays Sam Spade in *The Maltese Falcon* (1941) and Philip Marlowe in *The Big Sleep* (1946).''
4. DICK POWELL (1904–'63)
   "I always liked him as a detective. He created a wonderful continuing character, Willie Dante, on his 'Four Star Playhouse' ('52–56). And his Philip Marlowe characterization in *Murder, My Sweet* (1944) is an absolute classic.''

WILLIAM "CANNON" CONRAD RATES 13 TV DETECTIVES

William Conrad popularized a new kind of private detective in "Cannon" ('71–76). Quite different from traditional, suave, and handsome detectives, Frank Cannon was portly, balding, middle-aged—and very popular. Popular enough, in fact, to be reprised in a 1980 TV Movie, "The Return of Frank Cannon."

Conrad's next series, "Nero Wolfe," based on the classic whodunit mystery novels by Rex Stout, is awaiting scheduling at NBC. Conrad: "I think I'll like doing this show more than 'Cannon.' On 'Cannon,' I was always chasing fugitives and had a physical fight in every show. It was more physical that I wanted. Nero Wolfe is a crime-solving genius, but he does it while lavishing attention on his prize-winning orchids, while his assistant does all the legwork. That's my kind of show. Especially since I've been a Nero Wolfe fan for years. There are over 285 million copies of the Nero Wolfe books in print. I guess you could call the character well-established."

Conrad rates thirteen familiar TV detectives this way:

1. COLUMBO ('71–77), Peter Falk
   "The best. Numero Uno!"
2. HARRY-O ('74–76), David Janssen
   and . . .
3. RICHARD DIAMOND ('57–60), David Janssen
   "David was wonderful. I've always liked his work. I thought both 'Harry-O' and 'Richard Diamond' were good. I liked 'The Fugitive,' too . . . I did the narration on that one."
4. MANNIX ('67–75), Mike Connors
   "Very good. Mike is one of my favorite people."
5. THE ROCKFORD FILES ('74–80), James Garner
   "Jim is awfully good. His show was a lot of fun."
6. BARNABY JONES ('73–80), Buddy Ebsen
   "I love Buddy, but the show was mediocre."
7. CANNON ('71–76), Conrad
   "A little better than mediocre. The lead had a good voice, though."
8. KATE COLUMBO ('79–80), Kate Mulgrew
   "She was quite good, but they didn't seem to know what they wanted to do with the show. It didn't get very far."
9. MIKE HAMMER ('57–59), Darren McGavin
   "This wasn't great, but for its time, it wasn't that bad."
10. HONEY WEST ('65–66), Anne Francis
    "Annie was the first lady TV private eye, and the last one, unless you

"Hawaiian Eye," a private eye series with Robert Conrad and Poncie Ponce, was "same as '77 Sunset Strip,' not very interesting," says William "Cannon" Conrad.

count 'Charlie's Angels,' which I've never seen . . . and that tells you something right there."

11. THE THIN MAN ('57–59), Peter Lawford
    "William Powell was magnificent in the movies, but this TV show was . . . forgettable."

12. 77 SUNSET STRIP ('58–64), Efrem Zimbalist, Roger Moore, and Edd Byrnes
    "Not really very interesting." Conrad, while under contract to Warners, produced this show in its last season.

13. HAWAIIAN EYE ('59–63), Anthony Eisley, Robert Conrad, Connie Stevens
    "Same as 'Sunset Strip,' not very interesting."

LINDA KELSEY'S LIST OF THE 10 MOST SOCIALLY SIGNIFICANT EPISODES OF *LOU GRANT*

Linda Kelsey, who costars with Ed Asner and Robert Walden in the much-honored "Lou Grant" series (1977–present), is justly proud that the program explores timely areas of concern in both public and personal matters. Says Kelsey: "Many of our episodes are very relevant socially, and some, like the following, stand out for me as being particularly thought-provoking."

1. HOUSEWARMING
   "Dealt with the subject of wife beating."
2. HOME
   "This was the much-discussed episode about abuses in nursing homes for the elderly, encompassing the entire issue of aging in this country, in or out of a home."
3. VET
   "This was the Emmy-winning segment about the problem of re-entry into normal life of the Vietnam War veteran, dealing with the emotional as well as the physical scars."
4. HOOKER
   "The show took an insightful look at prostitution, especially the underlying motivation of the woman who chooses that life."
5. DOGS
   "This was a brutal, revealing show on the subject of dog fighting for sport in this country."
6. ROMANCE
   "It showed how the teenage pregnancy crisis is everything but romantic."
7. INHERITANCE
   "It explored the misuse of the drug DES as a miscarriage preventative and its carcinogenic effects on the offspring of its users. This episode was in the news.
8. DYING
   "This delved into the subject of the rights of a person to choose to die at home with his/her family."
9. COP
   "We looked into homosexuality on the police force, in a profession where it is least expected."
10. ANDREW, Parts 1 and 2
    "This was a two-hour show that dealt with the rights of the criminally insane."

CLINT EASTWOOD'S 5 CLASSIC TV WESTERN SERIES

Before he rode off into international stardom in his first spaghetti Western, "A Fistful of Dollars" (1966), Clint Eastwood was second banana Rowdy Yates for seven seasons on "Rawhide." Strangely, considering the name value of its star, "Rawhide" has never been syndicated.

Says Eastwood, about "Rawhide": "They were fun years, and they were frustrating, too. I grew to hate exposition and lots of dialogue because on 'Rawhide,' we had to explain everything in the dialogue. Also, we operated under a lot of taboos left over from the Hays Office. You couldn't, for example, do tie-up shots of a gun going off and a man getting shot. It was frustrating, too, because I wanted to direct a show or two, but they always found some excuse for me not to. I was pigeonholed as an actor. It was pretty restrictive, but I sure learned a lot. And I gotta tell you, I really enjoy the freedom of making movies."

1. GUNSMOKE ('55–75)
   With James Arness, Milburn Stone, Amanda Blake, and Dennis Weaver, who left the series in 1964, to be replaced by Ken Curtis. Its success spawned the wave of TV Westerns in the late '50s and early '60s: "This is *the* classic TV Western—no doubt about it. And it's certainly the longest-running."
2. THE WESTERNER (1960)
   With Brian Keith as an anti-heroic figure who, like his dog, would rather not fight unless there was no way out. Only made thirteen episodes. "This was some of director Sam Peckinpah's better work, before he got into all that slow-motion stuff. It was way ahead of its time."
3. RAWHIDE ('59–65)
   With Eastwood and Eric Fleming: "With all due lack of prejudice, it was a good show."
4. HAVE GUN, WILL TRAVEL ('57–63)
   With Richard Boone: "It had a real interesting style."
5. BONANZA ('59–73)
   With Lorne Green, Michael Landon, Dan Blocker, and Pernell Roberts, who left the series in 1965. "It was the best of its kind, but more of a Western soap sort of thing."

MARIO ANDRETTI'S LIST OF 3 TV SERIES WITH THE BEST CAR CHASES

If ever there was a guy who can tell a good car chase when he sees one, it's Mario Andretti. Born in Montana Trieste, Italy, in 1940, Andretti has become one of the truly great race car drivers of our times. Notable among his hundreds of titles and awards are: National Champ, U.S. Auto Club in 1965, 1966, 1969; winner of the Indianapolis 500 in 1969; and recipient of the ABC Athlete of the Year Award in 1969.

1. THE DUKES OF HAZZARD ('79–present), John Schneider, Tom Wopat, Catherine Bach, Denver Pyle

160

Clint Eastwood's first taste of fame came as cow-puncher Rowdy Yates on "Rawhide," here with co-star Eric Fleming. "With all due lack of prejudice," opines Eastwood, "it was a good show."

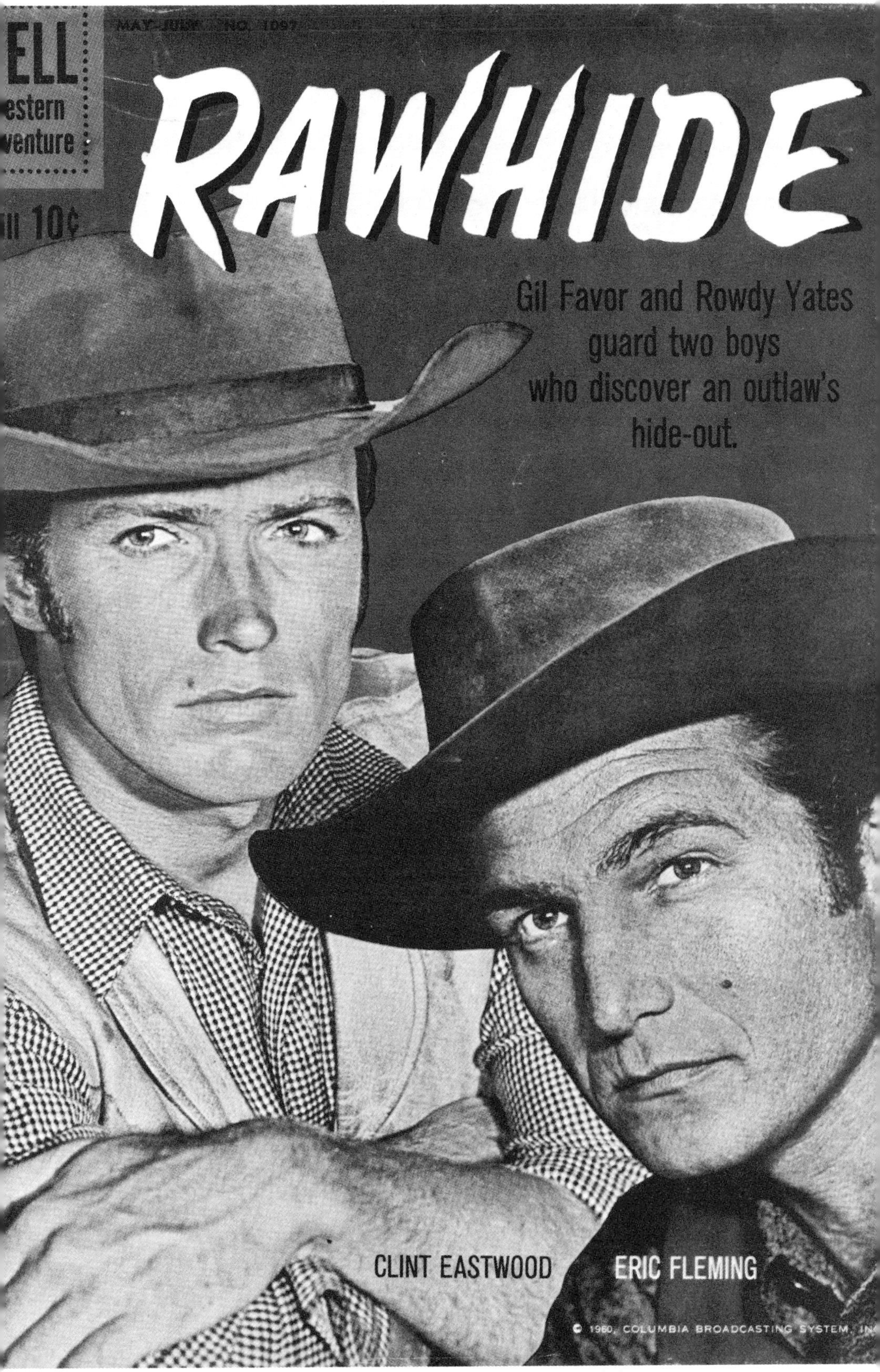
MAY-JUNE NO. 1097
ELL
estern
venture
10¢
RAWHIDE
Gil Favor and Rowdy Yates
guard two boys
who discover an outlaw's
hide-out.
CLINT EASTWOOD
ERIC FLEMING
© 1960, COLUMBIA BROADCASTING SYSTEM, IN

2. STARSKY AND HUTCH ('75–79), David Soul, Paul Michael Glaser
3. THE ROCKFORD FILES ('74–80), James Garner, Noah Beery, Joe Santos.

REX ALLEN'S LIST OF 8 B-WESTERN STARS WHO MADE THE TRANSITION TO A TELEVISION SERIES

With the advent of television, the B-Westerns and low-budget matinee features being cranked out by the hundreds in better years began to lose ground. TV literally ate up their market, and by 1955, the

Rex Allen, second only to Roy Rogers as the most popular B-Westerner, came to TV in 1957 in "Frontier Doctor." And he wasn't the only sagebrush hero to give TV a tumble.

B-Westerns had disappeared from theatres. Which is why so many producers and movie studios were at war with the small screen. It was direct competition . . . and it was winning.

Rex Allen, a rangy Arizona cowboy whose movie career as a sagebrush hero blossomed on the dawn of TV, remembers, "We all had a clause in our contract that we couldn't do TV. None at all. It was the enemy. I was one of the last contract cowboys at Republic, so I was one of the last ones to get into TV work. And when I did, it was old Republic who produced my series, 'Frontier Doctor' (1957–58)."

1. WILLIAM BOYD, "Hopalong Cassidy" ('48–54)
   "He was the first Western hero to go on TV. Between 1935 and 1948, he made some sixty-six movies as Hoppy, and wisely retained TV rights. He edited these into thirty- and sixty-minute shows, and went on the air with the first outdoor action series. Hoppy was such a hit that Boyd filmed an additional fifty-two episodes especially for TV in 1951–52."

2. GENE AUTRY, "The Gene Autry Show" ('50–56)
   "Gene was the first cowboy star to actually film a series for TV. Under his own Flying A Productions, he produced and starred in 104 half-hour episodes, all of which afforded him lots of opportunity to sing. His theme song, one he co-wrote, was 'Back in the Saddle Again.' "

3. ROY ROGERS, "The Roy Rogers Show" ('51–57)
   "With Gene and Hoppy on the tube, Roy was anxious to get into the act. He refused to renew his contract at Republic so he could set up Roy Rogers Productions and film 100 episodes with his lovely wife, Dale Evans, Pat Brady, the jeep Nelliebelle, his dog, Bullet, and, of course, Trigger. Who can forget their closing song, 'Happy Trails'? He later did 'The Roy Rogers and Dale Evans Show' (1962), a Country and Western musical variety show."

4. ROD CAMERON, "City Detective" ('53–55)
   "He did sixty-five episodes in syndication, which were sold to 171 stations across the country—a record at the time—and attested to the popularity of Western stars. His second series, 'State Trooper' ('56–60), 104 episodes, was filmed in Nevada, mostly around Las Vegas."

5. ROCKY LANE, "Red Ryder" ('56–57)
   "Lane had played Red Ryder in twenty-one B-Westerns, with Bobby Blake as Little Beaver. In the thirty-nine TV episodes, based on the comic strip character created by Fred Harmon, Louis Letteri was Little Beaver. Rocky later did the voice for television's talking horse, 'Mr. Ed' ('61–65). And this was something he wasn't too fond of telling people. To my mind, it showed that he was a good actor, creating character with only a voice."

6. DUNCAN RENALDO, "The Cisco Kid" ('51–57)
   "Duncan had been playing The Cisco Kid in films since 1946, with Leo Carillo as his sidekick, Pancho. This was O. Henry's Robin Hood of the

West. It was a pretty good little series, and, if you can believe it, it was the first series to be filmed in color, years before color was used on TV. That's smart thinking."

7. BUSTER CRABBE, "Captain Gallant of the Foreign Legion" ('55–57)
"Buster was an athlete, a swimmer, and that's how he got into pictures. Of his over 100 films, 67 were Westerns, including 42 'Billy the Kid' features for PRC. He also played Tarzan, Flash Gordon, and other heroes. His TV series is interesting because it was the first one to be shot on location in North Africa, and then toward the end in Northern Italy, where the political climate was safer."

8. JOEL McCREA, "Wichita Town" ('59–60)
"Joel turned one of his movies, *Wichita* (1955), into a series. His son, Jody, played his deputy. One of the reasons he did the show was to help his son get launched in TV."

8 ELUSIVE CONTINUING CHARACTERS WHO WEREN'T/AREN'T SHOWN ON THE SCREEN IN THEIR SERIES

(This list title reads like an Emmy Award category, doesn't it? Hope we didn't give them any ideas.)

Anyway . . . an interesting, albeit contrived, device that has worked repeatedly on television is the use of a continuing character who is never seen, or seen only in shadows, or over the shoulder; and who that elusive character really is, is never revealed. The mystery surrounding that character, according to the rationale, will keep viewers turning in, hoping perhaps to someday get a full glimpse. And it did happen—twice. And if you can think of which two series actually showed their mysterious character—before you read it below—you get a star for really knowing your television.

1. THE INVISIBLE MAN ('58–59)—The Invisible Man
This is the classic example of this type of character. There was so much secrecy afoot that not only did they never show him, but the name of the actor in the part was never revealed. These guys knew how to take a mystery seriously. If only they had devoted as much energy to producing a good show, it would have been around longer than just thirteen episodes. But a show like this has built-in problems. How can you root for, or identify with, someone you can't see, and consequently aren't even sure really exists?

2. THE PLAINCLOTHESMAN ('49–54)—The Lieutenant
This show is a real classic, too. The title character, a police detective referred to in the series only as "The Lieutenant" was never seen. But the

real gimmick was the subjective camera technique that had been more or less pioneered by Robert Montgomery in "The Lady in the Lake" (1946), in which the viewer saw everything exactly as the main character. If the Lieutenant lit a cigar, a hand (his) came toward camera with a lighted match to the tip of his cigar on screen; if he was knocked down, the viewer looked up from the ground level. It was interesting enough to last five years. Other than the novel camera technique, it was straightforward crime drama, and there were no bones made about the fact that the unseen title character was played by Ken Lynch.

3. THE MILLIONAIRE ('55–60)—The multi-billionaire
The mystery character in this anthology series was named John Beresford Tipton, a hugely wealthy man whose hobby was giving away a million bucks to people he didn't know, and remaining anonymous. Some hobby, huh? Each recipient was then the title character for that week's show. The million-dollar cashier's check was delivered by Tipton's executive secretary, Michael Anthony, played by Marvin Miller. The actor whose physical body was used for Tipton's back and hands was never revealed; although the producer, Don Fedderson, disclosed that Tipton's voice was provided by Paul Frees.

4. RICHARD DIAMOND ('57–60)—"Sam"
Private detective Richard Diamond, played by David Janssen (his first series), got his messages from "Sam," a lady who ran his answering service. Only Sam's gams were ever seen on screen, and they were the Mickey Spillane type of legs that "started here and went all the way to there." Sam's legs were first played by Mary Tyler Moore until May 1959, when Roxanne Brooks took over, displaying a set of just-as-lovely-to-look-at stems.

5. THE FUGITIVE ('63–67)—The one-armed man
Another David Janssen series, in which he portrayed a man wrongly convicted of the murder of his wife, and, by chance, escaping from custody, he spent four seasons tracking the elusive, only-rarely-seen one-armed man who was the actual murderer. Played by Bill Raisch, the one-armed man was finally fully shown to the viewers in a dramatic two-part finale, which producer Quinn Martin had the decency to film after the series had been canceled. And he got his money's worth. The final "Fugitive" episode is one of the highest-rated programs of all time; which goes to show you that viewers will hang in there with you if you finally deliver.

6. BRACKEN'S WORLD ('69–70)—John Bracken
Head of the fictional Century Studios, John Bracken, though never seen, dominated the lives of the principals in the series through his executive secretary, Sylvia Caldwell (Eleanor Parker). Since only moderately successful in its first season, major surgery was performed for the second. Bracken became visible, played by Leslie Nielsen, who had done his voice in the first season; he tried to guide the studio through troubled economic

times. But the series only made it halfway through the season. And this time, it looks like viewers didn't care once they saw who the mystery character was. Perhaps that's the moral: Don't reveal who the elusive character is until you're ready to kiss off the show.

7. MORK AND MINDY ('78–present)—Orson, the Orkan leader
Mork, a misfit on his own planet of Ork because of his unstylish sense of humor, was sent to Earth to learn about the planet. After landing in a spacecraft that looked suspiciously like a large egg, Mork (Robin Williams) is befriended by Mindy (Pam Dawber), who takes him in. As Mork learns things, he reports to his unseen Orkian mentor, Orson, whose voice is played by Ralph James.

8. CHARLIE'S ANGELS ('76–present)—Charlie
By far the most successful series to use this device, "Charlie's Angels" has succeeded more because of the Angels than because of Charlie. The Angels, who are sexy, lovely to look at, and change every season as yet another Angel flies the coop, are private investigators working for an unseen boss, Charlie, who is played by John Forsythe. The Angels are assisted by Bosley (David Doyle), Charlie's visible assistant and cost accountant.

ANTON LA VEY'S LIST OF 13 OF THE MOST SATANIC TV SHOWS EVER

Anton La Vey, an energetic, philosophical, and multi-interested individual, enjoys a good thriller or well-done occult piece on television as much as the rest of us. But for different reasons. In 1966, he founded the international Church of Satan, of which he is the High Priest. What he enjoys most is a production that treats a Satanic theme with insight and perception, even if unintentionally.

Says La Vey: "The medium of TV is in itself quite satanic, much more so than movies, in that it reaches such a vast number of people on a daily basis. The bulk of television occult and spook shows are not satanic in themselves, but are merely entertainment. Shows about devils and devil worship may be fun, but are not satanic, and often are sloppily made, totally unrealistic, and ridiculous. For a TV Movie or episode to be satanic, it doesn't have to deal with Satan, but rather must have a satanic parable or message. These would be about the supreme ironies in life, about victims of circumstance, about destiny, about exploiting the exploiters, and with retribution, because inevitably we reap what we sow."

1. DEVIL'S DAUGHTER (1972), TV Movie
This had a great *Rosemary's Baby*-ish theme, and starred Joseph Cotten,

Boris Karloff, who created more than his share of satanic portrayals, was the star of "Thriller." With him are cameraman Ben Klein, producer Douglas Benton, Richard Hall, and director Robert Florey. This was Florey's last production, an episode entitled "Dr. Markis."

Shelley Winters, and Belinda Montgomery. What made it special was the marvelous satanic portrayal by Cotten. His physical embodiment of a satanic image was superb. Though he walked with a limp and played a kindly family attorney, he shows up at the end in all his glory for who he is.

2. GARGOYLES (1972), TV Movie
   There were a number of weak spots in this film about anthropology and unusual skeletons, but the premise and the makeup were quite good. The subject hadn't been handled on TV before quite like this. Cornel Wilde starred, with Jennifer Salt and Bernie Casey.

3. HORROR AT 37,000 FEET (1973), TV Movie
   William Shatner, Roy Thinnes, and Buddy Ebsen were in this story about an ancient evil encased in huge stones in the cargo of a trans-Atlantic flight. Their unknown power holds the 747 motionless in the sky and produces strange voices, freezing cold, and a bizarre headwind, which forces the plane to return to its point of takeoff.

4. SATAN'S TRIANGLE (1975), TV Movie
   The best thing about this interesting movie set in the Bermuda Triangle was that there was no cop-out at the end. It literally left you hanging—

like the thing on the yardarm of the yacht. Alejandro Rey's performance was exceptional, right to the kicker at the end. Kim Novak and Doug McClure were also quite good.

5. TWILIGHT ZONE—"A World of His Own" ('59–60)
   Keenan Wynn is a playwright who creates true-to-life characters, so true that they appear in the room with him by conjuring them up from his imagination. And he can also make them disappear when he wants. Truly satanic in its use of magic through the power of imagination.

6. TWILIGHT ZONE—"The 16mm Shrine" ('59–60)
   Ida Lupino as a fading movie queen, a la *Sunset Boulevard,* who shuts out the world and retreats into the past by literally escaping into her old films. Written by Rod Serling.

7. TWILIGHT ZONE—"The Chaser" ('59–60)
   George Grizzard plays a man who buys a love potion in this traditional story; and the kicker is that the antidote costs $1,000. The satanic parable is that you have to be careful what you seek, because you might find it.

8. TWILIGHT ZONE—"The Old Man in the Cave" ('63–64)
   Fine satanic actor James Coburn is the callous leader of a small band of nuclear holocaust survivors who live by following the advice of the unseen Old Man in the cave. When Coburn decides to take over, he unwittingly destroys the old man—who turns out to be a computer, and the only thing that stood between them and inevitable death. Written by Rod Serling.

9. TWILIGHT ZONE—"Number 12 Looks Just Like You" ('63–64)
   Suzy Parker is a young woman who causes problems in a future world by refusing the cosmetic operations that will make her physically flawless. Her strong-willed determination to maintain her individuality in the face of strong opposition is very satanic.

10. NIGHT GALLERY—"The Academy" ('70–71)
    In his only satanic role, Pat Boone plays a wealthy man looking for a school that can handle the tough discipline problems of his son. The one he finds is a little more than he bargained for. Rod Serling, who wrote this episode, handled satanic irony with brilliance. He was the best in his field.

11. NIGHT GALLERY—"A Death in the Family" ('71–72)
    Another Rod Serling story about a wounded fugitive from the law, Desi Arnaz, Jr., who stumbles into a mortician's house seeking safety. Instead he finds the mortician's family embalmed and propped up around the dinner table.

12. NIGHT GALLERY—"The Sins of the Fathers" ('71–72)
    This is one of the most macabre and powerful of all the "Night Gallery" episodes ('70-73). Based on an old Welsh legend about the sin-eater, it tells of a young boy, Richard Thomas, who is doomed by his circumstance, as the son of a sin-eater, to follow in his father's footsteps. Geral-

dine Page provides a sinister and moving satanic portrayal as his mother, who, choiceless, has to trick him into his destiny.

13. TWILIGHT ZONE—"Eye of the Beholder" ('60–61)
Another Serling teleplay, and again one of the best of the entire run of "Twilight Zone" ('59–64). This deals with a team of plastic surgeons making a last-ditch attempt to improve a young woman's face so that she can live a normal life. When the final bandages come off, we see that she is beautiful, but when she sees herself, she breaks into tears. The operation didn't work. Another failure. Then, for the first time, we see the doctors shaking their heads sadly, and removing their surgical masks and they're all hideous grotesque monsters. Supreme satanity about our values.

STEPHEN KING'S LIST OF 8 OF THE MOST MACABRE TV SHOWS EVER TELECAST

The undisputed modern master of the macabre, best-selling author Stephen King writes highly visual tales of terror. His unforgettable novels *(Carrie, Salem's Lot, The Shining, The Stand,* and *The Dead Zone)* bear testimony to the influence that television and films have had on his arcane art. He explores this influence in an upcoming book, *DanseMacabre,* which deals with horror in the media. Like us all, King enjoys a good thriller on television. His favorites:

1. THE JAR, "Alfred Hitchcock Presents" ('55–60)
2. THE HUNGRY GLASS, "Thriller" ('60–62)
3. PIGEONS FROM HELL, "Thriller" ('60–62)
4. A WIG FOR MISS DeVORE, "Thriller" ('60–62)
5. IT CAME OUT OF THE WOODWORK, "The Outer Limits" ('63–65)
6. THE INVADERS, "The Twilight Zone" ('59–64)
7. I KISS YOUR SHADOW, "Bus Stop" ('61–62)
8. DUEL, "ABC Movie of the Week" (1971)

NBC PUBLICITY LIST OF 17 INJURIES SUFFERED BY "TARZAN" STAR RON ELY DURING THE FIRST SEASON OF PRODUCTION

According to a 1966 NBC publicity release: "Ron Ely, title star of the NBC Television Network color adventure series, 'Tarzan,' insists on doing all his own stunts and animal fights. The results have been at least seventeen wounds and injuries, as shown here".

1. Seven stitches in head from lion bite

2. Broken nose in water fight
3. Dislocated jaw in fight
4. Wrenched neck and disc in vine-swinging accident
5. Right shoulder broken from vine breaking mid-swing
6. Left shoulder broken from vine breaking mid-swing
6. Left shoulder separation in vine-swinging accident
7. Three broken ribs from same accident
8. Right biceps muscle torn in lion fight
9. Claw marks from leopard and puma fight
10. Sprained wrists from action scenes
11. Left leg hamstring muscle pulled
12. Right thigh muscle pulled
13. Bites and claw marks from jungle animals
14. Both ankles sprained from hard landings after leaps
15. Tops of both feet badly scratched in stunt fall downhill
16. Cracked left heel from fall
17. Bottom of right foot torn, slipping down rocky mountain

NBC: "All that and more from only the first season (September 1966 to September 1967)." "Tarzan" remained on network television for two seasons, filmed on location in Brazil and Mexico, against incredible production problems, delays, accidents, and some of the worst weather ever encountered by a film company.

Congenial and ruggedly handsome, Ron Ely, who has replaced Bert Parks as the Miss America Pageant emcee, is currently host of the syndicated "Face the Music." And he doesn't particularly like to rehash his loincloth days.

Says Ely: "When that picture appeared in *Life* magazine, I resented it terribly. They didn't begin to chronicle the things that happened to me. If they were going to do something like that, they should have done it in depth. I was injured constantly, and was always recovering from an injury. Some of them were quite serious. I had a broken shoulder, and a separated shoulder. I probably had four shoulder injuries. There was a helluva lot that they didn't even touch on, broken bones that they didn't know about. I don't even remember all of them. And I don't want to. I didn't want any special attention called to it at the time because I didn't want the show to be watched because of them."

In my *Tarzan of the Movies* (which Ely generously considers the most factual chronicle of the character in films), I wrote how he manfully continued work despite his wounds. The morning after the first vine-swinging accident: "Ron's separated shoulder bones were wired back together in a two-hour operation. And after a week's rest,

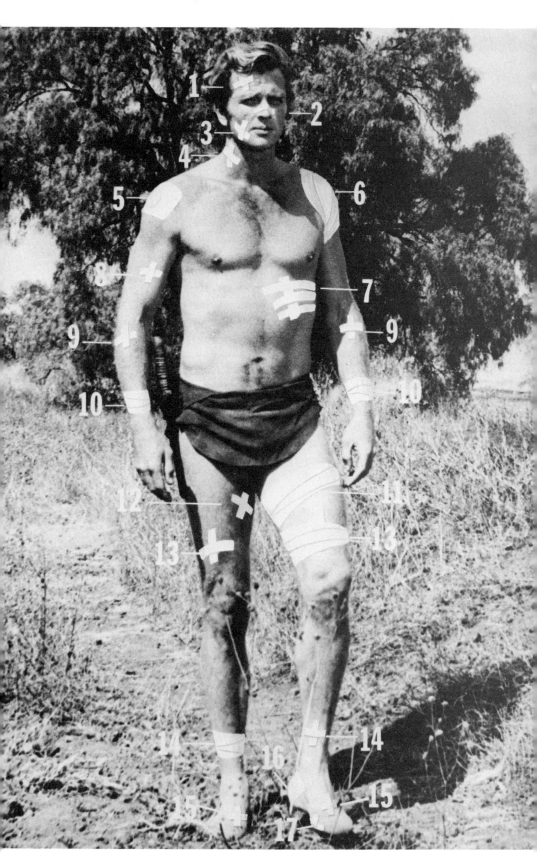

he was back on the set, adhesive tape protecting the surgical scar. The script had been rewritten to incorporate the fall, which had been recorded by two color cameras. A scene was inserted to show a villain shooting Tarzan from the vine.''

Ely: "I'm way beyond those years, and I don't really enjoy looking back. I enjoy books that deal with nostalgia, I just don't enjoy being nostalgic about my own life. It's wasted effort. I don't really enjoy my own memorabilia. I enjoy today, and looking forward. And that's it.''

Yet, he does have a bemused sense of humor about himself, and Tarzan. Guest-hosting "The Merv Griffin Show" in 1980, he quipped, "You know, they haven't done anything with Tarzan since I did that series in the late sixties. . . . I must've really ruined the character.''

There is, however, a new Tarzan project in the air, with Bo Derek as Jane and John Derek as director/producer. Former Tarzan Jock Mahoney is the stunt co-ordinator. And the picture, entitled *Me Jane,* is to be the story from Jane's point of view.

MELVIN BELLI'S LIST OF THE 5 BEST LAWYER SERIES

One of the most celebrated lawyers of our time, Melvin Belli is probably best known for his defense of Jack Ruby, on trial in Dallas for the murder of Lee Harvey Oswald, who assassinated President John F. Kennedy. Belli is best known by "Star Trek" fans for his portrayal of the cosmic villain in an episode entitled "And the Small Children Shall Lead.''

In his nearly fifty years of law practice, this colorful attorney has become a genuine legend. He has fought most of his well-documented battles on behalf of individuals against establishment powers—the insurance companies, the medical profession, the giant corporations. His spellbinding inventiveness in the courtroom, his imaginative use of demonstrative evidence, and his spectacular success in raising the levels of injury settlements have made him the most widely imitated lawyer in the world.

Says Belli: "I've always enjoyed watching lawyers on television, and many have indeed well represented my profession. Many were good, and many were not so good. I like to think that the best series about a lawyer is just now in the process of being developed. I have signed a contract with Columbia-TV who will produce 'The Belli Files,' based on my life and trials. They've put their top creative people on it, and we're hoping for a great show.

"The following is the best that's been on the air to now.''

1. THE DEFENDERS (1961–1965)

   "This high-quality series with E.G. Marshall and Robert Reed as a father-and-son defense team attracted much controversy, as well as critical acclaim during its four-year run. The series was a ground-breaker, dealing weekly with such sensitive issues as euthanasia, abortion, blacklisting, and civil disobedience. And if you can believe it, they even lost a case or two, something that TV lawyers never do. This show is my personal favorite in this genre."

2. PERRY MASON (1957–1966)

   "This fictional criminal lawyer, who was created by Erle Stanley Gardner (who himself was an attorney), achieved a record number of acquittals. Though Gardner did no writing for the series, he had script approval which helped to insure the quality of the show. Raymond Burr's portrayal was that of an aggressive advocate of justice who was blessed with superb powers of deductive reasoning. The series survived the longest of all lawyer shows, an incredible nine years, during which time Perry Mason won some 271 cases."

3. JUDD FOR THE DEFENSE (1967–1969)

   "A year after 'Perry Mason' went off the air, this series premiered with Carl Betz in the lead as a high-priced, high-powered criminal attorney based in Texas, and modeled, I'm told, on F. Lee Bailey. Though only lasting two seasons, the show had a contemporary ring to it, dealing with cases which mirrored newspaper headlines, such as draft evasion and civil rights murders."

4. THE TRIALS OF O'BRIEN (1965–1966)

   "Though it was only on for one season, this was an interesting series, and featured Peter Falk as a New York attorney whose personal life was sometimes more trying than his professional life. He was behind in the rent on his luxurious penthouse, behind in alimony payments to his beautiful ex-wife, and was a rotten gambler. Somehow, no matter how much money he made, it went out just as quickly as it came. His cases were treated seriously, but his personal problems were not. Falk's wonderful characterization in this series layed much of the foundation for his later Lt. Columbo."

5. OWEN MARSHALL, COUNSELOR AT LAW (1971–1974)

   "Arthur Hill played a compassionate defense attorney in this popular series, in which the cases were always marked by a warmth and consideration for the accused. Marshall was the courtroom equivalent of the kindly doctor, 'Marcus Welby' (Robert Young) and in fact the two series sometimes had overlapping episodes since both were produced by David Victor for Universal. In 1972 he defended one of Dr. Welby's patients against a murder charge, and in 1974, he defended Dr. Kiley (James Brolin) in a paternity suit. The series was well-regarded in legal circles and won several public service awards."

12
CHAPTER

"SMALL FRY CLUB":
Kid Stuff
Or: How Do Kids Always Manage To Select the Worst Show?

PANEL OF EXPERTS PICK THE TOP 16 CHILDREN'S SHOWS

A panel of ten top educators, pediatricians, child psychiatrists, and communications experts was assembled by *TV Guide* to watch and rate children's programs. Their conclusion was that substantially more than half the Saturday and Sunday morning shows were not worth watching; and that the best programming for children is during the week; and that much of the best is on PBS rather than on the three commercial networks.

Each of the shows was rated from one to ten, ranging from excellent to dreadful. Scores were given for both entertainment values and for educational and social values, as was a final overall score, which reflected but wasn't an average of the other scores.

1. ONCE UPON A CLASSIC ('76–present), PBS, overall rating: 9
   Comments by panel members: "Outclasses all the others." "Handsome format, first rate dramas. We could use more of these."
2. THE CBS FESTIVAL OF LIVELY ARTS FOR YOUNG PEOPLE ('79– present), overall rating: 8.7
   "The best idea of all, the best execution of all." "A program adults can enjoy as well as children."

10. ABC WEEKEND SPECIALS ('77–present), overall rating: 7.8
    "Good dramatic productions. Done with real respect for kids."
11. ¿QUE PASA, USA? ('76–present), PBS, overall rating: 7.85
    "This is actually funny! Fine bilingualism and biculturalism for English- and Spanish-speaking kids."
12. SESAME STREET ('69–present), PBS, overall rating: 7.7
    "An electronic baby-sitter. Too fast, too frenetic, too many cheap tricks."
    "Lots to criticize but it tries to teach kids—and it does."
13. ANIMALS, ANIMALS, ANIMALS ('76–present), ABC, overall rating: 7.5
    "Splendid and informative. A program adults as well as children can enjoy." "Really geared for kids who want to learn."
14. CAPTAIN KANGAROO ('55–present), CBS, overall rating: 7.5
    "A classic concept for preschoolers." "After twenty-five years—it's the longest-running network kid's show—it may look tired to grown-ups, but maybe not to a new batch of kids."
15. VILLA ALEGRE ('74–present), PBS, overall rating: 7.4
    "A weak imitation of 'Sesame Street,' but two cheers for the bilingualism."
16. CARRASCOLENDAS ('72–present), PBS, overall rating: 7.4
    "Good bilingualism, not-so-good role-modeling. Why do adults do such foolish things on this show?"

... THE 10 WORST CHILDREN'S SHOWS

1. CAPTAIN CAVEMAN & THE TEENANGELS ('77–present), ABC, rating: 1.7
   Comments: "No redeeming social values."
2. CASPER AND THE ANGELS ('79–present), NBC, rating: 1.9
   "Boring. A silly takeoff on 'Charlie's Angels.' An excuse to show girls in tights."
3. JASON OF STAR COMMAND ('79–present), CBS, rating: 2
   "It aspires to a low level—and succeeds."
4. THE GODZILLA/GLOBETROTTERS ADVENTURE HOUR ('78–present), NBC, rating: 2.2
   "Worthless, pointless, awful."
5. THE SKATEBIRDS ('77–present), CBS, rating: 2.4
   "Terrible! What a waste of any child's time."
6. FRED AND BARNEY MEET THE SHMOO ('79–present), NBC, rating: 2.4
   "Basically quite dreadful, though it does show friendly, warm relations between people more often than other cartoons."
7. THE ALL-NEW POPEYE HOUR ('78–present), CBS, rating: 2.4

"All new? Nothing new! Violent, destructive behavior is rewarded constantly."
8. THE MIGHTY MOUSE/HECKLE & JECKLE SHOW ('79–present), CBS, rating: 2.5
"Monotonous and mindless. Relentless violence-based humor."
9. THE DAFFY DUCK SHOW ('78–present), NBC, rating: 2.5
"Old cartoon favorites cut up into unintelligible segments. Surely the kids will notice."
10. PLASTIC MAN ('79–present), ABC, rating: 2.6
"Discombobulated activity presented as 'adventure.' Too frightening for many children."

HANNA & BARBERA'S LIST OF 6 MILESTONE ANIMATED TV SERIES

When soaring costs of theatrical cartoons forced the closing of most animation studios in Hollywood, William Hanna and Joseph Barbera, who had won seven Oscars for their "Tom and Jerry" cartoons at MGM, developed a less expensive product for television. This new, limited animation stressed plot and action, and abandoned much of the time-consuming and expensive detail of movement and backgrounds. They single-handedly ushered in a new era of Saturday morning children's programing.

1. RUFF AND READY ('57–60)
"This was the first Hanna-Barbera series using the limited animation process; it led to our domination of Saturday morning programing."
2. HUCKLEBERRY HOUND ('58–62)
"Launched the first animated TV series not bridged with a host, and introduced many characters who had spinoff series. We won an Emmy Award in 1960 for Outstanding Achievement in the Field of Children's Programing."
3. THE FLINTSTONES ('60–66)
"This was the first animated series for prime-time. It won several awards, including the Fame's Annual Critics Poll TV's Golden Dozen Award and the Golden Globe Award for Outstanding Achievement in International Television in Cartoons. In 1967, the show went to Saturday mornings for a couple of years, and returned in 1979 with all new shows. And now for the 1980–81 season, it's going back into prime-time after an absence of fourteen years."
4. ROCKY AND BULLWINKLE ('59–61)
"This series, created by Jay Ward, and not by Hanna-Barbera, attracted a minor cult following, because the show downplayed the animation and the art and emphasized story and dialogue, and often had humor subtlety aimed at an older audience."

5. SCOOBY-DOO ('69–present)
"With eleven consecutive years of new episodes, this is the longest-running cartoon series in network history."
6. THE NEW ADVENTURES OF HUCKLEBERRY FINN ('68–69)
"For the first time in a series, we combined animation and live action. Michael Shea played Huck, and Kevin Schultz was Tom Sawyer. We employed the techniques we'd developed on our Emmy Award-winning hour-long special, 'Jack and the Beanstalk,' in 1966, which starred Gene Kelly."

MEL BLANC'S 10 MOST DISTINCTIVE VOICES ON TELEVISION

In much the same way that Lon Chaney, Sr. was known as the Man with a Thousand Faces, Mel Blanc is known as the Man with a Thousand Voices. He has given life to literally hundreds of cartoon characters and inanimate objects by creating voices for them. His most famous vocal characterizations include Bugs Bunny, Elmer Fudd, and Daffy Duck.

1. LUCILLE BALL
2. GEORGE BURNS
3. PHYLLIS DILLER
4. SANDY DUNCAN
5. FARRAH FAWCETT
6. BOB HOPE
7. DAVID JANSSEN
8. JAMES EARL JONES
9. DON RICKLES
10. JACLYN SMITH

MEL BLANC'S PERSONAL FAVORITE TV CARTOON VOICES HE'S DONE

1. We have to include all the cartoon voices I've done for the movies, because most of them have since become Saturday morning television stars in their own right. (See the companion volume, *Movie Lists.)*
2. BARNEY RUBBLE
3. CAPTAIN CAVEMAN
4. DINO THE DINOSAUR
5. HEATHCLIFF THE CAT
6. MR. SPACELY
7. SPEED BUGGY

. . . AND 1 LIVE-ACTION ROBOT

8. TWIKI on "Buck Rogers" . . . whose personality was crystallized in the scene where the diminutive robot watches Princess Ardala (Pamela Hensley) dancing in the opening segment, and says "Biddi biddi biddi . . . whatta body!"

Mel Blanc, the man of a thousand voices, supplies the voice for Twikki, the robot on "Buck Rogers," which is also one of Gary Coleman's favorite shows. Here, Buck (Gil Gerard, a soap opera refugee) chats with guest stars Vera Miles and Kelley Miles.

GARY COLEMAN'S 10 FAVORITE TV SHOWS

"Diff'rent Strokes" (1978–present) has made its diminutive star, Gary Coleman, the most recognizable twelve year old in America. Coleman, who calls himself a "budding mellow comedy actor," got his break when a talent scout for Norman Lear signed him for a pilot film for a TV revival of "The Little Rascals." It didn't sell, but Lear liked the engaging youngster, and said: "We have gold in that kid." Lear signed him to a contract, put him in several episodes of "Good Times," "The Jeffersons," and "America 2-Night," before putting him in his own series.

Although precocious, Gary, like any kid his age, prefers cartoons over other TV fare, with science fiction as a close second.

1. Vintage BUGS BUNNY cartoons from the Golden Age of the late '40s and early '50s
2. FLASH GORDON, Saturday morning animated show
3. DAFFY DUCK, again the vintage stuff
4. TOM & JERRY
5. BUGS BUNNY, the newer stuff

Gary Coleman is not a thirty-year-old midget. He's just precocious. He's also the best-known kid on TV, and star of "Diff'rent Strokes." Todd Bridges plays his brother.

6. PORKY PIG
7. WOODY WOODPECKER
8. BUCK ROGERS, live action (on which he has guest-starred)
9. STAR TREK reruns
10. BATTLESTAR GALACTICA

BATMAN'S LIST OF 21 TREACHEROUSLY VILLAINOUS GUEST STARS WHO DECIDEDLY BEDEVILED THE DYNAMIC DUO

The first superhero series in prime-time to be a runaway hit with both adults and the younger set was "Batman" (1966–68), the ultimate "camp" show of the '60s. Borrowing from comic book and movie serial origins, "Batman" aired in two-part half-hour segments: the first part on Wednesday, ending in a cliff-hanger, and the conclusion on Thursday. Said Executive Producer William Dozier: "The silliness and absurdity caught the public's imagination. It was the only situation comedy on television without a laugh track."

Both the Wednesday and the Thursday night segments ranked in the Top 10 for the 1965–66 season, in a unique testament to the show's immense popularity. Appearing as a guest villain on "Batman" became a sort of status symbol, and many big-name celebrities who normally didn't do episodic television guested on this show. Some of the more celebrated foes were:

1. EARTHA KITT, JULIE NEWMAR, and LEE MERIWETHER—all played Catwoman
2. TALLULAH BANKHEAD—played Black Widow—she'd been urged by a friend to make this rare TV appearance because it was so camp. Retorted the irrepressible Tallulah: "Don't tell me about 'camp,' dahling. I invented it."
3. JOAN CRAWFORD—The Devil
4. MILTON BERLE—Louie the Lilac
5. CLIFF ROBERTSON and DINA MERRILL—Shame and Calamity Jane
6. ANNE BAXTER—Zelda
7. GEORGE SANDERS, OTTO PREMINGER, and ELI WALLACH—Mr. Freeze
8. BURGESS MEREDITH—The Penguin
9. CESAR ROMERO—The Joker
10. FRANK GORSHIN, then JOHN ASTIN—Riddler
11. ETHEL MERMAN—Lola Lasagne
12. VINCENT PRICE—Egghead
13. ART CARNEY—The Archer

Burt Ward and Adam West roared to fame in the Batmobile on "Batman," which was the first show to air its episodes on two nights each week. The Dynamic Duo were such high camp that big name film stars vyed to portray guest villains.

14. JOCK MAHONEY—Loud Leo
15. IDA LUPINO and HOWARD DUFF—Dr. Cassandra and Cabala
16. LIBERACE—Chandell
17. SHELLEY WINTERS—Ma Parker
18. VAN JOHNSON—The Minstrel
19. JOAN COLLINS—The Siren
20. ZSA ZSA GABOR—Minerva
21. RUDY VALLEE—Lord Marmaduke Ffog

5 WAYS TO IMPROVE YOUR CHILD'S READING SKILLS THROUGH TV

Unfortunately, television has been a negative influence on reading. Why should a child curl up with a book, which requires active participation, when he can sit passively in front of the old boob tube? According to statistics, by high school graduation, a child will have spent 15,000 hours watching TV, as compared with 11,000 hours in school. Elementary school age children average nearly thirty hours a week; and it drops only slightly for high school.

Rather than being overwhelmed by such statistics and the resulting apathy toward the printed word among his own high school English students, a visionary teacher in 1970 turned to TV for new reading tools—the printed script. That former high school teacher, Dr. Michael McAndrew, developed a reading program for grades 3 through 12 using television scripts from popular shows like "Mork and Mindy" and "Happy Days." His "Television Reading Program" (TVRP) now markets eight scripts a year on a nonprofit basis to schools across the country. McAndrew also developed a similar program at CBS, which has been in operation since 1978. It has been a huge success.

However, even without TV scripts, you can turn a passive TV viewing session into an active learning and reading skill development experience. Reading specialist Nina Hopp offers these five ways:

1. Build vocabulary by using the newspaper's TV section. Find three words that are not in your child's spoken vocabulary and encourage him to look them up in the dictionary. Because the words are in the TV section, the child's interest will be aroused.
2. Help your child differentiate between fact and opinion during a show by asking questions such as: "Can that be proven?" "Is this someone's opinion?" Understanding a writer's point of view is critical in reading comprehension.
3. Develop analytical skills by asking your child to explain why a character behaved in a certain way. This will improve comprehension as connections are made between actions and causes.
4. Stimulate creative thinking during station breaks by asking your child to guess what will happen next in the show. This helps a child to realize that there is more than one way to tell a story or to solve a problem.
5. Uncover propaganda techniques and influential words and phrases in commercials by discussing with your child the effect a commercial is having on him. Understanding how words are used to persuade will make him a more careful reader, whether of labels on cereal boxes or of newspaper articles.

For further information about TV script-reading programs contact: Dr. Michael McAndrew, TV Reading Program, Capital Cities Communication, 4100 City Line Avenue, Philadelphia, Pennsylvania 19131

13

"AMERICAN BANDSTAND":
The Sponsor Derby
Or: *How To Sell Anything in Sixty Seconds Or Less*

CHAPTER

MARTY INGELS' LIST OF THE 10 BEST (CELEBRITY AND NONCELEBRITY) COMMERCIALS*

Former comedian and now president of the world's largest Celebrity Brokerage, Marty Ingels went from flat broke to the head of a $6 million-a-year business. Most visible in "I'm Dickens, He's Fenster" (1962–63), a zany sitcom on ABC, he found himself in a financial and emotional downspin following the cancellation of his series. By 1971, he was divorced, his car repossessed, and his house sold out from under him. "It was then that I decided I had to make my living other than by performing," he says.

"I know seventy-five actors who would be glad to work in commercials for $25,000, but their agent asks for $100,000, so they don't get the job. And they often never hear about their having been considered until much later. What I do is go to the star direct and avoid the middleman."

As an illustration of his effectiveness, Ingels cites his toughest bonafide assignment: find Orson Welles for a French cognac ad. "Orson Welles has a fetish about being unreachable," says Ingels. "Garbo is easy by comparison. After finally tracing his homes in Spain and London, he's not there. In desperation, I called his business manager

185

Marty Ingels, former comedian and now president of the world's largest celebrity brokerage, puts an unabashed arm around Hugh Hefner, a recent client acquisition. Ingels once starred in the ill-fated "I'm Dickens, He's Fenster" sitcom.

in New York. He yawned and said he would tell Welles. Meantime, I remember that he and Dean Martin are pals. I call Dino, and fifteen minutes later Orson calls me, and we agree on the deal. Two days later, Welles' business manager in New York sends me a telegram saying: 'No deal. Not enough money.' He was unaware that I had gotten through to Welles and made the deal already. What could be a better representation of what's been going on in this business?"

Since then, Ingles, Inc. has become the key connection between advertising agencies and celebrities.

1. The James Garner/Mariette Hartley POLAROID spots
   Not only sold zillions of cameras, doubled Garner's popularity, and made Mariette a star (after twenty years of trying), but it put light comedy on the map for an industry that's been traditionally afraid of it, and has always gone in favor of the tried-and-true boring six-year-old-level garbage.

2. Bill Cosby's JELLO spots with the kids
   Not only got Cosby a kids'-oriented TV series, but is the best example of utilizing a "free-wheeling, improvisational, spontaneous genius" who usually stumps the ad-writing guys.

3. The James Coburn SCHLITZ LIGHT spots that ran in 1977–79
   Sexy, effective, beautifully shot (like a movie), and utilizing an absolute minimum of dialogue from the star.

4. Orson Welles' "Not till its time" PAUL MASSON wine spots
   While it is admittedly difficult to misuse an Orson Welles genius, this particular series had the perfect marriage of product, copy, and star—so much so that it appeared Welles himself created the commercial. It has also sold mucho vino because the "Not till its time" slogan proved to be one of the most memorable on the air, the goal of all ad men.

5. The Jimmy Stewart FIRESTONE TIRES spots
   Beautifully produced, lavish appointments, taking us back to Mr. Firestone's early manufacturing days with Stewart narrating in a kind of "Our Town" flavor; and another splendid utilization of the 100 percent sincere believability (one of the top five in that crucial category) of the great American stumbler. (I daresay that Mr. Stewart's fee set Mr. Firestone back a bit more than a bit!)

6. The Jack Klugman, Loretta Swit, etc., YOPLAIT YOGURT spots
   The stars eat the stuff and then pour out with a flood of French praise. Very visual, courageous enough to have much eating, without talking, time—a commercial rarity—and most memorably amusing with the unlikeliest Frenchmen.

7. The nonceleb (unless you want to count Charlie Pride over there on the side playing the piano, and Ron Guidry becoming a Pepper) DR. PEPPER "Be a Pepper" spots
   Does the almost impossible: they manage to grab you with the instant *whap* usually reserved for a star face, and they do it with sheer music and genuine catchy enthusiasm that urge you to get the hell out there and be a goddamn Pepper! In a world of celebrity-hungry advertising, this one stands out for its very successful lack of one.

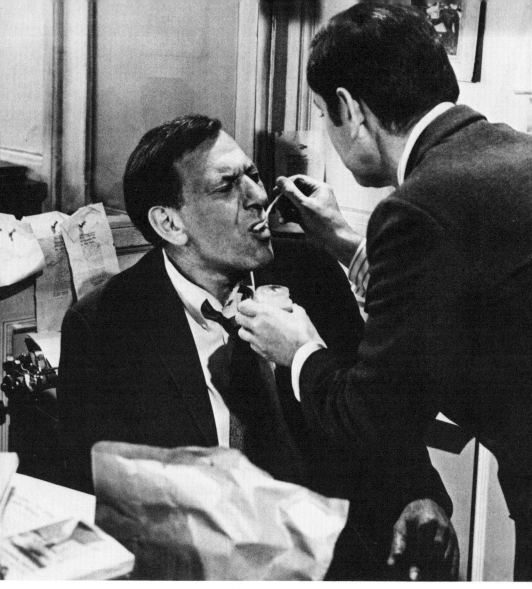

Jack Klugman protests, "It's not Yoplait," as Tony Randall shoves the spoon into his mouth. That's why they're called "The Odd Couple."

8. The sensational Joe Green/little boy COKE spots
   An award winner! And how could it have missed? It takes King Kong, the great beast, and adds Beauty, the little Elf, the Fawn . . . blending them in such an incredibly heart-tugging, poignant, a story-in-every-look fashion that we're about to run out for a Coke just from the love in that commercial! It's not easy to sell a product and humanity at the same time, as this one does.

9. One of my (and *the*) all-time favorites, though it ran in the early '70s: the wild and raucous Ann Miller CAMPBELL SOUP spot

Had the ever-preserved Miss Miller tap-dancing the house down in an outrageously extravagant Busby Berkeley-type Hollywood musical of the '40s set (giant bedecked chorus, floating pianos, disappearing staircases and all) . . . only to dissolve downstage into a modest apron and an All-American kitchen, squeamishly touting the simple virtues of nice hot soup! A daring use of tongue-in-cheek for its time, by the master, Stan Freberg. And the most expensive commercial ever shot till then.

10. The nonceleb, too-damn compelling WINCHELL'S DONUTS spots
With little more than a dynamic camera scan across some trays of unbearably mouth-watering donuts of every conceivable description, and a simple unannouncery voice-over expressing our very thoughts, they manage to break 98 percent of all current diets in America. A perfect example of a commercial that doesn't have to be expensive, lavish . . . or have Angie Dickinson . . . to grab you.

*NOTE: *I didn't include the sensational John Wayne GREAT WESTERN SAVINGS spots, which were dynamite in their perfect complement of star image, product, quality, and just general beautiful scenery. These were a favorite, but were only regional, rather than national.*

MARTY INGELS' LIST OF THE 10 WORST COMMERCIALS ON TV

1. Alas, the Rula Lenska HAIR SPRAY spots (and I can't remember for the life of me the name of the stuff—which is the important commercial measure).
Either it was some brilliant ad man's insidious joke on America (vigorously touting the fervent testimonial of a "super star" nobody's ever heard of) . . . or it's the best damn attention-getter ("Who the hell is Rula Lenska?" T-shirts are flooding the market) ever devised.

2. The JORDACHE JEANS spot with the kids
Not since the Nazi-oriented commercial that Hertz made the disastrous mistake to run (with all the busy car-polishers sporting boots and whips and chanting "Vee only take orders!") have I really been offended by a commercial. I'll even sit still for those feminine hygiene jobs; but the Jordache jeans spot, sexual overtones and all, showing us a mini-disco scene of eight-year olds bumping Jordache-logo'd derrieres, for me gets the Tackiest-Commercial-on-the-Air Award.

3. My God, that little white-suited son-of-a-bitch in my toilet screaming TIDY BOWL up at me
Don't ask me why—and maybe it even sells the product—but, if you took a national poll on who every American would secretly like to murder, I'm positive it'd be a 100 percent vote for that curiously irritating S.O.B. on the raft in my toilet!

4. The Bert Parks and "Lady Friend" singing the virtues of CHOCK-FULL-OF-NUTS COFFEE spot also rubs me (and everyone I talk to) the wrong way

   Here we're shown a terribly unattractive lady in her sixties who we don't know from Adam, singing about a mile and a half off-key, and perched directly next to the handsome perennial favorite who we've come to associate with your American beauty. (Word has it that the lady in question is *Mrs.* Chock-Full-of-Nuts—and wouldn't you know it.)

5. Call me un-American, but . . . the Joe DiMaggio MR. COFFEE spot just leaves me colder than cold.

   The man has made them absolutely Numero Uno in the field, but I just don't believe that super-macho Joltin' Joe knows which end of a coffee-maker is up.

6. There's something about luscious Suzanne Somers slinking around in a skin-tight sequined jump-suit that just doesn't make me wanna run out and buy an ACE HARDWARE drill-and-bit set.

7. For me, the all-time commercial miscast was done by the genius who put Sophia Loren (a sensational acquisition to start with) into an American kitchen, with an American apron, selling us an American WATER-PURI-FIER—accent and all!

8. Talk about intimidating. There's something about Robert Conrad continually daring me to knock the EVEREADY BATTERY off his shoulder that makes me wanna leave the battery intact, and knock him somewhere else!

9. I know Madison Avenue still has the entire country at about the eight-year-old mentality level, but I really do think we're past the point of believing those agonizingly belabored "moments" at Robert Young's house saving patient after patient from the nervous jitters with his SANKA.

10. My credibility tolerance is about at the exploding point when I see the suave and worldly Lauren Bacall selling us Chryslers, or whatever that is . . . but they've lost me completely when they try to convince me that bejeweled Sammy Davis serves his most precious guests $2.79 MANIS-CHEWITZ WINE!

MARTY INGELS' 9 "I'M GONNA GET 'EM SOMEDAY" LIST

INGELS: "Keeping in mind that the three commercial qualities that spell success are beauty, credibility, and stature, here are the celebrities I'd most like to sign . . . with the one-word reason they've been able to hold out this long, and refuse me."

Celebrity	Reason
1. BO DEREK	Success
2. HENRY KISSINGER	Prudence
3. JONAS SALK	Ethics
4. JACKIE KENNEDY	Image
5. WALTER CRONKITE	CBS
6. BILLY GRAHAM	God
7. JOHNNY CARSON	NBC
8. MARLON BRANDO	Policy
9. BARBRA STREISAND	Sense

MARTY INGELS' 10 MOST GRATIFYING ACQUISITIONS

Ingels: "Since divulging confidential fees is prohibited by contract in my field, I'll just list the most gratifying acquisitions I've made in my relatively short time (three years) in business as America's foremost 'arranger.' "

1. JOHN WAYNE
2. BURT LANCASTER
3. ROBERT MITCHUM
4. JACK PALANCE
5. RED SKELTON
6. SHIRLEY JONES
   (for more than one reason)*
7. GEORGE PEPPARD
8. HOPE LANGE
9. HELEN REDDY
10. REX REED

*Shirley Jones is Mrs. Marty Ingels.

16 TV COMMERCIAL STARS AND WHAT THEY GET (GOT) PAID

The name of the game in TV commercials these days is the name value of the celebrity that you can get to pitch your product. In the early days of advertising, long before TV commercials got to be big bucks, it was called "product endorsement." And, often, popular stars would endorse a product for a modest fee, coupled with publicity, free products, a new car, or movie tie-ins. But today, it is a billion-dollar-a-year business, and name-value celebrities from Sophia Loren to Bob Hope, Helen Hayes to James Garner, all are spokesmen for products on the tube.

The best blending of product and star is usually one in which the celebrity hawks an item that falls into his particular field of expertise. For example, Mickey Spillane extolling the virtues of Schlitz Light is

It's not widely know, but the main reason that Mr. Roarke (Ricardo Montalban) has all those guests to "Fantasy Island" is to sell them a Cordova; with spit-shine by Tatoo (Herve Villechaize).

more believable than Sophia Loren exclaiming the wonders of a water softener.

But whatever the product, the celebrity gets well paid to do the pitching:

1. CANDICE BERGEN
   $1 million for three years from Cie ('80–82). This includes print ads as well as commercials.
2. JOHN WAYNE
   A $1-million deal with Great Western Savings as its spokesman for a three-year period.
3. SIR LAURENCE OLIVIER
   $500,000 from Polaroid in 1978.
4. HENRY FONDA
   $275,000 a year from GAF Cameras (1978).
5. KIRK DOUGLAS
   $150,000 from Bulova (1978).
6. JACKIE GLEASON
   $150,000 a year from Pillsbury (1978).
7. BOB HOPE
   $300,000 a year from California Federal Savings (1980).
8. JOE DiMAGGIO
   $100,000 a year from Mr. Coffee (his own company).
9. JOHN HUSTON
   $50,000 a year from Great Western Savings (1980).
10. GLENN FORD
    $50,000 a year from Great Western Savings (1980).
11. BARBARA STANWYCK
    $50,000 a year from Great Western Savings (1980).
12. REGGIE JACKSON
    $35,000 a year from Rawlings Sporting Goods (1978).
13. DON KNOTTS
    $25,000 a year from a Midwestern Hardware Chain (1977).
14. HOWARD COSELL
    $25,000 for one Canada Dry cameo (1976).
15. GREGORY PECK
    Worried about the 600,000 jobs hanging on the survival of the Chrysler Corporation, he has volunteered to become an unpaid TV pitchman; as he has for Energy Conservation.
16. FRANK SINATRA
    Has made the same deal with Chrysler, and his commercials are already running on the air.

... AND THE MOST LUCRATIVE CELEBRITY COMMERCIAL DEAL OF ALL TIME

1. GLENN FORD has a highly controversial deal with Academy Life Insurance Company, which, in addition to a fee, stipulates that he will receive a commission from all of the policies generated from his TV commercials.

His estimated earnings from these spots, over the long run, could be as high as $2.5 million, which would make it the most lucrative single deal ever for a celebrity commercial. The controversy that has erupted over the deal is whether or not Ford is eligible to collect commissions from insurance policies without being a licensed insurance agent. If he has a good business manager, by the time you read this, Ford will not only be a licensed agent, but will have his own insurance agency.

EMMY MAGAZINE'S LIST OF THE 5 BEST TV COMMERCIALS OF ALL TIME

Emmy, The magazine of the Academy of Television Arts and Sciences, took an informal poll in the summer of 1979 to determine the five TV commercials that were most memorable. The most memorable are the best, because they give us a new, simple, undeniably logical reason to buy what they sell. We remember them because they present situations we instantly recognize as universally funny, romantic, or human. We remember them because they are like nothing we have seen before.''

1. ALKA-SELTZER, "Groom's First Meal," 1970
   Over the years, Alka-Seltzer, like Volkswagen, has always been in the forefront with simple, memorable, and often entertaining and amusing commercials. In this highly recallable outing, the dialog went like this: WIFE: "Our first home-cooked meal!" HUSBAND: "Honey, I've never seen a dumpling that big." WIFE: "What would you like for tomorrow? Stuffed crab surprise? . . . creamed duck delight? . . . Marshmallowed meatballs? Poached oysters!" ANNOUNCER: "What love doesn't conquer, Alka-Seltzer will."

2. BAN ROLL-ON DEODORANT, "Documentary #1; Ban Takes the Worry Out of Being Close," 1960
   With Leonard Bernstein's "West Side Story" musical score, and a gritty, rough-verite New York-style, it captured the tenseness of the moment using virtually no narration.

3. VOLKSWAGEN, "Snowplow," 1963
   NARRATOR: "Have you ever wondered how the man who drives a snowplow drives *to* the snowplow? This one drives a Volkswagen."

4. RC COLA, "Skateboard Pizza Delivery Girl," 1978
   There was something very sensual, attractive, and extremely wholesome about this commercial that featured lovely Kelly Moran as the lissome lovely we'd most like to have deliver our pizza. The catchy background jingle about "Me and My RC," in a light tribute to American ingenuity ends with the lyric: ". . . and they pay me by the mile."

5. LEVIS, "Taking the Levi Logo for a Walk," 1977
According to Burke Research, this rather fantastic trip down the block with a trusty Levi's logo was remembered by 59 percent of the audience the day after; more people recalled it than any other sixty-second commercial they had tested. Producer Bob Abel achieved his memorable effects with an innovative blend of live-action and animation.

PHYLLIS DILLER'S "8 THINGS ON TV I DEPLORE"

Zany and outrageous, Phyllis Diller's off-the-wall comedy has baffled critics and delighted TV addicts on scores of variety shows and specials; in her own series: "The Beautiful Phyllis Diller Show" (1968), and "The Pruitts of South Hampton" (1967–68); and as a regular on "The Colgate Comedy Hour" (1967) and "The Dean Martin Comedy World" (1974).

1. "Sanitary protection commercials. The one about the vinegar douche you can carry dangling from your belt. Makes you never want to eat a salad again.
2. "The tampon ads that have girls doing things that would tire Arnold Schwarzenegger: lifting trucks, folding the Great Wall of China, hanggliding from a 747, racing Amtrak.
3. "The commercials where the dumb broad from next door, whose laundry is dark gray, walks into your kitchen unannounced and tells you how to run your house and cure your kid of bed-wetting by feeding your family Stove-Top Stuffing. I'd like to stuff her with the Stove Top!
4. "The soap operas where things move like glue. The cast acts as if they'd swallowed enough tranquilizers to put the entire Mormon Tabernacle Choir into a coma.
5. "The commercials where they wash one side of their face with Brand X, and the other side with Panacea Pudding and immediately rave over the difference. It stretches my credulity further than Orson Welles' pot-holder. (That's a girdle for a male person.)
6. "The news stories that tell all about the attention-grabbing beginning, how the Synanon people put a snake in a mail box and it nearly killed a guy, but you never hear what happened to the head of the organization. Did he sober up enough to go to court? Did he run away with Aunt Mary? Did he marry a priest so he could plead insanity? Did he go back on dope? Did he swim the Atlantic? Did he wade into a bed of tulips and pollinate himself to death? What happened?
7. "The weather reports where they predict Hurricane Hilda as scattered showers. . . . Why don't they call it like it is: scattered landscape!
8. "When the newscasters giggle and become jocular and make inside jokes

at the end of a newscast that has just covered the war in Afghanistan, the famine in India, the flood in Mississippi, the plague in Hungary, the slide in Hollywood, the earthquake in Peru, the volcanic eruption in Washington, the cannabalism in Uganda, the fire in Turkey, a divorce next door, a murder in the Vatican, and the death of my cat."

WILLIAM CONRAD'S LIST OF 6 SUCCESSFUL VOICES ON TV COMMERCIALS

Long before people could recognize Bill Conrad on the street, they knew his distinctive voice. He created the role of Matt Dillon on the hugely popular CBS radio show, "Gunsmoke," in 1952, three years before James Arness would bring the character to life on TV.

Conrad's voice has been his fortune. Conrad: "When I was under contract to Warner Brothers in the late fifties and early sixties, as a producer, my boss, Jack Warner, didn't like anybody on his pay working for anybody else. But when I made my deal, it wasn't exclusive because I was making at least half a million dollars a year, and have been for years, doing voiceovers and commercials.

"We used to have lunch in a private dining room, and he'd sit at the head of the table with ten people on either side, and I'd be down at the foot of the table. So there was considerable distance between us. And everyday he'd take somebody on. It was his little game. One day, I was late, and I knew I was in for it when the room quieted down as I entered. And he said, 'Young man . . .' I knew I was in trouble whenever he called me that. 'Young man,' he said, 'I understand that you do a lot of voiceovers.' And I said, 'Yes, I do.' He nodded disapprovingly, and went on: 'My wife was watching something called 'Rocky and His Friends' the other day. She recognized your voice. Do you have anything to do with that show?' 'Yessir,' I said, 'I'm the announcer on that show.' Again he nodded blankly, and said, 'I was watching the World Series the other day and I thought I heard your voice on the Chrysler commercials.' And I said, 'Yessir, I do the Chrysler commercials.' And he went on and on, through about twenty-five things he'd prepared on a list. Finally, there was a long pause, and he took a slow spoonful of his soup. Then he put down the spoon, and said sternly, 'Young man, it seems you're doing a lot of moonlighting.' To which I responded: 'Yessir. But what you don't understand is that the voiceovers—that's what I do for a living. And what I do for you—that's my moonlighting.' He broke up, and never mentioned it again."

Even today, Conrad does more voiceovers and narrations than any other actor. "The style of voices that they want in commercials changes from year to year. Now it's the era of the common man, who doesn't sound like an actor. I think Eddie Binns does more commercials than any man alive. He has a most unusual voice, which has a very ordinary sound."

1. EDWARD BINNS
   "He's the busiest today."
2. ORSON WELLES
   "One of the most distinctive voices ever."
3. REX ALLEN
   "The greatest of the cowboy voices."
4. ROD SERLING
   "What a voice. Today we have a Rod Serling soundalike."
5. LORNE GREEN
   "No mistaking his voice."
6. LLOYD BRIDGES
   "He's got a real warm, mellow voice that you trust."

Lloyd Bridges, of "Forrester" and "Sea Hunt" fame, has turned to doing TV commercial voiceovers. "He has a real warm, mellow voice you can trust," says voiceover king, Bill Conrad.

20 MULTIPLE CHOICE QUESTIONS ABOUT COMMERCIALS—QUIZ #2

We warned you earlier in the book that there were two other participation lists. Here's number two, designed by the staff Advertising Experts to test your *commercial quotient:*

1. Rula Lenska has been showing out-of-town friends around London and executing difficult dance steps, while keeping her hair in perfect place with
   a. STICK-UPS
   b. KRAZY GLUE
   c. ALBERTO VO-5

2. Josephine the plumber, a lifelong busybody, has been trying forever to get us to clean up our acts with
   a. PHILLIPS
   b. LANACAINE
   c. COMET

3. Mr. Whipple continually accosts lady shoppers in his supermarket because they keep squeezing his
   a. BALL PARK FRANKS
   b. CHUNKY
   c. CHARMIN

4. Little cute-as-could-be Rodney Allan Rippy couldn't quite get his mouth around
   a. GAINES BURGERS
   b. FRUIT LOOPS
   c. JACK-IN-THE-BOX HAMBURGER

5. Jessie White, the idle repairman, would love to come to your house and work on your
   a. TWINKIES
   b. UNDERALLS
   c. MAYTAG

6. Mrs. Olson, a sixteen-year TV institution, has saved more marriages then Dr. Joyce Brothers, with her special mountain grown
   a. JIFFY POPS
   b. MAIDENFORM
   c. FOLGERS

7. Karl Malden has warned time and again not to leave town without your
   a. KAOPECTATE
   b. MEOW MIX
   c. AMERICAN EXPRESS

8. If you ever have athlete's foot again, you can't blame
   a. NO NONSENSE PANTY HOSE

b. PREPARATION H

c. DESENEX

9. Next time you get diarrhea, you can thank

a. HORMEL CHILI

b. MR. COFFEE

c. PEPTO BISMAL

10. When that obnoxious bellhop dumps your luggage in the hall so that he can point out the ring around your collar, you want to soak the little wiseacre in

a. PROPA PH

b. OXYDOL

c. WISK

11. If you're rough and rugged, you ain't gonna drink none of that sissy city beer; you reach for

a. BLACK FLAG

b. STP

c. COORS

12. Euell Gibbons, the late naturalist, used to confess that he was reminded of wild hickory nuts by

a. RONALD REAGAN

b. HOWARD COSELL

c. GRAPE NUTS

13. If your dog has been around as long as Lorne Green's, you can be grateful for

a. HUSH PUPPIES

b. GERITOL

c. ALPO

14. After carefully placing it on his shoulder, Robert Conrad dares you to knock off his

a. LEGGS

b. BAGGIES

c. EVEREADY

15. Madge, the manicurist, has been soaking all of her customers in

a. MOP 'N GLO

b. LYSOL

c. PALMOLIVE

16. That bossy, bigoted Southern sheriff with the pot belly, mirrored sun glasses, and cigar shore looks cool driving his

a. ROACH COACH

b. GRAVY TRAIN

c. DODGE DART

17. When Jack Klugman and Harry Guardino (at different times) have told you that you don't have time to hurt, you want

a. GREASE RELIEF

Former "Marcus Welby, M.D." star Robert Young examines a patient, and patiently advises: "What you need to get those eyes open is a nice cup of __(fill-in)__ ."

      b. SCHLITZ MALT LIQUOR
      c. BROMO-SELTZER

18. If your mother-in-law checks out your wine glasses before the party and finds ugly spotting, you have obviously not used
      a. CLEARASIL
      b. TIDY BOWL
      c. CASCADE

19. Mother Nature has been shaking the earth because she's been fooled one too many times by
      a. FRUIT OF THE LOOM
      b. STOVE TOP STUFFING
      c. IMPERIAL MARGARINE

20. Robert Young has been soothing nerves and keeping marriages out of deep water with his
      a. CHOCO-DILES
      b. GRANNY GOOSE
      c. SANKA

21. If when you go to the market, you bother the butcher, you're after
      a. DING DONGS
      b. TURTLE WAX
      c. BŌNZ

ANSWERS

As I'm sure you've already noticed, the correct answer to all of the above is, in every case, the letter b . . . er . . . no, wait a minute . . . that is, the letter c!

14
CHAPTER

THE MYSTERY CHEF:
Programing, Pilots, Spinoffs
Or: *Network Programers Work in Mysterious Ways*

16 OF THE MOST-AWAITED TV SHOWS
OR EPISODES OF ALL TIME

1. DALLAS (November 21, 1980) "Who Shot J.R.?"
    Without doubt, this was the most-awaited, and consequently most-watched, television show of all time. In the final episode of the 1979–80 season, J.R. Ewing (Larry Hagman) was shot and seriously wounded, leaving the question open for speculation as to who shot him. The incident gained international proportions when over the summer contests were held in England for the most interesting solutions to the mystery, with Hagman himself doing the judging. Even Queen Elizabeth was caught up in the mystery and held an audience with Hagman. The topic had been discussed on the news, been the subject of hundreds of magazine stories and items in the gossip columns; Las Vegas odds-makers had a field day. Hagman said, "I've been offered thousands of dollars in bribes to tell who the culprit was, and I'd have done it in a minute, but the truth of the matter is, I don't know."

    It was such a highly-guarded secret that four different possibilities were actually filmed, and the correct one wasn't revealed until airtime. CBS charged advertisers a record $500,000 for every 60 seconds of commercial time during this milestone episode, a price tag which has been matched only by the Super Bowl.

Who shot J.R. Ewing? was the most asked question of the TV season. "Dallas" star Larry Hagman just grins and won't tell. "You'll just have to watch the show," he said. The revealing episode got the highest rating of all time.

The revelation ending the ten-month mystery came near the end of the November 21 telecast, when J.R.'s wife, Sue Ellen (Linda Gray), fingered her sister, Kristin (Mary Crosby), as the trigger-person of the year. She was a woman scorned, having had an affair with J.R., only to be slapped with a phony prostitution rap when she pressed for the wedding bells he'd promised her. Her bombshell was the disclosure that she was pregnant by J.R., and that his baby would be born in jail if he sent her there.

2. THE FUGITIVE (August 22 & 29, 1967), "The One-Armed Man!"
The second next most-awaited, and consequently most-watched television series episode of all time was the final two-part "Fugitive," in which David Janssen, as Dr. Richard Kimble, finally caught up with the one-armed man who was responsible for making him a fugitive from the law. Kimble had been convicted of murdering his wife and sentenced to death, and yet had protested his innocence all along. A fortuitous train wreck allowed him to escape custody, so that he could spend the next four seasons searching for the one-armed man who was the actual killer. Complicating his task was *his* pursuer, Lieutenant Gerard, played by Barry Morse. The series climaxed in a special two-part episode after the summer reruns in 1967, with the final hour on August 29 attracting enough viewers to rank the show sixth in the Top 50 Programs of All Time.

3. I LOVE LUCY (January 19, 1953), "Lucy Has Her Baby!"
When Lucille Ball became pregnant during the production of "I Love Lucy," it was decided to make this new development a part of the show. And work like a charm it did. Over a long series of episodes, all of America shared in Lucy's pregnancy. And it was a national event when, on January 19, 1953, Lucy Ricardo gave birth to Little Ricky on the air, and as fate would have it, it was the same night that Lucille Ball gave birth to her second child, Desi Arnaz, Jr. As proof that Lucy's baby was the most popular infant in the nation, *TV Guide* featured him on the cover of their premier issue in April, 1953. And how that happened is a story in itself: Seems that when *TV Guide* went to Desi Arnaz for an exclusive picture of the most-celebrated baby of the decade, Desi regretfully informed them that all the photos he had were promised exclusively to *Life Magazine*. Then he took the prized photos out of a desk drawer and spread them out on the desk top, and left the room—after he'd made it clear that if one was missing by the time he got back, he'd never notice it. He didn't notice, and that's how Desi, Jr. ended up on the first *TV Guide* cover.

4. THE ED SULLIVAN SHOW (January 6, 1957), "Elvis Presley's 3rd Appearance."
In the summer of 1956, Elvis Presley, then the hottest entertainer in the world, was signed for three appearances at the then unheard-of fee of $50,000. His first two guest spots in September and October, 1956, created such a furor among the clergy, educators, and critics, all of whom attacked the young singer as being not only a lewd and suggestive performer, but also as being a corrupting influence on the morals of the youth of America. Despite great pressure to cancel Presley's final appearance, Sullivan refused, stating that Elvis would go on as scheduled. CBS, in trying to placate all of the would-be do-gooders (never mind how closed-minded they were), exercised its censorship powers to force Sullivan to show Elvis from the waist up only.

5. THE JERRY LEWIS SHOW (January 19, 1957)
After breaking up with partner Dean Martin in 1956, Jerry Lewis was anxious to show who the *real* talent of the comedy team was. Martin and Lewis was the biggest comedy draw in the business for just shy of eight years prior to their celebrated breakup. Lewis' first special, which was carried by NBC, wasn't bad, but not quite anything to build a TV career on; and he appeared little on TV for the next seven years, concentrating instead on films. Few would have predicted that Martin would have the more successful solo career. In addition to appearing in some thirty films on his own, Martin also became an enormously popular TV personality, by not taking himself too seriously, something that's always been difficult for Lewis to do.

6. THE ED SULLIVAN SHOW (February 9, 1964), "The Beatles Debut."
At the heart of the English rock and roll invasion of America was the Beatles, the legendary quartet of musician/singers who remain the most potent influence of rock music through their work in the '60s. As their fame spread to the States in the fall of 1963, Sullivan signed them for their first U.S. TV appearance. On February 9, everyone in the country tuned in to watch John, Paul, George, and Ringo for the first time, and took them to their hearts. They performed "All My Lovin'," "She Loves You," "This Boy," and "I Wanna Hold Your Hand," their current number one record. And Beatlemania was on its way. That show got the highest ratings Sullivan had ever had; ranking the telecast number 14 on the Top 50 Programs of All Time. Sullivan was no dummy, and demonstrating how he kept his show on the air for 24 seasons (longer than any other show of its kind), he promptly signed the Beatles for a return appearance the following week. That show, telecast February 16, 1964, got the second highest ratings Sullivan ever had, and is number 21 on the Top 50 Programs of All Time.

7. GUNSMOKE (September 1964), "So Long, Chester"
At the end of the '63–64 season, Dennis Weaver, who had played Chester Goode, Matt Dillon's (James Arness) deputy from the onset of the show in 1955, quit. Weaver had begun talking about leaving in 1962, and when his third series pilot sold, he left to become a leading man. The curious TV audience wondered, not only why a man would want to leave a hit series—it seemed like such an odd thing to do; no one had ever done it before—but they were also curious about what "Gunsmoke" would be like without old Chester. As it turned out, "Gunsmoke" was the same, and a new character, Festus Haggen (Ken Curtis), was added to perform the same function on the show as Chester. Nevertheless, it was the end of an era, and after the curiosity seekers had had their fill, the show's ratings began to sag, and continued in a doldrum for several seasons.

8. ELVIS (December 3, 1968), "Elvis' Return to TV"
Elvis Presley had been inducted into the U.S. Army at the height of his popularity in 1958. Following his two-year hitch, fans were eager to see their long-lost idol, but his only TV appearance was as a special guest star on a 1960 Frank Sinatra Special. Though he kept grinding out an endless string of mindless musical films, he stayed off TV until 1968 when he finally agreed to do a show his way. Half of the program, and the best part by far, was the jam session, where Elvis with four musicians played on a raised platform, encircled by his audience. True to his image, he wore black leather. It was a great show, with several show-stopping tunes, especially the closing number, "If I Can Dream," which had been written for him two days before the special was taped.

Carol Burnett unintentionally frames Tom and Dick Smothers, who said that the CBS censors "framed" them on a bum rap when they were branded trouble-makers during the controversial two-year run of "The Smothers Brothers Show." Their return to TV a year later was widely anticipated for its expected satire. Their return was toothless. 205

9. THE SMOTHERS BROTHERS SUMMER SHOW (July 15, 1970), "Return to TV"

While on CBS for two seasons ('67–69), the Smothers Brothers got a reputation. They were branded as troublemakers, two guys who wouldn't do it the way the establishment wanted. The public seemed to respond to their brand of comedy, satire, and especially to the way they fought the censors, even though they usually lost. They were the underdogs, albeit controversial, and they gained quite a following. They were the first CBS show to dent the popularity of "Bonanza." However, after two seasons of scrapping, tooth and nail, CBS decided the last straw was the Smothers' attempt to avoid censorship by turning their taped program in to the network too late to be cut up. When they were finally axed in 1969, neither of the two other networks was interested in them. It was a year later that ABC decided to give them a tryout as a summer replacement. All their old fans tuned in to find a toothless version of the old Smothers Brothers, and soon tuned them off.

10. RHODA (October 28, 1974), "Rhoda's Wedding"

As played by Valerie Harper, Rhoda Morgenstern was an engaging character on "The Mary Tyler Moore Show," engaging enough to get her own series in 1974. Her wedding got a big sendoff on the eighth show as Rhoda married Joe Gerard (David Groh). But it was not a match made in heaven; and the ratings proved it. From a high on the wedding, the ratings began to dissipate, and so did Rhoda's marriage. They eventually separated, began seeing other people, and by then the fans wanted something to hold onto; they wanted . . .

11. RHODA (September 11, 1977), "Rhoda's Divorce"

And they got it. The trial separation that had begun the previous September worked out, and Joe made only infrequent appearances on the series in the '76–77 season. He hung around long enough to sign the final papers. He divorced Rhoda. And so did CBS at the end of the season. They figured that if Joe's trial separation worked out that well, why not . . .?

12. M*A*S*H (September 9, 1975), "So Long Henry and Trapper"

At the start of the '75–76 season, both McLean Stevenson, who had played Colonel Henry Blake, and Wayne Rogers, who had been Trapper John, were gone to chase different fortunes. The question that the diehard "M*A*S*H" fans wanted to know was, how is this going to affect my all-time favorite TV comedy series? Well, the first show of the season, in which Frank Burns (Larry Linville) was the temporary camp commander and Trapper was shipped out and left without having a chance to say goodbye, was a fine show. Then came two new faces: Harry Morgan as Colonel Sherman Potter, the new commanding officer, and Mike Farrell as B.J. Hunnicutt. After a few shows, it seemed that they had been there all the time, and the high quality of the show never wavered, not even for one episode. In fact, "M*A*S*H" is a true television rarity, in that it gets better season by season.

13. ALL IN THE FAMILY (January 19, 1976), "Archie's Grandson Is Born"
The '75–76 season was the fifth year in a row that "All in the Family" was the number one show in the ratings. So, when little Joey Stivic was born, the son of Gloria (Sally Struthers) and Mike (Rob Reiner), giving America's favorite bigmouth bigot, Archie Bunker (Carroll O'Connor), his first and only grandchild, it was a national event, almost as newsworthy as when Lucy presented TV-land with Little Ricky. It was the highest-rated show for the series that season.

14. THE SONNY AND CHER SHOW (February 1, 1976), "Reunited!"
"The Sonny and Cher Comedy Hour" ('71–74) was the highest-rated variety series in the '73–74 season, but it was soon ended, as Sonny and Cher got divorced after nine years of marriage. Each went separate ways, and into their solo-starring shows. "The Sonny Comedy Revue" lasted four months, September through December, 1974. Cher had a little more to sell—namely sexy and outrageous costumes, often quite revealing—so she remained on the air for almost a year: February 1975 through January 1976. They returned to the air in the much bally-hooed "The Sonny and Cher Show," which reunited the star-crossed lovers, amid rumors that Cher had tired of Greg Allman's drug problems and that she and Sonny were getting back together again—at least for the show. Unfortunately, the first big surge in their ratings didn't continue; and neither did the show beyond August 1977. And neither—for that matter—did Sonny and Cher. It was over.

15. CHARLIE'S ANGELS (September 23, 1977), "The First New Angel"
The most popular new show of the '76–77 season was "Charlie's Angels," a high-profile and trend setting show. Stylish and mindless, with an enormous visual appeal, the Spelling-Goldberg production featured three stunning young ladies: Kate Jackson, Jaclyn Smith, and Farrah Fawcett, who by far became the most popular of the trio. So popular, in fact, that she quit the series at the end of the first season. In a three-month long, highly-publicized talent search, Spelling-Goldberg sought a replacement. It was the kind of publicity you can't buy. And when the new Angel was found—Cheryl Ladd, the sister-in-law of the then head of production at 20th Century Fox, the studio where "Charlie's Angels" is filmed—she made the cover and/or interior of practically every magazine in the country. Great looking, but can she act? Ladd had a lot to live up to, and, to her credit, she has. She not only satisfactorily replaced Farrah, but has built a following of her own, a following she started to gather on her very first show on September 23, 1977.

16. SOAP (Semtember 14, 1978), "The Real Killer Confesses!"
At the conclusion of its first season ('77–78), "Soap's" Jessica Tate (Katherine Helmond) had just been convicted of murder—a murder she

didn't commit. In the last episode, an off-screen narrator informed viewers that the truth would come to light, and sure enough, in the first episode of the '78–79 season, the real culprit confessed: It was Chester (Robert Mandan), Jessica's husband, who had killed Peter (Robert Urich—reportedly so that he could go on to "Vega$"). The whole scheme seems to have been borrowed by the "Dallas" folk, in a rather sophisticated update for their highly successful tease campaign about who shot J.R. (And that's what TV is really all about. The chief operating word is *imitation;* it's the sincerest form of flattery, or haven't you heard?)

BILL DANA'S LIST OF 7 TV SERIES THAT— HONEST TO GOD—ALMOST MADE IT

Comedian Bill Dana shot to international fame with his creation of the easily confused Latin American character, José Jimenez, on "The Steve Allen Show" of the late 1950s. This led to his own series, "The Bill Dana Show" (1963–65), in which he continued to play Jimenez, now employed as a bellhop in a New York hotel. Since then he has written and produced extensive comedy material for television and the movies, and is currently chairman of Dana/Corwin Enterprises, which produces celebrity humor books in association with Bantam Books.

In his many dealings with the networks, he overheard—not intentionally, you understand—various top-level conversations, in which some promising series were rejected, even though, it seems, the Un-Soda, 6 UP, was willing to sponsor several of the shows. Just goes to show you how uncreative network brass can be.

1. Mendel Morgenstern, in his desire to be a coroner pathologist, works part-time in the morgue washing Formaldehyde bottles. Heartwarming, true, but was rejected nonetheless. Its title: MORGUE AND MENDY.
2. The misadventures of Vernon Vye and Chuck Knott, who leave the farm for the lights of Los Angeles, hoping to make it big as Vye and Chuck. They never got the chance; they got rejected as: L.A. VERN & CHARLIE.
3. Domestic troubles constantly plague the Archer family of Bunker Hill. Then they acquire a wise old pet bird, and things get better—but not good enough to sell as a series called: OWL IN THE FAMILY.
4. One episode of this almost-made-it nonfiction series deals with an American businessman who pays his taxes all his life and finally passes away dead broke. Rejected as: THAT'S CREDIBLE.
5. A bunch of good ol' boys, who spend most of their time fishing, decide to turn their hobby into a big splash in the movie-making business. Just when they thought they'd caught the big one, they were tossed back in, as: REEL PEOPLE.

6. Thirty female and thirty male impressionists form a theatrical company and try to fake it big. But the networks just didn't want: 60 MIMICS.
7. Tennessee Irving Fine, Minnie Pearlman, and Nitty Gritty Schmutzig Band tried, but failed, to garner giggles from Noshville in HOO HA!

VERA MILES' LIST OF 17 TV SERIES PILOTS SHE'S DONE

In the past two decades, Vera Miles has become a unique TV persona, often referred to on the network level as "pilot insurance." That is, her presence in a pilot for a television series maximizes the chances for it to be sold as a series. And since 1961, she has appeared in and helped sell more TV series than any other television star.

1. ALFRED HITCHCOCK PRESENTS
   "Revenge." 1955, NBC. Sold. Half-hour suspense series, which ran through 1962.
2. ASPHALT JUNGLE
   "The Lady and the Lawyer," 1961, ABC. Sold. Crime drama with Jack Warden; ran for thirteen episodes.
3. ALFRED HITCHCOCK HOUR
   "Don't Look Behind You." 1962. CBS, Sold. Sixty-minute suspense series; ran through 1965.
4. ELEVENTH HOUR
   "Ann Costigan's Duel on a Field of White." 1962, NBC. Sold. Wendell Corey as a psychiatrist. Ran for two years, made sixty-two episodes. Says Miles: "This began as an episodic spinoff from 'Dr. Kildare,' and after the pilot sold, we shot some extra footage so Kildare (Richard Chamberlain) could be edited out of the film."
5. FUGITIVE
   "Fear in a Desert City," 1963, ABC. Sold. David Janssen as a man on the run trying to prove his innocence of murder. Ran for four seasons through 1967; 120 episodes.
6. COURT MARTIAL
   "The Case against Sgt. Ryker," 1963, NBC. Sold. World War II lawyer drama starring Peter Graves and Brad Dillman, shot in England; one season, '65–66, twenty-six episodes. Miles: "The pilot was a two-hour episode of 'The Kraft Suspense Theatre,' and five years later, in 1968, it was released as a movie to theatres . . . it was that good . . . talky, but good."
7. OUTER LIMITS
   "The Forms of Things Unknown," 1964, ABC, was a spinoff pilot from "Outer Limits," intended for a new series to be called TALES OF THE UNKNOWN. Though created by Joe Stefano, who wrote *Psycho* and was executive producer on "Outer Limits," the pilot didn't sell.

Actress Vera Miles was willing to star in "Gentle Giant," the TV-movie pilot for the "Gentle Ben" series, but was unwilling to commit to the series. The series sold, and Beth Brickell co-starred with Dennis Weaver and Clint Howard.

8. I SPY

"Affair in T-sien-Cha." 1965, NBC. Sold. International spy drama with Robert Culp and Bill Cosby. Ran through 1968, eighty-two episodes. Miles: "Bill Cosby was the first black performer to have a starring role in a dramatic series . . . he was a ground-breaker."

9. GENTLE BEN

"Gentle Giant," 1966. CBS. Sold. Adventure series set in the Everglades with Dennis Weaver; '67–69, fifty-six episodes. Miles: "I agreed to do the pilot on the condition I would not be committed to the series. I had nightmares of chasing that damned bear through the endless Florida swamps." The pilot was so good that it was released as a theatrical feature, "Gentle Giant"; and when the series kicked off Vera Miles' role was played by Beth Brickell.

10. NAME OF THE GAME

"Man of the People," 1970. NBC. Sold . . . sort of. Miles: "Universal, who produced this on-going series, was having problems with Tony Franciosa, who was one of three revolving characters on the show. They shot this particular episode to establish me as a newspaperwoman, and Gary Burghoff as my assistant, and intended to hold this over Franciosa's head. If he didn't play ball, they were going to pull him from the lineup, and replace him with my new character. The network approved. So, Universal built permanent sets, tied Gary Burghoff up for eight episodes . . . but I refused to sign an eight-segment commitment. I said that I would do it one script at a time, but wouldn't commit to anything I wasn't sure I wanted to do. Fortunately, it never got any further."

11. CANNON

   TV Movie pilot, 1971. CBS. Sold. William Conrad as an overweight, squinting, and somehow charismatic gumshoe; 1971– 77, ninety-six episodes. Miles was asked to co-star in the 1980 telefilm, "The Return of Cannon," but declined.

12. IN SEARCH OF AMERICA

   Movie of the Week pilot, 1971, ABC. Didn't sell. Miles: "This was the first time I had ever committed to doing a series, and, strangely enough, it didn't go. I had mixed emotions about that. The only reason I agreed to the series was that an old friend, Bill Froug, was the producer, and he had assembled a marvelous cast. There was Carl Betz, Ruth McDevitt, and Jeff Bridges."

13. OWEN MARSHALL

   TV Movie pilot, 1971, ABC. Sold. Arthur Hill as a counselor-at-law for

Vera Miles is being set up for the kill by Ralph Meeker in "Revenge," 1955, the pilot for "Alfred Hitchcock Presents."

three seasons, sixty-nine episodes.

14. JIGSAW
    TV Movie pilot, 1972, ABC. Sold. James Wainright as a police detective in Missing Persons; was one of three rotating segments of an overall series called "The Man." The other two segments were: "Assignment: Vienna," with Robert Conrad, and "The Delphi Bureau," with Laurence Luckinbill; 1972–73, twenty-four episodes.

15. THE UNDERGROUND MAN
    Movie of the Week pilot, 1974, NBC. Sold . . . sort of. Miles: "This was Peter Graves as Lew Archer and the network liked it and bought it. But before it was put on the schedule, 'The Rockford Files' with James Garner came in and the programing guys bumped Archer in favor of Rockford. They were probably right."

16. STATE FAIR
    TV Movie pilot, 1976. Unsold. Ironically, this was the only other series to which Miles has ever committed herself. "That commitment was contingent on producer Bill Self staying on the show if it sold. He's a dear, longtime friend."

17. MacNAUGHTON'S DAUGHTER
    TV Movie pilot, 1976, NBC. Sold. Susan Clark as a Los Angeles attorney was short-lived. Only three episodes. Miles: "I just do the pilots. The rest is up to the regulars on the series."

26 TV SERIES AND THEIR SPINOFFS—QUIZ #3

Well, you found it! This is the third and final mind-bender in the book. To get a perfect score, proving that you are a semi-conscious TV addict, just match up the hit series with its respective, not-always-successful spinoff.

1. THE GENE AUTRY SHOW	a.	HONEY WEST
2. THE DICK POWELL THEATRE	b.	PHYLLIS
3. ALL IN THE FAMILY	c.	ENOS
4. THE MARY TYLER MOORE SHOW	d.	RICHIE BROCKLEMAN, PRIVATE EYE
5. SIX MILLION DOLLAR MAN	e.	TRAPPER JOHN, M.D.
6. SOAP	f.	FISH
7. DUKES OF HAZZARD	g.	POLICE WOMAN
8. B.J. AND THE BEAR	h.	S.W.A.T.
9. HAPPY DAYS	i.	GOMER PYLE, USMC
10. ALICE	j.	THE ROPERS
11. PETTICOAT JUNCTION	k.	DIRTY SALLY
12. THE ANDY GRIFFITH SHOW	l.	ZORRO
13. M*A*S*H	m.	SURFSIDE SIX
14. POLICE STORY	n.	MORK AND MINDY

15. THE ROOKIES
16. THREE'S COMPANY
17. GUNSMOKE
18. THE ROCKFORD FILES
19. BARNEY MILLER
20. BEWITCHED
21. BURKE'S LAW
22. THE MAN FROM U.N.C.L.E.
23. BOURBON STREET BEAT
24. WONDERFUL WORLD OF DISNEY
25. MAUDE
26. DALLAS

o. TABITHA
p. KNOTTS LANDING
q. SHERIFF LOBO
r. THE BIONIC WOMAN
s. SAINTS AND SINNERS
t. CHAMPION
u. GOOD TIMES
v. GREEN ACRES
w. FLO
x. BENSON
y. THE GIRL FROM U.N.C.L.E.
z. THE JEFFERSONS

ANSWERS

1t, 2s, 3z, 4b, 5r, 6x, 7c, 8q, 9n, 10w, 11v, 12i, 13e, 14g, 15h, 16j, 17k, 18d, 19f, 20o, 21a, 22y, 23m, 24l, 25u, 26p.

"Zorro," with dashing Guy Williams and Dick York, was a spinoff from what series?

13 POPULAR SHOWS CANCELED DURING THE GREAT DE-RURALIZATION PURGE OF 1970–71

In the late 1960s, the concept of a hit show began to change.

As demographics became more sophisticated, sponsors were able to determine who the people were that they were reaching with their commercials. The new demographics were unsettling. For instance, "Mayberry R.F.D." (1968–71), a Top 10 program, had an audience that ostensibly contained too many people who could not afford to buy the advertiser's products. Suddenly, high ratings were no longer enough. A hit show was newly defined as a program that reaches a mass of young adults, preferably those who live in the big cities. These are the real consumers.

At the time, CBS had the biggest lineup of Top 20 shows, which suddenly fell into a marginal category, as having great ratings, but an audience that was all wrong, demographically speaking, for the needs of the sponsor. Most of the offenders were rural-oriented programs, or had strong rural appeal. Consequently, CBS became known as the "Hillbilly Network." It was not a welcome reputation, under the circumstances.

There was only one thing to do. Clean house and ax all the shows that were too country to draw the big advertising dollars. The CBS purge began in 1970, and climaxed within the following year. When the dust had settled, the face of programing had changed drastically. Not only on CBS, but also, to a lesser degree, on ABC and NBC, as well.

It is also important to note that the then upcoming season of 1971–72 was the first to fall under the new FCC prime-time access rule, which was aimed at giving local stations access to prime-time 7:30–8 P.M., Monday thru Saturday. In effect, the rule reduced each network's weekly programing schedule by three hours. This meant that nine hours of shows had to be cut to comply with the new FCC rule. CBS, some say, took the opportunity to rid itself of most of the rural appeal shows.

The casualties:

1. PETTICOAT JUNCTION ('63–70)
   Bea Benaderet, Edgar Buchanan, Jeannine Riley, Linda Kaye, Pat Woodell, Smiley Burnette, June Lockhart. Bea Benaderet left "The Beverly Hillbillies" to star in her own successful series. Her death in 1969 left the show without a unifying element. And when ratings took a dip, CBS took the opportunity to cancel it, in a preview of things to come.

2. GREEN ACRES ('65–71)
   Eddie Albert, Eva Gabor, Pat Buttram. This was a companion show to "Petticoat Junction," and one of CBS's biggest rural sitcoms. But it was too much country, and not enough rock and roll, so out it went, Arnold the pig and all.

3. THE BEVERLY HILLBILLIES ('62–71)
   Buddy Ebsen, Irene Ryan, Donna Douglas, Max Baer, Jr., Nancy Kulp. One of the most popular shows ever on the air, it was number one two years running, and in the Top 10 for most of a decade. But when it dipped below the Top 20 for the first time in its successful run, CBS sent it to Hillbilly Heaven.

4. MEN FROM SHILOH was actually THE VIRGINIAN ('62–71)
   Despite the confusing name change, this classic adult Western, the first drama to go ninety minutes, held onto its rating points, and was number eighteen on the Hit Parade when NBC put it out to pasture with its rural demographics. The stars were James Drury, Doug McClure, Lee J. Cobb, and Stewart Granger, who joined the series for its final season as the new owner of the Shiloh Ranch, hence the title change: Granger would not do the show unless he had the title role. He could be one of the men from Shiloh, but he couldn't be the Virginian. Drury already had that part, and wouldn't give it up.

5. MAYBERRY R.F.D. ('68–71)
   Ken Berry, Frances Bavier, George Lindsay. This successor to the "Andy Griffith Show" was in the top four shows during its first two seasons, and still in the Top 20 when CBS axed it in their extensive de-ruralization. It finished number fifteen in its last season.

6. HEE HAW ('69–71)
   Buck Owens, Roy Clark, Junior Samples, Granpa Jones, Cathy Baker. This pure corn-fed Country version of "Laugh-In" was a respectable number sixteen when CBS shucked it from the schedule. It promptly went into syndication with all new shows, rather than reruns, and has been a major hit ever since on a non-network basis. Apparently, some sponsors think that "Hee Haw" is reaching the right audience.

7. LASSIE ('54–71)
   Tommy Rettig, Jan Clayton, Jon Provost, Cloris Leachman, June Lockhart, Robert Bray. Although not a real high-rating program (it had been the '64–65 season the last time it was in the Top 20), "Lassie" was a perennial fixture, a constant favorite in children's programing. It had survived three format changes, but it couldn't survive its rural demographics, coupled with the prime-time cutback.

8. CIMARRON STRIP ('67–71)
   Stuart Whitman, Percy Herbert, Randy Boone. Although patterned on NBC's successful ninety-minute "The Virginian," "Cimarron Strip" had originally been intended to replace the faltering "Gunsmoke." But the

following season, "Gunsmoke" picked up and shot back into the Top 10, while "Cimarron Strip" pulled a constant, and not unrespectable, spot on the Top 30. Being now marginal, under new CBS policy, it was stripped from the boards.

9. FAMILY AFFAIR ('66–71)

Brian Keith, Sebastian Cabot, Anissa Jones, Johnny Whitaker, Kathy Garver. Though not a rural comedy as such, demographics showed that it was popular with the wrong audience. It had been number five for three seasons, just prior to its last year, when it was knocked out of the Top 20 by "Flip Wilson," who was number two in that deadly season.

10. THE JIM NABORS SHOW ('69–71)

Nabors went into a comedy/variety show right on the heels of his great success with "Gomer Pyle USMC" ('64–69). In the first season he was number twelve, but dropped out of the Top 20, opposite NBC's "Flip Wilson Show," and was dropped out altogether by CBS.

11. THE RED SKELTON SHOW ('51–71)

After twenty years on CBS, then NBC, Skelton was an institution, one of the genuine superstars of TV. In his opening season, he was the number four show; and for the next eighteen years he was always in the Top 15, reaching as high as the number two spot in '66–67. In his final season, his ratings were still better than marginal, but Red was tired; the production costs of his show were getting too high; and his demographics were no laughing matter.

12. THE LAWRENCE WELK SHOW ('55–71)

Lawrence Welk's champagne music had a phenomenal sixteen-year run on ABC, and though his ratings, like his show, were not dynamic, they were solid. And when ABC canceled the show, it was primarily because demographics said that his audience was—not too small, but—too old. Welk, like "Hee Haw," then assembled a syndicated network of his own and even today continues to attract a bigger audience than many high-rated network shows.

13. THE JOHNNY CASH SHOW ('69–71)

Although Cash was the first to bridge the gap between Country and Western music and the mass audience, the rural demographics and "Medical Center" on CBS opposite him, burned his bridge right out from under him.

14. THE ED SULLIVAN SHOW ('48–71)

TV's longest-running variety show ran on Sunday nights for twenty-four years. The host, Ed Sullivan, old Stone Face himself, couldn't sing, dance, or tell a joke to save his life, but he knew who could, and signed them all. His show was an institutional reliable in the CBS programing line-up. The ratings had been solid and consistent, though they slipped somewhat in the '60s, as "The F.B.I." and "Walt Disney Presents" made inroads. However, it wasn't the ratings that killed old Ed. He was canceled as part of CBS's attempt to change its image to *the* network with shows for youthful audiences. As it was, Sullivan, like Welk, attracted too many of the older viewers.

So, if one of these fourteen had been one of your favorites and you never knew what happened—now you know.

A BAKER'S DOZEN OF THE MOST SUCCESSFUL SERIES IN SYNDICATION

Syndication was, more or less, invented by "I Love Lucy," which pioneered the filming of each episode so that they could be rebroadcast endlessly. Once "I Love Lucy" finished its network run, the filmed episodes, all 179 of them, were available for licensing to local stations around the country. The thousands of dollars over the years are staggering when you stop to consider that "I Love Lucy" has been running nonstop in syndication since 1957.

Generally speaking, a TV producer doesn't get into the profit position until his series goes into syndication. And if he hits there, the pot of gold is limitless.

1. I LOVE LUCY ('51–57, 179 episodes)
   The pioneer, the leader of the pack, and the most successful show in syndication history.
2. STAR TREK ('66–69, 79 episodes)
   This show has unbelievable staying power. It's more popular in reruns than it was in prime-time. In some areas, the episodes have aired as many as forty times, but the Trekkies don't stop watching.
3. THE BRADY BUNCH ('69–74, 117 episodes)
   Robert Reed, Florence Henderson headline this surprise hit.
4. GILLIGAN'S ISLAND ('64–67, 98 episodes)
   This is the biggest surprise of all. Hard to believe that a juvenile show like this can be making more money today than it did five years ago. Its syndication popularity led to a movie-of-the-week reprise in 1979.
5. ALL IN THE FAMILY ('71–80, 221 episodes)
   Going strong in all markets.
6. M*A*S*H ('72–present, 208 episodes available)
   They expect it to be the next "I Love Lucy," with continuous reruns into the next century.
7. BEWITCHED ('64–72, 306 episodes)
   One of the biggest hits of all time. Liz Montgomery stars.
8. I DREAM OF JEANNIE ('65–70, 165 episodes)
   Has often run tandem with "Bewitched," though it has only half the number of shows.

9. MY THREE SONS ('60–72, 369 episodes)
   Another biggie, with a huge catalog of shows available.
10. TWILIGHT ZONE ('59–63, 134 episodes)
   This is by far the most popular of its genre, and is constantly being rediscovered by new generations. Many see it as timeless.
11. THE ODD COUPLE ('70–75, 135 episodes)
   Highly durable, due to the talents of Jack Klugman and Tony Randall.
12. SUPERMAN ('53–57, 104 episodes)
   Though half the shows are in black and white, it doesn't make any difference. Like "Star Trek," it seems to have a cult following; and like "Twilight Zone," it's also constantly being rediscovered.
13. PERRY MASON ('57–66, 271 episodes)
   Though starting to wane now, this Raymond Burr series has had one of the most impressive syndication runs ever.

7 OF THE MOST SURPRISING DISAPPOINTMENTS IN SYNDICATION

You'd expect that a hit prime-time series would also be popular in syndication. But it's not always true. Here are seven shows which were often in the Top 10 in their original runs, but somehow died in syndication, proving that the only predictable thing in this business is its unpredictability.

1. MARCUS WELBY ('69–76, 172 episodes)
2. THE BEVERLY HILLBILLIES ('62–71, 234 episodes)
3. GREEN ACRES ('65–71, 170 episodes)
4. PEYTON PLACE ('64–69, 514 episodes)
5. THE ROOKIES ('72–76, 104 episodes)
6. THE DORIS DAY SHOW ('68–73, 128 episodes)
7. THE FUGITIVE ('63–69, 120 episodes)

3 DISASTROUS ACCIDENTS DURING FILMING OF "THAT'S INCREDIBLE"

"That's Incredible" (1980–present) has been described as a kind of hybrid of "60 Minutes" and "The Gong Show," "designed by a network Dr. Strangelove." It could be an innocent TV throwback to the vintage "You Asked for It" (1950–59), if not for the fact that during the first few months of production for its opening season, there were several brutal accidents, which have transformed the show from mindless carnival-type entertainment to what some critics have called "snuff television."

The three stunts that were near-fatal disasters:

1. In March, 1980, thirty-six-year-old Stan Kruml, with four years of stunt experience, agreed to run through a 150-foot burning tunnel, constructed of chicken wire and burlap. With the tunnel aflame, and protected by a flame-retardant suit, Kruml made his run, only to stumble from the inferno, his suit afire, and his fingers nearly burned off. His pay was $8,000. He filed a multi-million-dollar suit against the show for negligence, and for the loss of a "fantastic career."

2. In July, 1980, twenty-five-year-old Steve Lewis, after trying for three months to get on the show, attempted a standing jump over two cars speeding bumper to bumper at him at 100 m.p.h. Drained by the 117-degree heat, he misjudged the stunt and his left foot smashed sickeningly into the windshield of the lead car. The impact shattered his foot and turned his lower leg twice around the knee. He may still lose his foot, and most certainly will never be able to walk normally again.

3. In September, 1980, twenty-three-year-old motorcycle daredevil, Gary Wells, hoping to be Evil Knievel's successor, attempted the jump over Caesar's Palace fountains, which had seriously injured his idol in 1967. During the stunt, before a crowd of 2,000 people and "That's Incredible" cameras, Wells lost control of his motorcycle some 180 feet in the air and ended up crashing into a concrete wall at 80 m.p.h. Suffering a ruptured aorta and severe pelvic, skull, and leg injuries, he was on the critical list for a week before his condition stabilized.

11 "REAL PEOPLE" SUBJECTS FOR THE 1980–81 SEASON

When "Real People" premiered in 1979, it not only shot to the Top 10 in popularity, but the show ushered in a new wave of Ripley's Believe-It-Or-Not-type reality programing. NBC's "Real People" was a trend-setting show, which was soon thereafter being cloned under various formats into a dozen imitation, trend-following programs. To prove that "Real People" still has the jump on its competition, NBC publicity released a list of upcoming subjects which are the goofiest of the goofy:

1. An Englishman who powers a motor with a lemon.
2. A Michigan woman who lives in a teepee guarded by a goose.
3. An Ohioan who collects tanks.
4. A Massachusetts man who lifts a 4,100-pound car with another man.
5. A Bostonian who makes chalk replicas of famous paintings on sidewalks.
6. A Californian who teaches Phillipine stick fighting to the elderly.
7. A Louisiana festival honoring a Cajun-type sausage.
8. A Miami psychic who conducts séances to reach Elvis Presley.
9. An Idaho man who says he can change the weather.

10. A sixteen-inch-tall Alabaman who attempts to live a normal life.
11. A gorilla that enjoys watching TV . . . he probably watches "Real People."

NBC's "Real People" with Byron Allen, Sara Purcell, John Barbour, and Skip Stephenson kicked off a trend toward "reality programing," which has been aptly criticized as "the goon show" and "the freak parade."

15

CHAPTER

"MATCH GAME":
The Movie Connection
Or: *How Movies and TV Became Kissing Cousins*

ROBERT STACK'S LIST OF 18 WELL-KNOWN MOVIE ACTORS WHO ACHIEVED THEIR GREATEST FAME ON TELEVISION

Discovered by producer Joe Pasternak while visiting the set of a Deanna Durbin film, Robert Stack began making films in 1939, and the next time he was on a Deanna Durbin set, he was her romantic lead and gave Miss Durbin her first screen kiss in *First Love.* Although perhaps too good looking and too personable to be taken seriously as an actor in his early career, Stack won a Best Supporting Oscar nomination in 1956 for *Written on the Wind,* and also made numerous classic films including *To Be Or Not To Be* (1942) and *The High and the Mighty* (1954). His movie career has been long and successful, yet his greatest fame came as a television superstar, playing Eliot Ness on "The Untouchables" (1959–63), which won him an Emmy, and later as editor Dan Farrell on "The Name of the Game" (1968–72).

1. RONALD REAGAN
    After a film career that began in 1937, peaked in 1941, and dwindled following WW II, he found new fame and fortune as host and occasional star of "The General Electric Theatre" ('53–61) and on "Death Valley Days" ('62–65).

Producer Doug Benton, Alan J. Miller, head of Revue Productions, and Ronald Reagan on the set of "G.E. Theatre" filming a segment called "A Turkey for the President." The episode, which ran in 1960, featured (inset) Reagan, Nancy Reagan (the First Lady) and Tommy Nolan. Sort of prophetic, don't you think?

2. LUCILLE BALL

A former MGM starlet whose career began in 1933 with *Broadway Through a Keyhole,* and after some sixty-seven films, she was still not a superstar. Entering TV with "I Love Lucy" ('51–58), she found true immortality, and ensured it with "The Lucy Show" ('62–74).

3. MILTON BERLE

A Vaudeville comedian, who began in films in 1937, but never found his true niche until "The Texaco Star Theatre" ('48–53), which he hosted and on which he became known as "Mr.•Television." A giant in the early days of TV, he continued with his own variety shows through 1967.

4. ROBERT WAGNER

A popular young leading man all through the '50s and early '60s, who achieved superstar status on TV in "It Takes a Thief" ('68–70), "Switch" ('75–78), and "Hart to Hart" ('79–present).

5. ROBERT YOUNG

A durable and well-liked leading man invariably cast in amiable dependable roles whose screen career spanned the years from 1931 to 1954, when he began his classic TV comedy series, "Father Knows Best" ('54–60), and ensured his superstardom with "Marcus Welby, M.D." ('69–76).

6. ANGIE DICKINSON

A former beauty contest winner who debuted in the movies with *Lucky Me* (1954) and went on to play romantic leads opposite such stars as John Wayne, Gregory Peck, and Burt Reynolds, only to find superstardom as TV's "Police Woman" ('74–78).

7. EVE ARDEN

Began as a Ziegfeld show girl, debuted in films with *Song of Love* (1929) and, following a long, successful screen career, was one of TV's first superstars as "Our Miss Brooks" ('52–56), "The Eve Arden Show" ('57–58), and "The Mothers-In-Law" ('67–69).

8. BUDDY EBSEN

A successful actor-dancer, he began making films with *Broadway Melody* (1936), later emerged as a solid character actor in scores of motion pictures, but achieved his greatest fame as Fess Parker's sidekick in Disney's TV version of "Davy Crockett" ('54–55); then superstardom on "The Beverly Hillbillies" ('62–71) and "Barnaby Jones" ('73–80).

9. BRIAN KEITH

Versatile, easy-going leading man who debuted in *Arrowhead* (1952) and earned fame in scores of films, only to overshadow it all with TV's "Family Affair" ('66–71). His other series include "The Crusader" ('55–56) and "The Brian Keith Show" ('72–74).

10. WARD BOND

He debuted in *The Big Trail* (1930), which was John Wayne's first starring film, and distinguished himself in a score of classic movies like

Gone With the Wind, Grapes of Wrath (1940), *The Maltese Falcon* (1941), *Fort Apache* (1948), *The Quiet Man* (1952), and *The Searchers* (1956). His superstardom came on television with "Wagon Train" ('57–65).

11. BOB CUMMINGS

A light-comedy leading man, whose career began in 1935 with *The Virginia Judge*. He firmly established himself in romantic comedies of the '40s and early '50s, which led to his greatest fame in "Love That Bob" ('54–59), "The Bob Cummings Show" ('61–62), and "My Living Doll" ('64–65).

12. RICARDO MONTALBAN

A suave Latin Lover leading man debuting in *Fiesta* (1947). His career was established in films like *The Kissing Bandit* (1949), *Latin Lovers* (1954), and *Sweet Charity* (1968). But everyone knows him best as the dapper Mr. Roarke, the man who owns "Fantasy Island" ('78–present).

13. ROBERT BLAKE

Began in films at age nine in *Andy Hardy's Double Life* (1943), survived the transition to adult parts with some difficulty, and became a leading man with *In Cold Blood* (1967), starting, in effect, a new career for the long-time actor. Superstardom, however, eluded him until "Baretta" ('75–78).

14. RICHARD BASEHART

Although a thoughtful leading man in a string of films that began with *Cry Wolf* (1947), he never achieved his expected stardom until ABC's "Voyage to the Bottom of the Sea" ('64–68), one of TV's most popular science fiction series.

15. LLOYD BRIDGES

Really versatile character actor and leading man, who plunged into an active screen career with *Here Comes Mr. Jordan* (1941), but got his biggest acclaim in "Sea Hunt" ('57–61), followed by "The Lloyd Bridges Show" ('62–63), "The Loner ('65–66), "San Francisco International ('70–71), and "Joe Forrester" ('75–76).

16. SHIRLEY JONES

A singer and leading lady who developed into a substantial actress during a fifteen-year Hollywood film career that began with *Oklahoma!* (1955). She won an Oscar as Best Supporting Actress for *Elmer Gantry* (1960), and superstardom was finally hers with TV's "Partridge Family" ('70–74).

17. ANN SOTHERN

A blonde comedienne and leading lady, who left the stage for the movies in 1934, debuting in *Let's Fall in Love*. After scores of films, she found greater stardom on television in "Private Secretary" ('53–57), which segued, supporting cast and all, into "The Ann Sothern Show" ('58–61).

18. GENE BARRY
    Debonair leading man, who began in films in 1952, won acclaim in *The War of the Worlds* (1953), lasting fame as TV's "Bat Masterson" ('57–61), in "Burke's Law," which became "Amos Burke, Secret Agent" in its final season ('63–66), and, finally, on "Name of the Game" ('68–72).

EARL HOLLIMAN'S LIST OF A DOZEN BIG-NAME FILM STARS WHO—FOR REASONS BEYOND THEIR CONTROL—DIDN'T MAKE IT IN A WEEKLY SERIES

In the early days of television, most big-name Hollywood stars, shunned appearing on the tube because it was considered a competitive medium. In fact, most studio contracts had a clause forbidding the actors from doing television. However, as time went by, it was finally realized that TV was not necessarily competitive, but rather a sister medium, and many film actors began to give it a chance. In fact, many movie actors didn't find their true niche until their TV work.

Earl Holliman and Angie Dickinson in "Police Woman," the series that made them stars.

Earl Holliman began his movie career in the early '50s, and built up an impressive list of supporting role credits in such features as *The Bridges at Toko-Ri* (1954), *Forbidden Planet* (1956), *Last Train from Gun Hill* (1959), *Summer and Smoke* (1961), *The Sons of Katie Elder* (1965), and *Anzio* (1968). Simultaneously, he kept busy on scores of television shows, which led to three series of his own: "Hotel de Paree" ('59–60), "The Wide Country" ('62–63), and "Police Woman" ('74–78), which finally gave him the recognition he so richly deserves and has worked so hard to achieve.

Having worked both mediums, and being a film and TV history buff, Holliman finds the back-and-forth transition of stars interesting. "It's a well known fact that many big TV stars have been unable to duplicate their success on the big screen, and at the same time, there have been some big-name film stars who—for reasons beyond their control—have not been able to find that same success in a weekly TV series.

"There are so many intangibles involved in making a hit series. The packaging has to be right; it has to be the right vehicle for the star; if you're scheduled against 'All in the Family' in your opening season, that's a bad time slot. These are some of the reasons why someone like Jimmy Stewart had a series that didn't last beyond the first season; it certainly wasn't because a star like him isn't talented or popular. Here are some of the big-name movie stars who didn't realize the TV series success they deserved."

1. JAMES STEWART—"The Jimmy Stewart Show" ('71–72); "Hawkins" ('73–74)
2. LANA TURNER—"The Survivors" (Sept.–Nov. 69)
3. GIG YOUNG, CHARLES BOYER, DAVID NIVEN—"The Rogues" ('64–65)
4. GEORGE KENNEDY—"The Blue Knight" ('75–76). Specifically, what killed George's series was being opposite "Charlie's Angels."
5. DEBBIE REYNOLDS—"The Debbie Reynolds Show" ('69–70)
6. MICKEY ROONEY—"The Mickey Rooney Show" ('54–55); "Mickey" ('64–65)
7. RONALD COLMAN—"Halls of Ivy" ('54–55). This is a classic example of being the absolutely wrong vehicle for the star.
8. JUDY GARLAND—"The Judy Garland Show" ('63–64). Judy's health problems and competition from "Bonanza" (the number two show then) stopped her series.
9. YUL BRYNNER—"Anna and the King" (Sept.–Dec. '72)
10. SHIRLEY MacLAINE—"Shirley's World" ('71–72)
11. GLENN FORD—"Cade's County" ('71–72)

12. ANTHONY QUINN—"The Man and the City" ('71–72)
13. BETTY HUTTON—"The Betty Hutton Show" ('59–60). Her competition was really rough: "The Donna Reed Show" and "Bat Masterson," both hits.
14. JULIE ANDREWS—"The Julie Andrews Hour" ('72–73)
15. TAB HUNTER—"The Tab Hunter Show" ('60–61)

...AND 13 MOVIE SUPERSTARS TO BECOME TV SUPERSTARS

Holliman: "However, there have been a lucky handful who have been able to achieve superstardom in both mediums, and this includes:

1. BOB HOPE—The "Bob Hope Christmas Shows" are among the highest-rated programs of all time. He's done it all.
2. ROCK HUDSON—"McMillan and Wife" ('71–77)
3. DICK POWELL—"The Dick Powell Theatre" ('61–63); "Zane Grey Theatre" ('56–62)
4. DONNA REED—"The Donna Reed Show" ('58–66)
5. WALTER BRENNAN—"The Real McCoys" ('57–63)
6. LORETTA YOUNG—"The Loretta Young Show" ('53–61)
7. BARBARA STANWYCK—"Big Valley" (65–69)
8. JACK BENNY—"The Jack Benny Show" ('50–65)
9. DORIS DAY—"The Doris Day Show" ('68–73)
10. FRED MacMURRAY—"My Three Sons" ('60–72)
11. GROUCHO MARX—"You Bet Your Life" ('50–61)
12. ERNEST BORGNINE—"McHale's Navy" ('62–66)
13. RED SKELTON—"The Red Skelton Show" ('51–71)

19 TV SERIES STARS WHO BECAME MOVIE SUPERSTARS

As many actors entrenched in a television series complain, you get stuck in a particular role, and it becomes hard to break out of that mold. Even harder is trying to make that huge leap from television to the silver screen. Only a handful of actors starring in TV series in the '50s and '60s, and a few since whose roots are TV-bound, have been able not only to make the transition, but to become filmdom's superstars.

1. CLINT EASTWOOD—"Rawhide" ('59–66)
2. BURT REYNOLDS—"Riverboat" ('59–60); "Gunsmoke" ('62–65); "Hawk" ('66–67); "Dan August" ('70–71)
3. CHARLES BRONSON—"Man with a Camera" ('53–54); "Empire" ('62–63); "The Travels of Jamie McPheeters" ('63–64)

TV's "Flying Nun" and "Gidget", Sally Field finally broke her typecasting mold with "Norma Rae" winning an Oscar and well-deserved stardom.

4. STEVE McQUEEN—"Wanted Dead or Alive" ('58–61)
5. ROGER MOORE—"Ivanhoe" ('57–58); "The Alaskan" ('59–60); "The Saint" ('63–69); "The Persuaders" ('71–72)
6. WARREN BEATTY—"The Many Loves of Dobie Gillis" ('59–60)
7. RYAN O'NEAL—"Empire ('62–63); "Peyton Place" ('64–65)
8. JACK LEMMON—"That Wonderful Guy" ('49–50); "Heaven for Betsy" ('52–53)
9. WALTER MATTHAU—"Tallahassee 7000" ('61–62)
10. JAMES GARNER—"Maverick" ('57–62); "Nichols" ('71–72); "The Rockford Files" ('74–80)
11. SALLY FIELD—"Gidget" ('65–66); "The Flying Nun" ('67–70)
12. GEORGE C. SCOTT—"East Side/West Side" ('63–64)
13. JOHN TRAVOLTA—"Welcome Back, Kotter" ('75–80)
14. LEE MARVIN—"M Squad" ('57–60)
15. ROBERT SHAW—"The Buccaneers" ('56–57)
16. BRUCE LEE—"The Green Hornet" ('66–67)
17. JAMES COBURN—"Klondike" ('60–61); "Acapulco" ('61–62)
18. MIA FARROW—"Peyton Place" ('64–65)
19. MARK HAMILL—"General Hospital" ('72–74); "The Texas Wheelers" ('74–75)

tunt actor Burt Reynolds cavorts on "Gunsmoke," on which he portrayed a half-
reed blacksmith for three seasons. He had four series before making a successful
ap to feature films and superstardom.

THE 8 MOVIES IN THE FIRST SEASON OF THE FIRST TV-MOVIES SERIES

Increasing demand for movies on television led to a major new development in the mid-'60s—the made-for-TV Movie. Universal was the first major studio to attempt producing a film expressly for television, for NBC during the 1963–64 season. That first film was "The Killers," with Lee Marvin and Angie Dickinson, and Ronald Reagan in a small role, directed by Don Siegal. However, it was deemed too violent for TV and went, instead, with some new scenes, into theatrical release.

The first made-for-TV film then became "See How They Run," with John Forsythe and Senta Berger, telecast on October 7, 1964. TV Movies began appearing sporadically thereafter, leading in a few years to the first series of TV Movies called "World Premiere," in which NBC unveiled a multimillion-dollar showcase of eight—count 'em—brand new films made expressly for television:

1. FAME IS THE NAME OF THE GAME ('Nov. '66) Director: Stuart Rosenberg
   Tony Franciosa, Jill St. John, Jack Klugman, George Macready, Susan St. James. This movie about a big-time magazine writer spawned a series, "Name of the Game" ('68–71).
2. THE DOOMSDAY FLIGHT (Nov. '66), D: Billy Graham
   Suspenseful Rod Serling script featured Jack Lord, Edmond O'Brien, Van Johnson, Katherine Crawford, John Saxon, Michael Sarrazin.
3. DRAGNET '66 (Dec. '66), D: Jack Webb
   Jack Webb and Harry Morgan in a two-hour pilot for the reprise of the original "Dragnet" series ('52–59). It worked, and "Dragnet" was back on the schedule as of January 1967 and ran through September 1970.
4. HOW I SPENT MY SUMMER VACATION (Jan. '67), D: William Hale
   Robert Wagner, Lola Albright, Peter Lawford, Walter Pidgeon, Jill St. John. The big suspense is trying to figure out why they made it.
5. THE BORGIA STICK (Jan. '67), D: David Lowell Rich
   Don Murray, Fritz Weaver, Inger Stevens, Barry Nelson. The suspense that was missing in the above movie can be found in this one.
6. THE LONGEST HUNDRED MILES (Feb. '67), D: Don Weis
   Doug McClure, Katharine Ross, Ricardo Montalban. Average and occasionally tedious WW II yarn set on the Philippine Islands.
7. WINGS OF FIRE (Feb. '67), D: David Lowell Rich
   Suzanne Pleshette, James Farentino, Ralph Bellamy, Juliet Mills, Jeremy Slate, Lloyd Nolan. Hokey story about floundering air freight service, but Pleshette is nice to look at.
8. WINCHESTER '73 (Mar. '67), D: Herschel Daugherty

Tony Franciosa and Jill St. John starred in "Fame Is the Name of the Game," the initial installment of the first season of TV Movies. It proved to be a pilot for a series called "Name of the Game."

Tom Tryon, John Saxon, Dan Duryea, Joan Blondell, John Drew Barrymore. Okay remake of 1950 James Stewart movie; good action sequences. Notable is Duryea, who was also in the earlier version.

JUDITH CRIST'S LIST OF THE TOP 10 TV MOVIES OF 1979

It's not unusual for film critics to publish their 10 Best Lists of Movies for any given year, but for the 10 Best TV Movies, it's more a rarity than tradition. But Judith Crist did just that in *TV Guide,* for which she's the resident film reviewer.

Writes Crist: "When NBC introduced its multimillion-dollar series of eight World Premiere made-for-television movies in 1966, it started with "Fame Is the Name of the Game," co-starring Tony Franciosa, his white teeth and his cleft chin in an incoherent sex-and-slaughter story that seemed like an overgrown pilot for a TV series—as, in fact, it proved to be. But it drew 40 percent of the audience and was a sign of flicks to come."

In 1979, there were 104 TV Movies. Here are Judith Crist's pick of the litter (in chronological order of their broadcasts):

1. MURDER BY NATURAL CAUSES, Richard Levinson and William Link, producer-writers
   Hal Holbrook, Katharine Ross, Barry Bostwick, Richard Anderson. "A sparkling whodunit in the *Sleuth* tradition, it is first-class entertainment."
2. TOO FAR TO GO, based on ten John Updike stories, written by William Hanley
   Blythe Danner, Michael Moriarity: ". . . a searing study of the disintegration of a twenty-year marriage."
3. THE JERICHO MILE, teleplay by director Michael Mann and Patrick J. Nolan
   "An offbeat and unpredictable story of a life-sentence prisoner, played by Peter Strauss, who hopes to qualify as an Olympic miler. It is told without compromise."
4. NO OTHER LOVE, by Edwin Francis Kaplan
   "With brilliant performances by Richard Thomas and Julie Kavner, this unsentimental drama about two marginally retarded young adults who fall in love is as enriching as it is engrossing and deeply affecting."
5. FRIENDLY FIRE, adapted by Fay Kanin, from the C.D.B. Bryan book
   True account of an Iowa farm couple seeking the truth about the death of their son in Vietnam. "With Carol Burnett and Ned Beatty as the couple, the film boldly considers questions of patriotism, integrity, and righteous wrath . . . with stunning effect."

6. I KNOW WHY THE CAGED BIRD SINGS, adapted by Leonora Thuna and Maya Angelou from Angelou's autobiographical book
"An excellent cast brings universal truth to the story of a black girl growing up in the South in the 1930s, and the adults who influenced her."

7. STRANGERS: THE STORY OF A MOTHER AND DAUGHTER, original teleplay by Michael de Guzman
"Gena Rowlands, as the prodigal daughter, and Bette Davis, as her embittered mother, provide us, beyond startling human insights, with that all-too-rare experience of watching two fine actresses work one-on-one."

8. THIS MAN STANDS ALONE, written and directed by Jerrold Freedman; Lou Gossett Jr., Clu Gulager
"This absorbing drama about the first black sheriff elected in the South since Reconstruction paints a vivid portrait of a time and place in turmoil, and the triumph therein of a nonviolent revolutionary."

9. UNDERCOVER WITH THE KKK, written by Lane Slate for producer Doug Benton, based on Gary Rowe's book
"Don Meredith is excellent as Rowe, in that the informant is not glorified; he is seen as a man who was out for the cash and the credit."

10. THE GIFT, adapted by Robert Mallory, from the Pete Hamill novel
"It's extraordinary as a period piece, a Christmas special, and a vignette of the beginning of manhood . . . in Brooklyn in the early 1950s. Gary Frank, Glenn Ford, and Julie Harris break our hearts a little without even a tug at a heartstring."

. . . AND 8 CONTENDERS FOR NUMBER 11

Crist: "TV film at its best. Stop at ten? There are a number of contenders for the eleventh spot:"

11. THE INCREDIBLE JOURNEY OF DOCTOR MEG LAUREL, Lindsay Wagner, Jane Wyman, Dorothy McGuire, Gary Lockwood

11. THE FAMILY MAN, Ed Asner, Meredith Baxter Birney, Anne Jackson

11. THE SACKETTS, taken from two Louis L'Amour novels, Sam Elliott, Tom Selleck, Jeff Osterhage, Glenn Ford, Ben Johnson, Gilbert Roland, Ruth Roman, Jack Elam, Mercedes McCambridge

11. DEATH OF OCEAN VIEW PARK, Mike Connors, Martin Landau, Diana Canova

11. BIRTH OF THE BEATLES, Stephen Mackenna, Rod Culbertson, John Altman, Ray Ashcroft, Mitchell Ryan

11. THE STREETS OF L.A., Joanne Woodward, Robert Webber, Michael C. Gwynne

11. MAYFLOWER: THE PILGRIM'S ADVENTURE, Anthony Hopkins, Richard Crenna, Jenny Agutter, Trish Van Devere

11. THE LAST RIDE OF THE DALTON GANG, Cliff Potts, Randy Quaid, Larry Wilcox, Jack Palance, Dale Robertson, Bo Hopkins, Sharon Farrell

THE 10 HIGHEST-RATED TV MOVIES OF ALL TIME

1. HELTER SKELTER, Part II (1976). Rating: 37.5; share: 60
   Director: Tom Gries; George DiCenzo, Steve Railsback, Nancy Wolfe, Christina Hart, Marilyn Burns, Cathey Paine
2. LITTLE LADIES OF THE NIGHT (1977). Rating: 36.9; share: 53
   D: Marvin Chomsky; David Soul, Lou Gossett, Linda Purl, Clifton James, Carolyn Jones, Paul Burke, Lana Wood, Kathleen Quinlan, Vic Tayback, Dorothy Malone
3. HELTER SKELTER, Part I (1976). Rating: 35.2; share: 59
4. THE WALTONS THANKSGIVING STORY (1973). Rating: 33.5; share: 51
   D: Phillip Leacock; Ralph Waite, Michael Learned, Richard Thomas, Jon Walmsleg, Ellen Corby, Will Greer
5. THE NIGHT STALKER (1972). Rating: 33.2; share: 48
   D: John Llewelly Moxey; Darren McGavin, Carol Lynley, Simon Oakland, Ralph Meeker, Claude Akins
6. A CASE OF RAPE (1974). Rating: 33.1; share: 49
   D: Boris Sagal; Elizabeth Montgomery, Ronny Cox, Cliff Potts, William Daniels
7. DALLAS COWBOYS CHEERLEADERS (1979). Rating: 33.0; share: 48
   D: Bruce Bilson; Jane Seymour, Laraine Stephens, Bert Convy, Laura Tewes, Pamela Susan Shoop, Katherine Baumann, Bucky Dent
8. BRIAN'S SONG (1970). Rating: 32.9; share: 48
   D: Buzz Kulik; Billy Dee Williams, James Caan, Jack Warden, Shelley Fabares, Judy Pace
9. WOMEN IN CHAINS (1972). Rating: 32.3; share: 48
   D: Bernard Kowalski; Ida Lupino, Lois Nettleton, Jessica Walters, Belinda Montgomery, John Larch, Penny Fuller
10. JESUS OF NAZARETH, Part I (1977).
    D: Franco Zefferelli; Robert Powell, Anne Bancroft, Ernest Borgnine, Claudia Cardinale, James Mason, Rod Steiger, Anthony Quinn, Peter Ustinov

AFTERWORD

I hope that this book was as much fun for you to read as it was for me to write.

Deadlines and space limitations would not permit us to publish all of the wonderful, nostalgic trivia and fascinating stuff that we've unearthed, so, as you might suspect, a second volume, a sort of *Son of the Book of TV Lists,* is a distinct possibility.

Any comments you have, corrections, additions, beefs, suggestions for lists, and trivia information, will be gladly received. And if you're interested in participating in a nationwide poll of All-Time TV Favorites, please enclose a self-addressed, stamped envelope so that we may send you a questionnaire.

Please address all mail to: Gabe Essoe, c/o Arlington House Publishers, 333 Post Road West, Westport, CT 06880. Thanks so much.

INDEX